British Campaigns
in the South Atlantic
1805–1807

British Campaigns in the South Atlantic 1805–1807

Operations in the Cape and the River Plate and their Consequences

John D. Grainger

Pen & Sword
MILITARY

First published in Great Britain in 2015 by
Pen & Sword Military
an imprint of
Pen & Sword Books Ltd
47 Church Street
Barnsley
South Yorkshire
S70 2AS

Copyright © John D. Grainger 2015

ISBN 978 1 78346 364 0

Typeset in Ehrhardt by
Mac Style Ltd, Bridlington, East Yorkshire

Printed and bound in the UK by
CPI Group (UK) Ltd, Croydon, CR0 4YY

Pen & Sword Books Ltd incorporates the imprints of Pen & Sword
Archaeology, Atlas, Aviation, Battleground, Discovery, Family History,
History, Maritime, Military, Naval, Politics, Railways, Select,
Transport, True Crime, and Fiction, Frontline Books, Leo Cooper,
Praetorian Press, Seaforth Publishing and Wharncliffe.

For a complete list of Pen & Sword titles please contact
PEN & SWORD BOOKS LIMITED
47 Church Street, Barnsley, South Yorkshire, S70 2AS, England
E-mail: enquiries@pen-and-sword.co.uk
Website: www.pen-and-sword.co.uk

Contents

List of Maps and Diagrams

Introduction

There is a theory that a chain reaction of events may begin with the beating of a butterfly's wings in Brazil and end with a tornado in Japan. In physics or meteorology this seems thoroughly unlikely, but in human affairs something very similar does seem to occur. In this book the proximate event which set events in motion was the meeting, more or less by chance, between a Royal Navy captain and an ex-prisoner-of-war army captain in Portsmouth; the end results were the independence of Latin America and the development of the *apartheid* regime in South Africa.

These ends may well be likened to Japanese tornadoes in their indifference to human life, but Captain Sir Home Popham is an unlikely butterfly. Yet there is a clear connection between his meeting with Captain Jones in Portsmouth and those ends. It is, however, the connection of accident and happenstance as much as deliberation. At the same time, Popham had long been interested in South America, and he had been to the Cape of Good Hope more than once, so the accidents and twists and turns of the story took place in a human environment already well prepared for them.

It is therefore tempting to ascribe the results of these military operations to chance, mere human actions, and absence of mind. But such an argument scarcely works. The expeditions of 1806–1807 came in the context of the war of Britain against the Napoleonic dictatorship in Europe, and took place simultaneously with the great extension of that dictatorship as a result of the victories of French arms at Austerlitz and Jena and Friedland and Eylau, and the peace treaty of Tilsit. Further, these expeditions were only the latest in a series of British attempts on both the Cape and the River Plate. When Popham met Jones, therefore, the political and naval and military context was ready.

But it is the Scottish dimension to these events which is perhaps the oddest part of all. Popham had already worked with the General Sir David Baird, and Baird always favoured using Scottish troops, so a situation developed where the revival of the moribund Calvinist Christianity of the Dutch of

South Africa was encouraged by the Scottish intervention at the Cape, and together these helped the development of the ideology of *apartheid*, with all its continuing consequences for life in South Africa; meanwhile across the Atlantic the imprisonment of a Scottish regiment, deliberately selected by Baird to undertake a hare-brained raid, as a favour, pushed forward the achievement of independence among the peoples of the River Plate. This was the first success of that movement and it led on to the eventual emancipation of the whole continent.

And yet it need not have happened at all. It was not necessary for Britain to control the Cape; in Dutch hands it would have been a nuisance, but no more. Popham did not need to go to the River Plate, against orders; Baird could have prevented him doing so without difficulty. The 71st Regiment of Foot did not have to be retained as prisoners-of-war by the reconquerors of Buenos Aires; if they had been released at once, unarmed, Popham would have had to sail away, and would have been glad to do so. In Dutch hands the history of South Africa would certainly have taken a different course; if nothing else the expansion of Dutch control would have been slower.

In South Africa, however, almost simultaneously with Popham's arrival in the River Plate, Francisco da Miranda was landing in Venezuela, hoping to provoke a movement for independence; and the revival of the Dutch Reformed Church in South Africa would probably have happened without the intervention of Scots ministers, once peace reopened connections with Holland. These developments, however, would have taken differing courses. If South American independence had begun in the north of the continent rather than the south, if the Dutch Church had reformed itself, the results would clearly have been different.

So this is the story of an armed expedition which was probably unnecessary, which was certainly unauthorized, and which had wholly unanticipated and unlooked-for results. And there is a sting in the tail (or tale): the absence of several thousands of young and vigorous Highland men surely had an effect on their homeland; had they been present, would their homes have been so comprehensively 'cleared' by their clan chiefs – who had persuaded them, in many cases, to join the army in the first place?

I have deliberately quoted repeatedly from the first-hand accounts of many of the participants, particularly the soldiers, who appear to have been an unusually literate set. Either that or they scented a journalistic opportunity. But it is necessary to distinguish between those which are diaries or were composed directly following the events they describe, and those which were composed some years later. The latter had the advantage of knowing the result and of hearing other versions, and thus are less to be relied on. Nevertheless they were composed in large part at a time of particularly vigorous English expression, and they usually describe events more clearly than anything which can be recomposed by historians two centuries afterwards.

Chapter One

The Expedition

The summer of 1805 was the most anxious time for the British government of any during the Revolutionary and Napoleonic Wars, not excluding 1797 and 1801. The new Emperor Napoleon with the Army of England was camped at Boulogne. Admiral Villeneuve with the French Toulon fleet had escaped from the shadowing British Mediterranean fleet under Vice-Admiral Horatio Nelson and had vanished into the wide Atlantic, followed by Nelson and his fleet. The second French fleet at Rochfort under Commodore Allemand had escaped confinement because the blockading fleet under Rear-Admiral Charles Stirling had been withdrawn. Off Brest Admiral William Cornwallis commanded yet another blockading fleet, and the assumption was that Villeneuve would try to drive Cornwallis and his fleet away, link up with the French fleet from Brest, and perhaps with Allemand's fleet, and then sail up-Channel to convoy the Army of England across the water to land in Kent.[1]

The British army was heavily concentrated in Kent, just in case, though both public and government confidence was strong that the fleet would prevent the landing. 'I do not say they cannot come,' the First Lord of the Admiralty Lord St Vincent pronounced in the House of Lords, 'but I do say they will not come by sea.'[2] But there were other possibilities. Villeneuve had sailed west, after all, and he might well have been sent to the West Indies to campaign there, where there were plenty of small and rich British islands which could be snapped up. French successes there would hurt, and would produce a great cry from the sugar planters and importers, who were well represented in Parliament. So a force was made ready in southern Ireland to be sent to mop up after him, to be commanded by the newly appointed governor of Jamaica, the distinguished General Sir Eyre Coote.[3]

In the midst of all this excitement, the captain of the 64-gun line-of-battle ship *Diadem*, Captain Sir Home Riggs Popham, arrived in Whitehall from Portsmouth. He had met Captain Jones, of the 29th Light Dragoons, who had landed at Portsmouth from a spell as a prisoner of war in the Dutch colony of the Cape of Good Hope. Popham was an inquisitive and imaginative fellow, and Jones appears to have passed on to him news, to the effect that the Cape was expecting to be the base for a French fleet.

This was scarcely a surprise. If a French fleet was at sea, at least one possible destination was the Indian Ocean, where there were islands under French rule, and the East Indian archipelago was under Dutch rule. Any ship or fleet heading east would wish to call at the Cape for fresh provisions, water, and for news, if it could. (British ships could not, since the Dutch were at war with Britain – instead they used St Helena.) Possession of the Cape, or at least its good harbours, would much facilitate connections with India, and would act as a forward defence for it as well. Popham, like any Royal Navy captain of the time, knew this perfectly well, and the prospect of a French fleet staging through to the Indian Ocean was not something he should keep to himself, even if Captain Jones was less excited about it.

Popham was a long-time acquaintance of the former First Lord of the Admiralty, Henry Dundas, Viscount Melville, and through him of the Prime Minister, William Pitt. Even though Melville had been driven from power in April, Popham could still use his political connections, and was able to see Pitt right away.[4] The news he brought – at least by his own account later, after Pitt was dead – galvanized the British government. Pitt consulted his Cabinet colleagues, and a decision was soon taken to send an expedition to capture the Cape. News had arrived that the West Indian islands had made good arrangements on their own behalf for self-defence against any French attacks, and the *Curieux* had arrived at Plymouth on 7 July with firm information that Villeneuve was actually on his way back to Europe.[5]

It followed that the expeditionary force which was gathered at Cork to be sent to the islands had not been required and had been reduced to only two regiments, and now it could be used elsewhere in the Atlantic. It may be, indeed, that Popham – not above pushing himself forward, even to the Prime Minister – suggested the name of the commander, Lieutenant-General Sir David Baird, for he was an old campaigning colleague of his. It is, however, quite likely that Baird's name suggested itself, partly by his being available and partly because he had experience at the Cape already. But, with Popham, this sort of assumption comes very easy.

Popham went back to his ship at Portsmouth. Baird, living at St Albans, was appointed to the command of the expedition. He immediately began a campaign to enlarge the force he was to take with him. He spoke to Captain Jones – no doubt handed on by Popham – and made some calculations. Jones apparently reported that the Dutch had about 3,000 troops at the Cape, of whom 2,000 were Europeans, 800 were Hottentots, and they had some artillery and cavalry. Baird sent Jones to London to report this to Viscount Castlereagh, the Secretary of State for War, whose responsibility it was to decide the size of Baird's expedition. Baird had then brought in General Sir David Dundas, who was the effective deputy to the Duke of York, Commander-in-Chief of the army.[6]

Already one can see a Scottish dimension to this story. Viscount Melville, as Henry Dundas, had been the political controller of Scotland for thirty years, and had been Pitt's closest colleague in the House of Commons for twenty. Even though he had recently fallen from grace in a political attack in the Commons, he was still a powerful figure in the background, and had long been as much a British imperialist as a Scotsman.[7] General David Dundas, not a relation of Melville's, but a vastly experienced military man was another Scot. Baird, as will emerge from these events, was a decided and patriotic Scot, perhaps more so than British. An Englishman might have scented a Scots conspiracy.

The Cape was not unknown to the British. As a Dutch colony it had become a useful refreshment point for ships on the long voyage to India in time of peace. The British had taken control of St Helena for that same purpose, though the Cape was more capacious and much more convenient. In 1795 the Netherlands, under the Batavian Republican regime, had become an active ally of France, and so were at war with Britain. A British expedition was sent to take the colony, which was returned to the Dutch at the peace of 1801. It took well over a year for the transfer to be accomplished, thanks to slow communication, and a degree of British reluctance. The commander of the forces at the Cape had been General Francis Dundas, Lord Melville's nephew, and he had been acting governor twice in that time while the appointed governors were absent; Baird had served as a Brigadier-General on the Staff there for a year, and so could claim to know what he was talking about when discussing how to capture the Cape.[8]

The colony was back in Dutch ownership from 1803, and the Dutch and the French were once again allies in a war against Britain. Nevertheless there were some doubts in Britain about the real need to retake the Cape. Admiral Nelson, presently chasing Villeneuve across the Atlantic, had been dismissive of its usefulness in the debate on the peace treaty in the House of Lords in 1802, calling it no more than a 'tavern on the passage' to India.[9] But with the British now firmly established in India as a territorial power – particularly after Sir Arthur Wellesley's victory over the Mahrattas at Assaye a year before – the Cape took on a greater significance. French or Dutch or Spanish ships at large on the seas could use it as a base to interrupt the rich British trade with India and China which had to pass that way, and this was not a comfortable thought for a British government which was largely dependent on customs revenues for financing its war-making capacity.

Somewhat later, in a letter to the governor general in India, Lord Castlereagh explained the government's reason for acquiring the Cape:

> … the true value of the Cape to Great Britain is its being considered and treated at all times as a post subservient to the protection and security of our Indian possessions. In our hands it must afford comfortable accommodation and facilities to our intercourse with those possessions; but its occupation is perhaps even more material as depriving the enemy of the best immediate position between Europe and India for assembling and preparing a large European armament for service in the East Indies, as well as of a more advantageous station for watching and intercepting our outward and homeward bound trade.[10]

In mid-July *The Times* reported news from the Cape, presumably much the same news which Jones had given to Popham a month or more earlier. A French corvette had called at Cape Town, and orders had then gone out that supplies of fresh food were to be sold at a fixed price to the colony's government.[11] It was assumed that this was in preparation for the arrival of a large naval force from Europe, probably French, and perhaps transporting a substantial military force. The British government's Indian nerve was instantly sensitized. To have the Cape in the hands of a hostile French force was a very different proposition from the Cape in the feeble hands of the Dutch, and the prospect of a French fleet based there was a matter demanding a British response; Popham's information was thus confirmed, and Baird's expedition was even more urgent.

The news of a French intention to reinforce the Cape added grist to Baird's mill. He could speak from knowledge of the difficulties of landing if Cape Town was hostile, and Baird at least would not minimize the problem. He had already pointed out that the Dutch had almost 3,000 troops there, and now he added in 1,500 French soldiers. These were the troops which were supposed to be on board the ships of the French squadron under Allemand which had come out of Rochfort. It was now known that Villeneuve had not headed east; where Allemand had gone was not known; his escape had been thought to be part of the grand invasion plan, but now his squadron was assumed to be the one intended for the Cape. These assumptions were almost all wrong, but at the time they looked likely.

Baird was thus able to make his case that the Cape would have at least 4,500 capable of defending it. He therefore required his attacking force to be larger than that, bearing in mind the likelihood of casualties on the voyage, or in landing through heavy surf, and the probably of fortifications having been constructed in preparation for an attack. He suggested a total force of 5,500 men, plus 500 recruits. He also had strong views of the composition of the force: he wanted riflemen and cavalry to be included, neither of which had been regarded as essential for an expedition to the West Indies. And he wanted a commission for himself as governor.[12]

Castlereagh was not totally convinced by Baird's calculations, but he juggled the figures and the regiments about, and came up with a scheme which was acceptable to Baird and dealt with several other matters at the same time. The regiments which Sir Eyre Coote had been left with, after his original force had been scaled down, could now be included, since they could then be sent on to the West Indies after being used at the Cape. One or two regiments intended for India could also be used, for they could first help at the Cape and then go on eastwards. A small cavalry detachment was available, and Baird could have the extra gunners and extra ammunition for the guns he asked for, since supplies would be difficult to come by at the Cape. Castlereagh disputed Baird's figures for the Dutch forces – and in this he was quite correct – but he also gave him the force he wanted.

The final decision to send the expedition was taken on 24 July at a Cabinet meeting. Baird was then informed that he would have a total force of over 6,600 men.[13] The Admiralty had already begun gathering ships for the escort. Popham, suitably enough, was to be in command, and was then to take command of the naval forces to be stationed at the Cape as the local commander-in-chief. A convoy of East India ships could be included, which added armed weight, and made the provision of a separate convoy escort for the Indiamen unnecessary. A total of four line-of-battle ships were provided, with two frigates and some smaller vessels. Popham's orders included how he was to distribute the ships after the Cape had been taken.[14]

Castlereagh also dealt with the most specifically colonial aspects of the expedition. Baird did not get his wish to be appointed as governor, but he was given the commission as lieutenant-governor, and it was clearly intended that he would be replaced as soon as news arrived that the military matters at the Cape had been dealt with. He was also made local commander-in-chief, so combining the two supreme authorities in the colony for the initial conquest, though this was quite normal. In this regard also, Castlereagh sent with him two officers with even more extensive experience of the Cape and Baird himself: Major Donald Campbell of the 40th Foot, and Captain Duncan Stewart of the 90th, both of whom were experts in the command of Hottentot troops (and both men, note, were Scots). One of the aims of the conquest was to recruit local troops so that the colony should begin to provide in part for its own defence, and Baird was told by the Commander-in-Chief, the Duke of York, to recruit as many of the Dutch soldiers at the Cape as he could into the 60th Foot, and also to form a regiment of Hottentots for local defence.[15]

Baird had been a soldier for over forty years, since he enlisted as an ensign at 15. He had spent much of his career in the east, and in particular he had three times been involved in the wars against Mysore in southern India, an experience which included surviving nearly four years as a prisoner as a captain, and having the eventual satisfaction of supervising the capture of that city as a major-general. He had served at the Cape, and in Egypt, where he commanded an expedition from India to attack the French from the south, and where the naval part of the expedition was commanded by Popham. Baird had even been considered a candidate for the command-in-chief in India, a post in the end given to Sir Arthur Wellesley; as a result he had always bore a grudge against Wellesley who was favoured by his brother the Marquess Wellesley, the governor of Bengal, and by other governors. He was a tough soldier, well over 6ft tall, but not a particularly intelligent one. He would never have won the Assaye campaign, for instance, and his experience in the command of large forces in the field was very limited. His frantic efforts to increase the size of the force for the Cape expedition may well be a sign of his insecurity in overall command. It had rarely emerged in his career so far, but he was also a patriotic Scot, and seemed to have harboured a certain resentment at the English establishment, a feeling which predated his failure to gain the Indian command, but which no doubt re-affirmed it.[16]

Baird was in Dublin by 30 July, and at Cork three days later. He said he expected to sail on 4 or 5 August, and made a great to-do about gathering supplies and men, complaining that he had not all the troops he had been allotted.[17] But his expedition inevitably became mixed up with the great naval campaigns going on in the seas about Spain, and he was alternately encouraged and forbidden to sail. He protested that he was ready, but he had no naval escort, and several of his transport ships were still missing, so we may presume that a good deal of this was bluster.[18] The escort arrived on 27 August, and by then both Baird and Popham had permission to leave, though it was not until 1 September that all the ships got out of the harbour.[19]

Baird had spent the month's delay in investigating his command, replacing rotten provisions with good, gathering up extra stores, and worrying about his numbers. He complained that one regiment was 100 men short, and that he had received only 200 recruits rather than the 572 he had been promised. He decided that he was 900 men short of the number he had been promised, and pointed out that another regiment, the 8th, was close by.[20] This received no answer, not surprisingly.

What he did have was a substantial force of over 6,000 men. In terms of European warfare this was a tiny army, less than Napoleon would have considered a decent casualty list for a small battle, but in terms of warfare in the rest of the world, Baird commanded a major force. Battles in India had been won by smaller forces, and fewer men had surrendered at Yorktown to lose an American empire. He had seven infantry battalions, three English, the 24th, 38th, 59th, one Irish, the 83rd, and three Scottish, the 71st (Baird's own old regiment), the 72nd, and the 93rd, plus a small cavalry force, a detachment of the 20th Light Dragoons, and a detachment of Royal Artillery and some Royal Engineers.

Most of the men had already been in the transports for several weeks, even months. Neither the original destination of the West Indies nor the change to the Cape had been announced to them. The 59th Foot was one of the regiments destined for India in the end, but could only be kept at the Cape briefly, and Baird was instructed to return the artillery, cavalry, and the engineers to Britain when the Cape was secured. The rest was to become his command at the Cape when he had conquered it and so forming the garrison. Similarly Popham's fleet was mainly to be kept on that station: the 74-gun line-of-battle ship *Belliqueux* was to go on to India with the 59th, and *Raisonable* (74) was supposed to escort the next India convoy home; after which Popham would command a small fleet of eight or nine warships. The earlier suggestion that Sir Eyre Coote's former regiments should be sent to the West Indies seems to have been dropped. Failure was also contemplated: in the event of being repelled Baird was to send the 38th Foot on to India with the 59th, and all the rest were to retire on St Helena. But in the event of success Baird was going to command a garrison of a substantial size.

A cover story had been given out that the fleet was destined for the Mediterranean. At Cork, Major John Graham of the 93rd Foot had written to his brother Robert at Fintry in Perthshire that he did not know where they were going, but that it was not to be the West Indies. That was on the 31st July; four days later he thought they were going to Spain. Captain

Robert Campbell of the 71st wrote to his father Archibald at Inverary that he did not know where they were going either, but he guessed it to be the Cape from the fact that several of the officers on the Staff had experience there.[21]

Among the cavalry, the opinions were just as various. Major Richard Dulane guessed it was to be either the Mediterranean or the Cape, and he inclined to the Cape only because they were setting out from Ireland, a flimsy basis for his guess; Sergeant Norbert Landsheit, a German mercenary serving in the Dragoons, had no idea, and commented in his memoirs that 'few took the trouble to enquire'.[22] This may be taken as representative of the attitude of the rank-and-file, whether the soldiers did not ask because they knew they would not be told, or simply did not care where they were sent, we cannot tell. On the *Diadem*, Royal Marine Captain Alexander Gillespie at first thought they were going to Constantinople on a diplomatic mission, but when Baird's horses were loaded, at Cork, he decided that they would be fighting, which apparently ruled out Turkey. His colleague Royal Marine Lieutenant Robert Fernyhough guessed it was to be Gibraltar.[23] In all of this speculation the Cape was no more prominent as a guess than anywhere else, though the consensus of opinion was probably the Mediterranean. And so any French spy in Cork would have gathered.

Probably no one on board any of the ships knew it, but the convoy was under constant threat all the time between sailing from Cork on 1 September and the rendezvous at Madeira. Commodore Allemand had called at Vigo in northwest Spain for supplies and had left there on 13 August. He moved into the northern part of the Bay of Biscay and stayed there until 6 September, by which time Popham's convoy was due south of Fastnet, moving fairly slowly. The forces moved south on converging courses, but Allemand, commanding warships only, moved faster. By 10 September he was off Lisbon, while Popham was delayed by contrary winds for several days northwest of Corunna. Allemand waited for several days off Cape St Vincent, and then on 14 September he set off for the English Channel, taking a roundabout route northwest from the Cape to get out into the Atlantic to avoid the heavy concentration of Royal Navy power off Brest. On that day Popham's convoy was off Vigo, and the two forces were again on converging courses. They crossed each other's courses on the 16 September, without sighting each other. Neither knew of the other's presence.[24] It is not only in retrospect that there was the possibility of a clash.

The assumptions and speculations as to the convoy's destination continued on the southward voyage, but as it sailed further and further south, however, most guesses had to be discarded. By the time the whole fleet gathered at

Funchal in Madeira and began replenishing with water and fresh food, and the officers restocked their wine lockers, both the West Indies and the Mediterranean were clearly no longer possible. Colonel Robert Wilson of the 20th Light Dragoons, Major Dulane's and Sergeant Landsheit's commanding officer, had at first thought that Gibraltar was the destination, but now he noted in his diary that he had learned that the convoy would next sail on to the Cape Verde Islands, and so the destination must be either the Cape or South America. On the whole he thought South America the more likely since he had been told by General Yorke of the artillery that he was adapting his gun carriages so that they could be hauled by bullocks,[25] though why he made the connection was hardly clear. Major Graham did not even guess any more.[26] That is, no one had any hard information yet; and if anyone would know, these officers would.

The warships in Popham's fleet were the two 64s, *Diadem* and *Belliqueux*, *Diomede* (50), and two frigates, *Narcissus* and *Leda*, but more ships were waiting to join at Funchal. *Raisonable* had been there a month, occupied in repairing the damage sustained in the battle with Villeneuve's fleet on 22 July. *Leda* had been sent on ahead by Popham to arrange for the reprovisioning, and was also waiting. Two more ships, the sloop *L'Espoir* and the gun brig *Encounter*, had arrived, and two days later the gun brig *Protector* joined.[27] It may have been this increase in the fleet which gave Popham the idea for the next move in his personal campaign, but it is more likely that he had planned it all along.

Popham was an unusual naval officer.[28] He had risen to lieutenant during the American War, but in the time of peace and unemployment which followed he had spent six years as a private trader, sailing to India out of Ostend. When he returned to England in 1793 his ship and cargo had been confiscated on suspicion of smuggling, for by that time there was another war on. He then simultaneously returned to his naval career as a lieutenant and began a long legal battle for restitution. He was employed in the Flanders campaign in 1794 and 1795, organizing transport along the rivers and canals, and he had done well enough in this difficult task for the Duke of York to exert his influence to get him promoted to post-captain by late 1795.

In all this several notable personal traits had emerged. He was famous as a navigator and as a surveyor, having been employed in surveys of the Kaffraria coast of South Africa, of Penang Island, and of the mouths of the Ganges. He was notoriously avaricious, as his trading ventures show, a trait which stuck with him all his life – though this was hardly unusual among naval officers, who were always greedy for prize money. He was unorthodox and much more adaptable than most naval officers, as his career as a merchant captain showed. He had gained valuable experience in co-operation with the army in combined operations in Flanders and later. In the ten years of his career since Flanders he had been employed in the Channel, on a diplomatic mission to St Petersburg – he had entertained Tsar Paul on his flagship, who requited this treat by knighting him – in the Helder campaign, in the Copenhagen fight in 1801, and in the Red Sea expedition later in that year, where he had been Baird's colleague, and had commanded the naval forces when the original commander died.[29] He was in Indian waters until 1804, and returned to England in that year, when he was once again involved in operations in the Channel. He had devised a greatly improved method of naval signalling and this was accepted by the Admiralty. In 1805 his campaign for restitution dating from 1793 was finally successful, and he was awarded a total of £16,000.

In all this he had made enemies within the service. When he returned to England in 1804 he had been accused of spending too lavishly on repairs to his ship, the *Romney* (74). It was only when Pitt returned to power, and had replaced Lord St Vincent at the Admiralty with Lord Melville, that the charge was dropped – for it had been a political job all through. He was accused in a privately written note which he probably never saw, of never having fought a battle or in a battle, yet he had gained command of Baird's expedition. Since this was an accusation by a clerk at the Admiralty, Benjamin Tucker, an adherent of St Vincent, it does not bear much weight.[30] But it is a fact that he never did fight a battle, and it is clear from his career that he was much more likely to use cunning to gain a victory than gunpowder.

He depended for his promotion and his appointments, therefore, not so much on battle-glory as on influence – the Duke of York, Lord Melville, William Pitt – but he was also technically a highly accomplished and very inventive sailing captain. Apart from the signal book he had devised, he also bombarded his acquaintances with ideas. A whole file of these is in the Melville Papers in the National Library of Scotland.[31] He was also not above exaggeration and even assuming a status to which he was not entitled; his knighthood from Tsar Paul was not recognized in Britain, but he always insisted on being addressed as if it was.

This was the man whom the Admiralty had put in command of this joint expedition, a project which involved great secrecy, careful preparation, speed of execution, and detailed co-operation with the Army. His experience and abilities were clearly being put to good use. But he was also a man with his own ambitions. As the fleet sailed from Funchal he showed this. Outside the harbour he hoisted a broad pendant, signifying that he was taking command of the fleet as a commodore. He had no right to do this. He clearly knew it, and so he carefully did not report it until 10 October, in a letter which he knew would not reach the Admiralty for months, since he had no way of sending it off. (It actually arrived on 22 February the next year.)[32] Then, as if to implicate his naval colleagues in his wrongdoing, he set about reshuffling the ship commands, for, as a commodore, he was entitled to have a captain under him in *Diadem*. The captains clearly knew what he was doing, for they greeted hoisting of the new pendant with a salute of eleven guns.[33] And in his exchanging of captains he carefully avoided involving the *Belliqueux*, which he had been ordered to send on to India from the Cape; only the ships and men he was to keep under his command after the Cape was conquered were involved in the transfers and promotions.

Baird was still bothered that he did not have enough men for the task he had been set. He had it fixed in his mind that he would face an armed force of 5,000 men – even more than he had calculated for Castlereagh. Popham was equal to the occasion. Already he had made Lieutenant Fernyhough of the Marines on *Diadem* adjutant of a 'sea-battalion' composed of all the Marines in the fleet, and he had obviously promised Baird that he could use these men as part of the landing force.[34] Baird had complained in a letter to the War Office from Funchal that the 8th Foot had not joined him, though there is no indication that this had ever been promised, except in his own mind.[35] But the Marines of the fleet numbered nearly 1,000 men, the equivalent of the 8th Foot he never had. Later Popham ordered that 100 seamen from each of the ships of the line, and smaller numbers from the smaller ships, should be armed and drilled as a half-battalion, capable of fighting as foot soldiers on land. The sailors made the uniforms for these men, called 'Blues', and the logs of the ships are full of references to the men drilling with small arms and pikes.[36] This provided another 400 men for Baird's landing party.

The fleet had to stop at San Salvador in Brazil for water, for the voyage was slow, and the large numbers of men consumed the water quickly. After that most of those who were interested assumed that their destination was the Cape. Since they were not going to stop anywhere else, there was no real attempt to keep the destination secret any more, and Colonel Wilson found out from a visit to Popham's cabin, as he gleefully recorded in his diary.[37] Popham sent the frigate *Narcissus*, Captain Ross Donnelly, on ahead to St Helena, both to gather the latest information about the condition of the Cape's defences – Baird sent Captain Snell of his staff with Donnelly for the same purpose – and then to go on to reconnoitre the Cape itself. Donnelly and Snell could also alert Governor Patten of St Helena to the approach of the expedition, for the island was the expedition's fall-back position, and Patten had to be warned that he might suddenly be overwhelmed by the arrival of the defeated remnants of a fleet and an army.[38]

This was a long, slow voyage, inevitably so with the large number of ships – over 100 when the fleet left Funchal – all of which had to sail at the speed of the slowest ship. The navigational problems were considerable. Two ships were lost when they ran into the Roccas, a group of low sandy islets off the northeast coast of Brazil. One was an Indiaman, the *Britannia*, the other a naval transport carrying some of the 20th Light Dragoons. Only two men were lost, General Yorke of the artillery and an artilleryman who was generally assumed to have been drunk.[39] Finding the Cape of Good Hope was just as difficult as avoiding such hazards, and it was important that the arrival should be accurate. A fleet arriving on the coast north of the Cape would then have a tedious southward passage of coastal navigation against wind and current, not to mention the complete loss of surprise, though this was not a condition which was counted on. Arriving too far south meant missing the Cape altogether and perhaps being driven eastwards into the Indian Ocean by the great world-circulating winds.

The accepted practice was to head south as far as the latitude of the Cape and then sail due east. The fleet was in the hands of one of the master navigators of the time, as was well recognized – it was one of the reasons for Popham's appointment – and this is what he did. Landfall was made at Martin Vas Island, a thousand miles off the coast of Brazil, and at Tristan Da Cunha in the middle of the South Atlantic, which were useful checks on the fleet's position, and then for two weeks the fleet headed due east.

In this time the officers digested the plan for the landing which Baird had issued on 6 December.[40] Baird now knew he would get no more troops, beyond those sailors who were being daily exercised at small arms on most of the warships. As a basis for the plan, he had his own knowledge of the Cape from his previous duty there, he had advice from members of the staff, such as Major Campbell and Captain Stewart, who also had experience of the place. He also had an account, unsigned and undated, which survives among his papers, which discussed the best approaches to the Cape, the best landing places, the problem of the surf, and the best place to anchor.[41] It is clearly a seaman's thoughts, probably Popham's, who had his own experiences of this land from his time surveying the Kaffrarian coast, and in fact Baird's plan followed the suggestions in this paper quite closely.

One regiment, the 24th, under Lieutenant–Colonel William Kelly, was to be loaded into the frigate *Leda* and sent towards Camp's Bay, a possible landing place south of Cape Town, but this was only intended as a demonstration in order to distract and divide the defenders. The real landing was to take place further north at one of the beaches on the north of Table Bay, well away from Cape Town, so as to give the troops time to get ashore and form up without enemy interference. The landing would be a slow process, using ships' boats, and would take time to complete. Each commanding officer was told the arrangements, and some officers were given particular instructions. Major Graham was given command of a light brigade, composed of the light companies of all the regiments brigaded together, and was to push forward in advance of the main body to form a picquet line to delay any attack. Colonel Wilson, whose 200 or so dragoons had only seventy-four horses between them, was to make his first priority the seizing of all the horses and draught cattle in the area. The artillery, commanded now by Major Spicer after the death of General Yorke, had to be got ashore in case the enemy put in a formal attack, or in case Cape Town had to be besieged. An elaborate set of instructions for marching and camping was drawn up and issued. And so on, covering all the details for an army on the march in hostile country.[42] It was a good, detailed, careful, and well thought out plan. It was not, of course, put into effect.

Chapter Two

The Cape – Conquest

The expedition arrived off the Cape on 4 January 1806, the men fully instructed in what they were to do. The day before the brig *L'Espoir* had scouted Table Bay and had captured a Portuguese brig, whose captain proved to be both talkative and informative.[1] But there was also the problem of the surf, which might prevent the small boats they would have to use for the landing from approaching the shore. At dawn on 5 January the soldiers of the light companies were sent in towards the shore in boats, while other troops waited to follow up any success. The surf was too powerful. The boats were recalled, and Baird had to recast his plans.[2]

The great problem was that he had now tipped his hand, and the Dutch had a good idea of where the landing would take place; he would therefore in all probability be opposed, and an opposed landing is one of the more difficult of military operations. It was, therefore, necessary to put part of the landing force ashore somewhere else, which could at least distract the Dutch, and maybe, if it could get to the landing place in time, even drive them off.

The new plan was for Colonel Wilson's 20th Light Dragoons and the 38th Foot to sail in their transports with *Diomede* and *L'Espoir* to Saldanha Bay, sixty miles to the north, where a landing would not be impeded, and where the surf was known to be partly blocked by the sheltering point which formed the bay. Captain Smyth of the Engineers, who knew the place from his time in the colony during the previous British occupation, would go first in *L'Espoir* to seize the person of the postmaster, to prevent any warning being given, and to secure as many cattle as possible. Then the main force would land and march south. Baird put the idea to his two brigadiers. Ferguson disliked it, and said so; Beresford then approved, and so Beresford got the command. The plan was made quickly and the troops were transferred to the ships during the 6th. *Diomede* set off with *L'Espoir*. The detachment would be ashore by the next day, assuming all was well. *L'Espoir* would return with the news.[3]

As it happened, on the morning of the 6th the surf in Table Bay was much calmer, so Baird decided to go ahead with the original landing without waiting for Beresford's detachment to seize the landing place from the north. The light battalion under Major Graham would lead. A better landing place had been located at Losperd's Bay, somewhat north of the original choice. The commander of the 59th Foot, Lieutenant Colonel John Laing Weir, described the situation in a letter to his friend Lieutenant Colonel Murray, the Deputy Quartermaster-General at Dublin:

> Until the following morning when the boats with the 1st Brigade were actually assembled opposite to the beach I believe no idea was entertained but that we could land at any point we chose from Craigstown to Losperd's Bay; yet along the whole of this shore that is just such a surf as runs to windward of Barbados. It is really astonishing that men who have lived for years at the Cape should be grossly ignorant of this and many other particulars of the country. It was only by means of some seaweed which has the effect of oil in preventing the water from breaking that we were able to land at last.[4]

Colonel Weir was, of course, wrong, for the surf had been known to be a problem from the very start, and Baird had mentioned it before he left England, indeed he had mentioned Losperd's Bay specifically because the land 'there forms a point to the southward to defend it from the natural surge and roll of the sea', and this is specifically said to have been information from officers and men who had served at the Cape.[5] Nor does Weir mention several other factors which assisted in the landing, for example that boats from the naval ships had buoyed the boat channel in advance. Captain Gillespie of the Royal Marines did not see the seaweed in so benign a light: he claimed that 'a dense tangle of seaweed … totally impeded the advance of our boats', but then he was landing later, when the skirmishers had been driven off and he could attend to relatively minor inconveniences.[6]

All this, of course, had warned the Dutch quite clearly where the landing would take place, and the day's delay had given more of their mounted infantry time to reach the place, though not yet the artillery, which set out later and had a much more difficult journey.[7] Graham's light battalion landed first, covered by *Leda* and *Diadem* and, closer in, by *Protector* and *Encounter*, whose gunners could reach the shore with their fire. One boat, carrying thirty-six men of the 93rd, struck unsuspected rocks and foundered with the loss of all the men. The rest came under fire from the Dutch light infantry on shore and from some Dutch light cavalry as they reached the shore, but the Dutch fire was neutralized by the heavier fire from the ships, which may not have been very accurate, but was distracting and frightening.

Major Graham saw the men of the 71st ashore first:

> About 100 yagers [light cavalry] threw themselves into the bushes and kept popping away until the 71st Lt Coy landed; they very soon made them scamper from the first ridge of sand hills to the second. I was in a boat by myself and so contrived to get some of our Lt Coy on shore, a part of the 72nd landing at the same time; on we went and as an attempt was made to surround the enemy's sharp-shooters, they immediately ran to the third range of hills. On arriving ... we were a good deal disappointed to find that they were mostly mounted riflemen and were galloping off.[8]

The Dutch interception force was thus driven off by the light battalion as planned and intended. There were some losses, particularly among the British officers, and no less than three colonels were wounded. Behind the screen thus set up, the rest of the troops were got ashore during the day, together with several pieces of artillery.[9] All this took until nightfall, and the soldiers did not have time to investigate their surroundings. Some, of course, did manage to locate the three farms in the area, break in, and loot them. One of the farmers, John Jacob Mostert, later claimed that they had caused damage valued at 685 *rixdollars*, and complained of the destruction of the furniture, the consumption of his provisions, and that his goods and utensils had been stolen.[10] It certainly sounds like the behaviour of British soldiers in enemy country. General Weir's men had no supply of water that night, though the morning showed that there was a supply just over a nearby hill.[11]

The swift Dutch response to the landing was a clear sign that the British arrival and invasion were not really a surprise. In one sense the British attack had been expected ever since the arrival of the news of the renewed war in Europe between Britain and France, with the Batavian Republic dragged in as well. The word of this had reached Cape Town in September 1803, and the more time which passed without an actual invasion the more likely it was. So, in a long-term strategic sense, the whole Cape was expecting to be attacked at almost any time. In the short term as well, the arrival of Popham's fleet was known to be imminent. The frigate *Narcissus*, sent ahead from the Cape Verde Islands, by way of St Helena, arrived in Table Bay a fortnight before the main fleet. Captain Donnelly had disguised his ship as a merchantman, and had sailed right into Table Bay as far as Robben Island, so as to count the ships at anchor there – a dozen, none of them large warships. He then cruised nearby until on Christmas Day a ship came out, hoisted French colours, and made a private signal. No doubt *Narcissus'* continued presence had been noted, and suspicions aroused. If so, they were quite correct. Donnelly chased the French ship, a privateer called *Napoleon*, and drove the ship onto the rocks of the Cape next morning, and then rescued the crew. Next, a Dutch sloop came out of Table Bay heading round for Simons Bay, and it was captured, together with its cargo of naval stores. It proved to be captained by another Frenchman, who had previously been the captain of the *Atalante* frigate, which had been sunken earlier.[12]

All of this grated steadily on the nerves of the Dutch authorities at the Cape and heightened expectations. Then an American vessel arrived with the news that it had passed through a great fleet in the Atlantic, which was heading south. And on 28 December another ship came in from Madeira and reported that Popham's fleet had been seen there back in October.[13] All these details were quite enough to alert the Dutch government to its danger. The presence of the *Narcissus* – clearly revealed to be a British warship by its conduct – only emphasized that the reported fleet was probably headed for the Cape, and so would arrive soon.

Beyond all this, the government of the colony had been back in Dutch hands for less than three years, and it was a very different government from that which had surrendered to the British back in 1796. That had been a Company government, for the colony was originally established as a refreshment station by the Dutch East India Company, for the use of its ships on the way to India and the East Indies. The new Dutch government was of revolutionary origin, still somewhat unsure of itself at the time, not surprisingly, given the continued political turbulence and repeated changes in regime at home. The colonial regime was also profoundly pessimistic about its chances of survival.[14]

Preparations had nevertheless been made to meet the expected attack. As soon as news arrived of the outbreak of the new war, a militia, comprising one in six of all able-bodied men, was established, and the new government showed its determination by shooting the first three men to desert. Then after a year, the liability to serve was extended to all men between the ages of 16 and 35, and an artillery battalion was added. This militia was intended to supplement the power of the regular garrison, which consisted of the 22nd Regiment of the Line, the Regiment of Waldeck (a mercenary force – both of these being infantry forces – a Malay artillery company, and a Hottentot light infantry battalion. A militia battalion of Jagers, light cavalry, was also established – these were the men Major Graham encountered at the landing. The problem was, of course, that the militia was still essentially untrained, and the approaching army was composed of professionals. Ensign Petrus Borcherds, for example, had virtually no training, and spent most of his time as secretary to the militia officers.[15]

The governor who was organizing all this was Lieutenant General Jan Willem Janssens, an old revolutionary, whose rise was due as much to his consistently pro-French and revolutionary politics as to his ability which, to be sure, was considerable.[16] He had been told, in June 1805, by the Pensionary Schimmelpeninck, writing from the Netherlands, that it was necessary to hold onto the Cape in order to impress the enemy, and to make sure that 'the Great Napoleon', as he called him, looked with favour on the Pensionary's government; the Cape was also a first line of defence for all the other Dutch colonies in the east.[17] It was hardly an inspiring exhortation. Reading between the lines, the Dutch clearly expected to lose the Cape, and soon, and Janssens could expect no help from home.

Nevertheless Janssens made plans with the aim of prolonging Cape resistance. The professional military force he commanded was now augmented by the burgher militia, but he had to assume that this force would be outnumbered and outfought by the British force. So he developed a strategy which, like that of Tsar Alexander in Russia later, would use the great open spaces of the interior of the colony under his control as a weapon. Janssens intended to retreat into the interior and fight on.[18]

This strategy made excellent sense, if it could be carried out, but it had to be properly prepared, and he needed the active support of the people. It meant that food stocks and military supplies had to be prepared in the interior for the army to use when it retreated inland, and this was the first difficulty. The harvest of 1803–1804 in the Cape had been poor, and that of 1804–1805 was worse.[19] British command of the seas had meant that few ships had called at Cape Town recently, and so Janssens could not import supplies, while the periodic visits of a few French warships had removed any surplus which did accumulate. Yet, given a firm popular resolve to fight on, there was certainly food enough in the interior, grain produced in the neighbourhood of Cape Town, game on the veldt, cattle on the farms. The main difficulty Janssens faced was the absence of any serious popular support for his policy, and for his regime.

The previous British occupation had not been at all onerous in social or political terms, and had not provoked much local opposition, while in economic terms it had been the cause of considerable prosperity. While the Royal Navy controlled the seas, it was clearly better, in economic terms, for such a relatively isolated station to be within the British Empire than to be at war with it. British troops, like all soldiers, might well be boisterous or even violent, coarse-mouthed, drunken, unwashed, but they had money in their pockets, and the commissary bought and paid for locally grown supplies. And in British hands, the harbour of Cape Town became open to all vessels, providing another market, and a source of goods. In 1803–1806, without the British military market, with its bad harvests and its withered trade, the Cape was fading away into economic self-sufficiency, to the level of the Iron Age tribes of the interior. The memory of the former prosperity provided by the presence of a British garrison contrasted strongly with the present misery.[20]

There were a number of British people, merchants mainly, still in the colony as a reminder of that earlier, recent, prosperity. They were more or less interned when news of the war came, usually being kept away from the coast, but the government judged that anything more rigorous than open arrest would be unpopular.[21] The property of the East India Company (the English one) and of the British government was, of course, confiscated, and the food stocks of the Agent Victualler were used to supply French warships, but this scarcely compensated for the lack of trade.[22]

The governor was not concerned only with the prospects of invasion. He had to deal with a colony which contained a great variety of peoples, and this would hamper his defence. In the immediate hinterland of Cape Town was a slave-owning society of white residents, merchants and farmers – the revolutionary ideals of the Batavian republican government had not extended as far as the liberation of those slaves. Further inland there were Dutch farmers, already widely known as Boers, who ran herds of cattle on the open veldt, as did the Hottentot pastoralists. Beyond them were groups of Bushman hunters. Further east, in the better-watered lands, there were various black tribes and kingdoms, who were farmers. All these groups were hostile to one another.[23] The only group which was important in Janssens' plan of resistance in the interior was the Boers, but he could not wholly ignore the others.

The Boer society which had developed in the lands east of the Hottentots Hollands Mountains was an odd mixture of nomadic and sedentary life. It was based mainly on rearing cattle, since the rainfall in most areas was thought to be too little and too unreliable for growing crops. Each farm, therefore, needed space, and each farm was a minor village, a group of buildings in the centre of an area of veldt, usually at a water source. This society both required plenty of space to operate in and spread itself very thinly, geographically speaking. The farmers, *boer* in Dutch, needed certain supplies from Cape Town: guns, powder and shot, and a few luxuries; otherwise their lives were little different from those of the black farmers with whom they came into increasingly frequent contact as they moved steadily further east.[24]

This contact was alternately hostile and indifferent, but the Blacks had recently generally had the best of it. They used the land better – though they also lived in the wetter area – mixing cattle herding with cultivation in the river valleys, and they were more self-sufficient, as a result.[25] By 1806 the conflict between Boers and Blacks had seen the frontier between them moving westwards. In particular the Blacks had successfully occupied an area called the Zuurveld, between the Sundays River and the Great Fish River. This had then become the base for the further expansion of black farmers into the Langkloof, a region of hills and valleys lying parallel to the southern coast, west of the Sundays River, though there were yet few of them there. But, as the black population density in the Zuurveld increased, so did the sophistication of their political order, and the emergence of a powerful Xhosa ruler, Ndlambe, in the Zuurveld both increased the power of the Blacks there, by providing them with a coherent political organization, and drove out those groups who had quarrelled with him. These inimical groups inevitably moved into the apparently near-empty lands of the whites. Perhaps a quarter of the white farmers along the frontier had been displaced during the last period of open conflict, which had ended in 1802.[26]

Janssens, who had made a tour of the interior, wished to push the Blacks, mainly Xhosa, out of their conquests, but he did not have the military power to attempt it, since the prospect of an invasion from the sea meant he had to keep what soldiers he had in or near Cape Town. So he concentrated on minimizing conflict. Gradually the people of the area calmed down, though this meant implicitly recognizing Xhosa occupation of the Zuurveld, which annoyed the Boers of the frontier area. Their concentration on their own narrow concerns sapped the support Janssens might have expected from them in the event of a British attack, particularly when his plans called for a retreat to the interior – into their area – and the waging of a long war.

The last war in the interior had been notable for the emergence of an alliance between the Xhosa and the Hottentots, not groups who were usually friendly with each other. Janssens had successfully eased that alliance apart, but the grievances of the Hottentots, related mainly to their treatment, or rather ill-treatment, by the Boers, were not removed.[27] In fact, one man, a missionary called J. W. van der Kemp, who had established a mission at Bethelsdorp west of the Sundays River, near to the newly established *drostdy*, or government centre, at Uitenhage, had vociferously taken the part of the Hottentots to such effect that the Boers of the area complained to Janssens about him. Janssens had first restricted his mission activities and had then removed him from his mission at Bethelsdorp to Cape Town. Van der Kemp's position was made the more awkward in that he, though Dutch, was supported by the London Missionary Society. Van der Kemp had been living in Cape Town since April 1805, and by the time the British fleet appeared he had decided to leave.[28]

Janssens had a force of about eighty soldiers at Fort Frederick on the coast at Algoa Bay, close to Uitenhage and to van der Kemp's Bethelsdorp, just west of the Xhosa-occupied Zuurveld, but he had no troops between there and the Cape Town area, and none in the northern frontier areas where raid and counter-raid between cattle-owning Boers and the hunting Bushmen were constant, if on a small scale. Again, the advantage, since the successes of the Xhosa-Hottentot alliance in the last war, tended to be with the Bushmen and the Hottentots. The only thing Janssens had been able to do was establish the new *drostdy* at Uitenhage in 1804, to go along with the other one on the frontier at Graaff Reinet in the north. This did provide a sketchy governing system – like Ndlambe in the Zuurveld – but without a fairly serious military presence administration was generally ineffective. For lack of resources and time, the Boers' cries for help to the government in Cape Town were largely ignored.[29]

Thus Janssens' government was scarcely popular on the frontier. Yet these were the people on whom he would have to rely for supplies if his strategy for combatting the British invasion by a withdrawal into the interior was to work. He would have to leave Cape Town and its people to the tender mercies of the British. Being a good revolutionary, he would be able to do that without too many qualms, even to the extent of regarding them as *bouches inutiles*, and removing all their economic resources – meaning their food and money – from them. Before this, however, the first necessity was to show fight, that is, to combat the British at their chosen landing place. This was also, of course, the easiest place to stop them. Supposing they did get ashore, the second necessity was to fight them as soon as possible. Unless the professional Dutch forces made a serious attempt to stop the invasion, the governor could not expect much support from the rest of his people. So Baird was perfectly correct in preparing his men for an early battle.

Janssens in Cape Town was warned on 4 January that the fleet was approaching, and when the lookouts on Table Mountain could see the ships they fired signal guns and put up all their flags. The militia was mustered. Next day, the invasion fleet anchored, and the militia cavalry arrived in Cape Town from the surrounding country. In the town itself Janssens had the Regiment of Waldeck, the 22nd Regiment of the Line, the Hottentot infantry battalion, a battalion of Jagers, and one of artillery, a squadron of light dragoons and three other small artillery units, all of them under strength, a total of less than 1,500 officers and men. To these were added the French sailors who had survived the wreck of the frigate *Atalante* and the sinking of the privateer *Napoleon*, who were formed into a disciplined body of 240 men, commanded by Colonel Gaudin Beauchene. The burgher militia brought the total of men under arms and present up to about 2,000, with sixteen guns. There were some other burgher cavalry detachments at Wynberg and Stellenbosch as well, but no more than a company at each place. There were no more troops Janssens could call up.[30]

He now had to predict where the landing would be attempted. Baird sent *Leda* with the 54th Foot towards Camp's Bay, south of the Town, as a decoy, and the ship's company had an enjoyable time firing guns, lighting flares, and making false signals.[31] Janssens was not deceived – though some of the guns in the Cape Town batteries banged away at *Leda*. Neither side seems to have hit anything. As early as 5 January, when the British fleet anchored, Janssens sent a detachment of Hottentot infantry north to the Blaauwberg Hills, and followed it up with the Malay artillery.[32]

The delay in the landing did mean that Janssens had time to get his light troops to the landing place, but they were not strong enough to have any real effect. The men retreated southwards. Janssens, meanwhile, with the main Dutch force, got out from Cape Town in the afternoon of 7 January and the army camped for that night at Riet Vlei, over halfway to the landing place. He marched on again at 3.00 am on the morning of 8 January. His one hope, now that the landing place was known, was to catch the British force still in a state of confusion. The advanced force retired to rejoin as the main force advanced, but at dawn Janssens saw that he was too late. The British had occupied the Blaauwberg Hills the previous day, and were now advancing towards him.

The British had, in fact, had a full day (7 January) to get ashore and organize themselves. But they knew that a battle was close. Private Balfour

Kennach of the 71st remembered that there was 'very little hardship to the soldier', but he also recalled pre-battle nerves:

> On the evening before the battle we were seated in small parties talking about the work of tomorrow, some making their last wills verbally, others giving instructions to their comrades to acquaint their parents or relatives if they should fall, and all seemed anxious to seek honour at the cannon's mouth. Among the party where I was seated was a corporal, a fine looking fellow, who entertained the idea that he was to fall. We exhausted all our eloquence to turn him from such a foolish notion but in vain; his spirits sank and no persuasion could arouse him.[33]

Baird had divided his force, of course, sending his cavalry and a whole infantry regiment to Saldanha Bay. This gave him scope for a little nepotism, as well as showing that he was perfectly well aware of the restricted numbers he would face. He formed his regiments into two brigades, the First and the Highland. The First contained the 24th, 38th, and 83rd, English and Irish; the Highland Brigade had the 71st, 72nd, and 93rd, and was placed under the command of one of the brigadiers, Ronald Crawford Ferguson, who had demurred at the plan for a landing a Saldanha Bay. He was yet another officer familiar with the Cape from the first British occupation, and yet another Scot, from Muirtown in Fife. He took his soldiering seriously, having attended the Berlin military academy as an ensign. His promotion, assisted by this education, by experience in Flanders, the Cape, France, and Spain, and lubricated by purchase, had been rapid, from ensign to lieutenant-colonel in four years. The First Brigade should have been the command of Beresford, the other brigadier, but he was at Saldanha Bay; instead it went to Baird's brother Joseph, who was lieutenant-colonel in the 83rd. He was to gain further favour later.

The approach of the Dutch force was known, and Baird was able to take his time. He marshalled his forces into brigade columns, the Highlanders inland and the First Brigade deploying away from the track between them and the sea (Map 1). Although when they were encountered by the Dutch they were advancing, the meeting took place fairly close to the British camp; Baird had sensibly let the Dutch do most of the marching. The going was unpleasant, dense brush, with loose sand underfoot. Water was short, and the British troops were soon complaining about the heat. Had Janssens realized all this, he might have tried a disciplined withdrawal, so as to wear out the British, but his own troops were hardly well enough trained for such a manoeuvre. Baird thrust Major Graham's light troops out in front while he deployed his two brigades. These were to advance, Colonel Weir reported later, in echelon of battalions at thirty paces distance, left wing in front.

The Dutch don't seem to have noticed this subtlety, but the slowness it imposed on the British did give Janssens time to deploy his troops as well. Graham's men had to race a group of Dutch Jagers for possession of a hill to the right of the battlefield, and the Dutch artillery came out in front of their line to bombard both Graham's force and the main British line. The sand was now an advantage, for the Dutch cannon balls simply buried themselves instead of ricochetting along the ground, though one ball killed the apprehensive corporal of the 71st, and another grazed Captain Duncan Mackenzie. Janssens had time to ride along the line, receiving cheers from most of his men. The exception was the men of the Regiment of Waldeck, who were in no mood to earn their pay. Baird ordered his men to advance as soon as they were ready, and while the light infantry skirmish to his right was still continuing.[34]

There was no battle, in the strict sense. The manoeuvre to advance in 'echelon of battalions' meant that the Highland Brigade was well in advance of their English and Irish colleagues of the First Brigade. Then the British line – that is, the Highland Brigade – was halted to deliver a volley at about 150 yards, which was far too distant to have any serious effect.[35] Against a more experienced enemy, all this would have been disastrous. Baird had effectively nullified all his work of establishing a numerical superiority, first by detaching his dragoons and the 38th Foot to the north, then by separating the two brigades of infantry. As a result he had brought into battle just three foot regiments, perhaps 2,300 men, against an enemy force almost equal in number, then he had – or his brother had – wasted the crucial first volley by firing too soon. The other three regiments of the First Brigade were so far off that they were out of reach, and they never did get involved in the fighting. The Dutch artillery began to have some effect, firing and then retreating to fire again in a very professional manner.[36] At least one officer, Captain Aeneas Sutherland of the 93rd, was so unnerved by this artillery fire that he trailed along behind his company so conspicuously that he was later court-martialled for cowardice.[37]

The British were in fact saved by the behaviour of their opponents. The distant volley was all the disenchanted Waldeckers were waiting for, and the whole regiment broke at once. (In fact, if they had advanced to fire from close range they would have done so into a force whose muskets were still being reloaded.) Janssens and the Waldeck officers pleaded with the men to stay and succeeded in preventing the panic from spreading to the 22nd Line Regiment and the militia, and for the moment one company of the Waldeckers was brought back into line.[38] The British advance continued to a distance of sixty yards, and then a bayonet charge was ordered. This is the moment when the Dutch volley should have torn into the ragged, hot, thirsty British line, while the charge was approaching through sand and brush over too long a distance, but the Waldeckers' desertion had made their position hopeless, and now the 22nd Line Regiment, clearly unnerved by that desertion, also broke and fled, as did the remaining Waldeckers. Once more the Dutch artillery was conspicuously gallant, even the British singling out the Malays – 'Chinese', they called them – as particularly good and disciplined fighters. Janssens in the end had personally to order one artillery company, under Lieutenant Pellegrini, to cease fire and retreat.[39] By that time the rest of the Dutch had got away.

This victory was a display of incompetence by the British commanders which deserved to be punished by more than a few casualties. Almost every possible mistake had been made, from advancing without proper supplies, to dividing the army, to separating the brigades, firing the volley too soon, to failing to secure the flanks, to beginning a bayonet charge at such a distance that the troops must arrive out of breath and with their formation disorganized. Finally Baird capped his ludicrous generalship by permitting the enemy forces to retreat unmolested. The British force followed the Dutch for just three miles – 'pursued' would be inaccurate – and Janssens was able to gather most of his forces at the overnight camp at Riet Vlei, hold a muster, and then, in good order, march off to the Hottentots Hollands Pass before the British arrived.[40]

All who wrote about these events commented on the heat and thirst. Ensign William Gavin of the 71st remembered a man who collapsed and died, and then turned black at once. But Captain Campbell of the 72nd also remembered that his regiment perked up at a brief halt when the pipers struck up the regimental quickstep. Some of those in the grenadier company were lively enough to dance a Highland reel on the spot. The following regiment, the English 59th, regarded this performance with astonishment – at least that was what Captain Campbell thought was their reaction.[41]

Baird seems to have been a prisoner of his notion that Janssens had many more troops at his disposal than had appeared in the battle. As early as the landing of the light companies, the rumour went around that the Dutch force was 5,000 strong; although his experienced, soldierly eye must have told him the truth before the battle, Baird afterwards maintained that Janssens' force was 5,000 in number.[42] In one sense, he had to justify his oft-repeated demands for more men, since the force he faced had been exactly what Castlereagh had told him he would face.[43]

But, believing that there were more troops than he had faced so far, he had to find them and the obvious place was Cape Town. So Baird now made yet another mistake. He ignored Janssens – if he actually knew what the Dutch were doing – and sent his army on the march for Cape Town. This, to be sure, was also the prime strategic target for the whole expedition, for, to the British, the main interest of South Africa was as a maritime base, or, in enemy hands, as a danger to their maritime communications, but to concentrate on its capture while the main enemy force was escaping was dangerous. To be sure, in Janssens' hands Cape Town might have posed problems for a besieger. It had several forts blocking the land routes along the coast, as well as a series of entrenched batteries facing the sea. The forts might be somewhat antiquated, but they contained several hundred guns, and Baird had few. If there was serious resistance from the Town, Baird might find himself trapped between the forts and Janssens' army, so seizing them made a certain sense, though he completely lost track of the main Dutch force. But there were few men to man the Cape Town forts, as it turned out; Janssens had sent the remains of the Regiment of Waldeck back to Cape Town, but a lot of the men had already disappeared, and those who remained were hardly a resolute and determined defensive force.[44]

The British army arrived at the outskirts of the Town the day after the battle at Blaauwberg. Baird had realized what Janssens was doing by now, and his force was disposed to face both ways. The First Brigade crossed the Liesbeck River, which flows across the front of the Town. The Highland Brigade was left to the east of the river, facing towards the interior, just in case Janssens' intention was to act as a hammer upon the Cape Town anvil, aimed at crushing the British between these forces. Baird's situation was not, in fact, very pleasant. If the Cape Town forts stood a siege, he would have to get more guns from the ships, as well as all the powder and shot and food and even water for an army of 6,000 men. Numbers of his soldiers had already collapsed from the heat and there were no supplies to be got locally. The Dutch had already shown a capability as sharpshooters and as mounted infantry, the sort of troops who would be ideal for harassing foraging parties, and Baird had no cavalry.[45]

It was, therefore, no doubt with some relief that he discovered that Lieutenant-Colonel Prophalau, the Dutch commander in Cape Town, had no intention of resisting. Baird made some military movements of a threatening nature and sent a summons into the Town: a truce was proposed during which Baird would occupy the most important of the town forts, Fort Knokke. Prophalau agreed – he had no choice – and surrender terms were then agreed, first with Brigadier-General Ferguson, and then with Baird himself. On 10 January the army occupied Cape Town, and the ships in the bay fired a royal salute on seeing the Dutch flags replaced by British in the forts and the castle.[46]

The main object of the expedition had thus been attained at a comparatively low cost. The British casualties in the landing and the battle were at least fifty-nine killed and 200 wounded; Dutch casualties were estimated by Baird at 700, but he was attempting to justify his exaggeration of their original numbers. Janssens' force certainly lost more men than did the British, but not many more, and nowhere near 700. Thirty-six of the British deaths were due to the foundering of the boat at the landing place; eleven of the dead were from the 71st, one corporal and the rest private soldiers.[47]

The capitulation of the Town was only the start, however. Most of the Dutch troops were still with Janssens, and certainly hostile. A sign of this came even during the final negotiations, when a ship in Cape Town harbour was scuttled, and a line-of-battle ship, the *Bato*, at Simon's Bay was burned. Popham insisted on adding an article to the capitulation terms whereby these ships should be raised at the expense of those who sank them. Popham had also made some cogent financial points, complaining that Ferguson had been too precipitate in agreeing terms. Apart from the two sunken ships, Popham pointed out that the situation of the British was now different from that during the first occupation. This time, he claimed, the British should have much greater powers of taxation, which were limited before, and over the use of paper currency. He also made the valid point that it would become more comfortable if the French prisoners could be sent to Europe as soon as possible. These points were thus incorporated into the final articles, signed at 4.00 pm on 10 January. It was characteristic of Popham to be thinking finance.[48]

By that time Beresford's detachment had rejoined contact, though only in a way. His troops had begun landing through the surf at Saldanha Bay, but before the disembarkation had been completed an Indiaman, the *Sarah Christina*, had arrived with the news that the landing had been successfully accomplished by the main force. Beresford had already sent off Colonel Wilson with his dragoons and the light company of the 38th to a farmhouse called Thefonteyn, reputed to be fifteen miles off. They were to requisition horses and draught cattle there, while the rest of the 38th marched south through sand and brush along the coast. Some had the additional complication of indigestion from eating ostrich eggs. All suffered from the heat.[49]

Wilson's group marched until dark, and on into the night. By midnight he was down to seventy men, having sent eighty back to Beresford. He reached a farm where he found one horse and discovered that he was in the wrong place. Next day this force marched to a place called Elandsfonteyn, reduced to his dragoons alone – carrying their saddles – and just two of the light infantry. He reached Thefonteyn next day, and found that all the cattle and horses had been driven off. It seems likely, from this performance, that the absence of British cavalry from Baird's main strike force was not really a serious deprivation.

Next day, the 9th (while Baird was negotiating surrender terms at Cape Town), Beresford took Wilson and those dragoons who were present and mounted, and went on ahead. This party reached Cape Town as the 59th was occupying Fort Knokke, by which time Beresford was almost alone. His troops were scattered in small exhausted groups all the way back to Saldanha Bay. It seems a good thing that Baird was not depending on the help of either Beresford or Wilson.[50]

Beresford's urgency had been due to his wish to be in on the action. He had failed in this, but now his keenness could be put to use; Baird gave him the job of finding and dealing with Janssens. Baird himself, as provisional governor, had to establish his authority in Cape Town, and get the administration operating again. This was the best way of convincing everyone from Janssens down that the conquest was successful. He administered an oath of allegiance to the existing public officials, and appointed W.S. van Rynefeld as chief civil magistrate to get the civil courts functioning again.[51]

The most urgent problem turned out to be food. It was found that there was only two days' supply in Cape Town, and with Janssens and his men still at large few local supplies could be expected.[52] Indeed, the British invasion had disrupted the harvest, and so there might well be a third bad harvest in succession. The Navy landed food from the storeships and transports, and ships were sent off to buy supplies abroad – *Leda* was sent to St Helena for flour, and a transport went to Rio de Janiero for rice – though these were going to take time to arrive.[53] The shortage of food was clearly due to Janssens' requisitions. William Maude, the Agent Victualler, who had been left in office when the British withdrew in 1803, turned up on 13 January. He reported that all his salt provisions, confiscated when the war began again,

had been used to supply French ships. Other supplies had been removed by
Janssens along with his army into the interior, but it does not seem that any
of the British realized this. There was also a suspicious shortage of cash in
the town, but no one remarked on it yet. Maude refused to take up his post
again, and Popham appointed William Robinson, his own secretary, as the
new Agent.[54]

The military and naval booty had to be reckoned up. Three hundred and
seventy guns of various sorts were counted to add to those already captured.
And there were prisoners, over forty officers, French and Dutch, naval and
military, more than 400 soldiers, and about 270 seamen. The soldiers were
of an immense variety. Most were from the Regiment of Walbeck; less than
fifty of these were actually Dutch, the majority being Germans, and most
of the rest were from all parts of Europe; there were also some Americans,
Indians, and one African.[55] Baird had been told to enlist as many of these into
the British 60th Foot as he could, but he had also agreed, by the terms of the
capitulation, not to press them into his forces. He therefore had to persuade
them, so that they could be classified as volunteers. His method was crude.
He locked them into the Amsterdam Battery, a thoroughly insalubrious
place, and then promised them a $20 bounty each if they enlisted in the
British army.[56]

Janssens' force had still to be dealt with. He had taken his command to
the Hottentots Hollands Pass. Baird knew by 12 January where the Dutch
army was and Beresford was ordered to take a force to Stellenbosch and
deal with it. Colonel Wilson was sent to deal with another force, reputedly
French, which was at Hout's Bay, but the surrender was actually effected
by Lieutenant MacArthur of the 72nd before Wilson arrived. MacArthur
had only thirty men and faced twice as many, but he spread his troops
out deceptively and the Dutch soldiers – there were no French there –
surrendered.[57] Baird issued a proclamation, urging Janssens to give in and
the civilian population to stay calm, and he ordered the 83rd Foot on board
ship to be taken round to Mossel Bay to be landed in Janssens' rear. This
would expose another flaw in Janssens' plan. As it happened, though it is not
known if Baird knew this, Mossel Bay was the place where the Scots farmer
John Murray from Aberdeen had settled. He also ran a whale fishery along
the shore and traded with the local farmers; he had been there since 1797,
and was thoroughly established by now.[58]

Beresford took three regiments with him, the 59th, the 72nd, and the
93rd. He left the first two at Stellenbosch and moved the 93rd to the foot
of the Hottentots Hollands Pass.[59] This was regarded as a major obstacle.

An English traveller had described it two years before as 'wild, awful, and steep to a very great degree', and thought it 'might be sufficient to deter the timid from ever entering the interior of the country'.[60] Ensign Gavin of the 71st, who marched to the foot of the pass on the 18 January, was certainly impressed by the strength of the Dutch position. He pointed out that its seaward side was protected by the coastal cliffs and that the land approach was narrow, though perhaps he diminished its size in memory when he thought it only wide enough for one person at a time. Major Graham agreed that it was 'impossible to force' Janssens out of his position, but Colonel Wilson decided that it was not 'unassailable and impregnable', though he only appears to have decided that after all possibility of fighting had ended and he was able to inspect the position closely. It seems as though the assumption on the British side was that Janssens had a very strong position, and they clearly did not relish the prospect of attacking it.[61] It can be assumed that Beresford shared their views.

Janssens had issued his own proclamation of defiance on 11 January, but this further display of force by the British disheartened him and his men. The farmers whose lands and homes were now in British occupation were allowed to go home, and this would remove the majority of the militiamen. He still had one company of the Regiment of Walbeck, but they were so downhearted at defeats and disgraced by the desertion of the rest of the regiment that twenty men are said to have committed suicide, though this came from Colonel Wilson, not a wholly reliable source for enemy numbers.[62] Beresford sent up a letter from Baird to Janssens; Janssens replied, asking that J.A. Truter, the Secretary of the Batavian colonial regime, be sent up for discussions. Baird agreed to this, and came himself to Stellenbosch. The 83rd Foot, on board their ships and bound for Mossel Bay, were meanwhile windbound in False Bay, Truter could point out the threat they posed to Janssens rear; the 83rd alone now outnumbered his remaining force. The longer he waited the more Janssens' position would deteriorate.

Beresford managed to initiate another exchange of letters with Janssens through Truter, who could also report on the size and determination of the British force below the pass. Having begun to negotiate, Janssens would clearly now soon give in. On 16 January he sent back two marines, called Hale and Cook, who had tried to desert to the enemy, a singularly ill-timed move on their part. He tried to gain a modification of Baird's terms, but by 18 January his weakness became so obvious that Baird refused any more concessions. Janssens capitulated.[63]

Colonel Wilson climbed the pass to inspect the Dutch position, and commented that the troops at the top looked miserable, which was scarcely surprising in the circumstances.[64] Janssens' gamble had not worked. With more men he would have had a chance, but the basic cause of his defeat was the lack of local enthusiasm for his cause. The Dutch colony gave in to an incompetent British attack without a serious fight being made by anyone except its governor and the Malay artillerymen. The Boers had been indifferent throughout.

Baird could exercise one more item of nepotism, and sent his brother Joseph to London with the dispatches describing his victory, a task which automatically brought promotion.

Chapter Three

The Cape – Defence and Control

Having seized control of the Cape, it became necessary for the British to defend the colony against any attack. At once, the problem facing them was altered and Janssens' dilemma became Baird's and Popham's: the place now became ringed with potential enemies. Although it was geographically part of the continent of Africa, in political and strategic terms the Cape was effectively an island. The sea to the south and west was controlled by the British, though occasional enemy ships could get through; to the north the land dried out to desert, and the authority of the government at Cape Town extended not much more than 100 miles along the coast and less inland; to the east were Boer pastoralist families, as far as the Sundays River and Graaff Reinet, and then various Black states and peoples who might or might not be hostile (Map 2). The colony was thus isolated between the sea, the desert, and the Blacks, without any support closer than Britain and India, except from St Helena.

The problems the British governor faced were three. First, was the need to control the colony. The capitulation of Cape Town and Janssens' army had only affected the immediate area of Cape Town; the rest of the colony, north of Saldanha Bay and east of the Hottentots Hollands Pass, might still be hostile. The Boers on the eastern frontier had a reputation for maintaining their independence of any government at Cape Town, at least until they needed help; and had staged a rebellion against the previous British regime. Secondly, was the possible hostility of the Bushmen, the Hottentots, and Xhosa. Their collective enmity had confined the Boers of the interior within their present boundaries for the past forty years, and had even pushed them back from their farthest expansion; they were clearly formidable and would need watching. Thirdly, there was the sea. If an expedition from Britain could reach the Cape, so could one from France, or the Dutch East Indies, or French Mauritius. And rumours abounded about French ships in the southern oceans.

Baird, as governor and commander-in-chief, shared the task of defence with Popham, who could concentrate on naval defence. Baird's was the more delicate task, but also the easier. The capitulation of the Dutch governor and all his armed forces left the government system, such as it was, more or less intact, and Baird had enforced continuity by his rapid oath of allegiance and by the appointment of van Ryneveld as civil magistrate. The imprisonment of the Dutch forces had reduced the security problem on land. The absence of money in the public treasury soon became obvious, but was also soon explained.

A slave girl of the Secretary, J.A. Truter, revealed in gossip that the money had been handed out to a variety of people to keep until the British were beaten. Janssens denied any knowledge of this, but it is reasonable to assume that it was part of his plan to continue the war after initial defeat in the field. He had already removed all food supplies from the town, and here was evidence that he had removed all the cash as well. No receipts had been taken, of course. Baird and Popham made demands, threats were breathed, and most of the money was soon handed back.[1] The money supply was to be a constant problem, which repeatedly concerned Baird as governor. Until the colony was clearly and securely in British control, it would be difficult to collect taxes, and few people would be willing to spend what money they had.

The army was, of course, the main defence of the colony, and Baird, confident in his numbers, kept most of the troops in the Cape Town area. The 71st Foot was posted at Wynberg, seven miles south of Cape Town, and the 72nd at Simon's Town on False Bay, with outpost garrisons at Muizenberg (where the British had landed in 1795) and at Hout's Bay and Olifant's Bay on the western side of the Cape Peninsula.[2] He thus made no attempt to occupy the interior, any more than Janssens had, but his defensive dispositions were clearly designed to combat an attack from the sea, either in the face of a landing in Table Bay or Simon's Bay. Logistically also it was easier to supply soldiers in the Cape Town area, for that was where such supplies as they had were concentrated: the ships were the main source.

One of Baird's problems was always going to be discipline. The tensions of the conquest were released, and the relaxations of peacetime soldiering took their place. In effect, the army had nothing to do while it was concentrated in the Cape Town area, and boredom soon set in. Baird's answer was a strict discipline. Sergeant Landshiet of the dragoons remembered him appearing on the drill ground, watch in hand, like a regimental adjutant. Landshiet was fortunate in that his commanding officer was Colonel Wilson, whose notions of discipline were more imaginative than Baird's; when Baird discovered that Wilson was organizing sports for his man, he stopped them and insisted on drill. Wilson's discipline and control of his small force was up to the challenge, but he himself was bored by inactivity. Only one of his men deserted while he was in command.[3]

One of Baird's major problems, and another reason for concentrating his troops in and near Cape Town, was the presence of the prisoners of war. His nightmare was the arrival of an invading force, and the liberation and rearming of the prisoners, of which there were about 2,000. He had two methods of dealing with them: recruit those who would join into the British forces, or evacuate them to Europe by parole and cartel. Baird combined these two approaches, by recruiting those he could – about 300 succumbed to his pressure – and then evacuating the rest.

His original instructions had been that enlistment should be into the 60th Foot, a regiment composed of foreigners, but he put only two men into that unit; instead the regiments which were with him at the Cape were given their choice, though even then he was selective in his distribution. The 59th, on its way to India, received none; the 93rd, recruited almost exclusively from the Sutherland estates, received none – anyone not Scots, and perhaps not Gaelic-speaking, would have been very unwelcome. Colonel Wilson got thirty-two men for the 20th Light Dragoons, and a few each went to the 24th Foot, the artillery, and the Staff Corps. The rest were roughly divided amongst the other four regiments: seventy-eight to the 38th, sixty-one to the 72nd, forty-two to the 83rd, and seventy-nine to the 71st.[4]

The men who were recruited were almost entirely from the Regiment of Waldeck, and so were mainly Germans. Little or no attempt seems to have been made to recruit any of the French or the Dutch soldiers, who had a stronger sense of patriotism; but the mercenaries were clearly seen as fair game. They were incarcerated in the damp and gloomy batteries, minimally fed, and promised a bounty for joining the British: most complied, though not all at once. But they were scarcely enthusiastic recruits any more than they had been enthusiastic warriors, and once out of prison they began to desert. The first group who did so and were caught were punished with a flogging, but the next group was sentenced to death. There was a widespread sense of shock when that sentence was actually carried out at once. As one man remembered: 'desertion was certainly stopped, but …'.[5] But desertion started again after a time: four of Colonel Wilson's dragoons deserted in March, one from the 24th Foot, and five from the 83rd. Of the Scottish regiments, neither the 72nd nor the 93rd lost any man, but three deserted from the 71st, though it is not possible to work out from the records just who they were.[6]

Not that the officers escaped Baird's discipline. Trials by court-martial came weekly during February; Captain Aeneas Sutherland of the 93rd was accused of 'misbehaviour before the enemy' at Blaauwberg and sentenced to be cashiered; Captain Samuel Pococke and Lieutenant James Clarke, both of the 71st Foot, were separately accused of conduct subversive of military discipline on the transport during the voyage south. Pococke was acquitted by the skin of his teeth, but Clarke had repeated the offence in camp at Wynberg on 10 March, and was clearly guilty. Baird remarked that 'the ill conduct ... appears to have in a great degree proceeded from ignorance and imbecility'. The solution, it was agreed, was that Clarke should sell his commission and leave the service. Private Samuel Ramsden of the 38th Foot was accused of murder, found guilty of manslaughter, and was sentenced to a month in solitary.[7] It is an odd kind of discipline which shoots a man for deserting from an army he has been hijacked into, yet gives another man a month in solitary confinement for killing.

Men fell sick. Six regiments stayed on at the Cape until April. When they had arrived, after months on board ship, only the 83rd had more than eleven men sick. Popham rightly pointed out with pride that the total sick list was less than seventy in the whole force at the beginning of January.[8] But, back on land, by the end of the month the lowest total sick in any regiment was ten, and that was in the smallest group, Wilson's 20th Light Dragoons. By the time of the February monthly return, over ten per cent of every regiment was noted as sick. By April the total was even higher: the 72nd had almost a third of its men on the sick list. Almost fifty men had died in March and April.

The 71st was as badly affected as any unit (Diagram 3). It was at the Cape for just fifteen weeks, and in that time thirteen men were in hospital for eleven weeks, and perhaps more. Given that the regiment's monthly returns do not cover April, these men had in effect been ill the whole time the regiment was in South Africa. In the three months for which records survive, 216 of the regiment's rank-and-file were admitted either to the Regimental Hospital, or to the General Hospital; the total man-days involved was 4,911, the equivalent of a reduction in strength of over sixty men for three months (the 71st had lost only eleven men in the fighting in January). Six of the sick died, and nine others were discharged after their illness as being too unfit any longer to continue in the service. Of course, the great majority – over 500 – of the men were not sick at any time, or at least not badly enough to be admitted to the hospital, but the net effect was a permanent reduction in the effective strength of the regiment by ten per cent.

The other regiments were as badly affected, or worse, and it would go on like this for years. The Cape was perhaps not so lethal a station as India or the West Indies, but it was clearly bad enough. Some things could be done, of course. Exercise, cleanliness, and decent food were all conducive to good health, but, above all, it took good officers to see to it that effective health measures were taken and enforced. It is very obvious that the 83rd had the worst officers, for it had the worst sickness record while at sea, the worst on land, the worst desertion record, and its death rate was as bad as any other regiment.

One group in the Dutch army which had fought the invaders was treated differently from the rest: the Hottentot Light Infantry Regiment was reconstituted as the Cape Regiment, part of the British army. Major Graham was given the post of commanding officer, with the local rank of lieutenant-colonel, and officers and NCOs were brought in from other regiments. The 71st contributed Ensign John Bell, Corporal James Ward, and Private John Alexander, all of whom, like Graham, received promotion. Graham wrote to his brother on 20 February about his appointment, in enthusiastic terms. His men, he said, detested the Dutch, which suggests it was partly due to their anti-Dutch sentiments that the men were recruited. But they were people of the colony, and inevitably they were going to be used in a local capacity.

Graham had just between 200 and 300 men at the beginning, and began recruiting more, so that he had over 500 by the end of January. The main problem was to prevent the Hottentots from casually deserting and returning equally casually, but sickness was also a concern – over forty men of his recruits died in the first three months. Late in March he commented to his brother that he did not wish to stay any longer because he feared he would be buried alive. But he made a condition – his regiment should be in tolerable order first, and that would take a long time.[9]

The control of the interior of the colony was not a major priority for Baird, but he had to take over the government installations there at least, and had to appoint a loyal administration. The main centre to establish control over, in view of the problem of defence against possible attack, was at Algoa Bay, 500 miles east of Cape Town. The Batavian regime had established a new *drostdy* at Uitenhage, just inland from the bay, only two years before. This was also close to van der Kemp's mission at Bethelsdorp, and even closer to the area which had been the scene of fighting in the recent past (the 'Third Kaffir War') – Uitenhage in fact had been founded on the site of a farm burnt in that war. A small garrison had also been placed at Fort Frederick on the coast nearby. None of these places was large, but the three together, along with Bethelsdorp, comprised a centre of power and administration in a sensitive frontier area, which it was necessary to control; given the intention of Janssens to carry on the fight from the interior, and the possible hostility of the Boers, it had to be done delicately.

Baird appointed a new landdrost for Uitenhage, and on 14 February issued his instructions. The new officer was a Dutch-speaking officer of the 59th Foot, Captain Jacob Glen Cuyler.[10] His Dutch is likely to have been strange to both the Boers – whose stripped-down dialect had many Bantu words in it already, and approximated to the later Afrikaans – and to the Dutch from Europe, for he had learned it from his parents, who were Dutch of New York. He had been born in Albany, New York, in the year the American rebellion began, and had been taken to Canada by Loyalist parents. He had been in the army since 1799, and his appointment to Uitenhage was the start of a long association with that place.[11] His appointment was partly common sense because of his language skills, but he was also chosen no doubt as a conciliatory gesture towards the Boers of this frontier; few if any of the locals would be able to speak any English, though there was an English colleague of van der Kemp's at Bethelsdorp, another missionary called Edward Read. Cuyler was to be the only British officer in any official position in the interior, replacing the Dutch Captain Alberti, and he was specifically instructed to listen to the missionary van der Kemp as a local expert. Neither man was especially anxious to plunge into the detail of life on the frontier for a time, and they were both still in Cape Town a month later.[12] The other *drostdy* on the frontier was at Graaff Reinet in the north, but no British replacement was sent there for the present. There were no troops in place there, and it was remote from the threat of a foreign invasion, which was Baird's primary concern in these first months.

The threat of invasion was in fact as much Popham's problem as Baird's. Popham knew that there was a French squadron under Rear-Admiral Linois based at Mauritius, but he had not been sure of its size when he sailed. He also knew that the combined fleets of France and Spain had been at Cadiz when he left Europe, but since then he had heard nothing. Linois' squadron was however known of at the Cape. It consisted of the 86-gun line-of-battle ship *Marengo* and the frigate *Belle Poule*. The ships had been at the Cape until early in November, and one of them had then sailed north into the Atlantic, not into the Indian Ocean.[13]

Then one of Linois' captures, a Liverpool slaver called *Resource*, was retaken by *Diomede* and *Encounter* when it approached Table Bay.[14] By examining the people on board, and from some private letters he found, Popham was able to work out that Linois had sailed north, capturing *Resource* and another ship, a brig, off Loango, and had then watered at the Portuguese island of Sao Thome in the Bay of Biafra. *Resource*, under its prize crew, was detached at that point, but it seemed that Linois himself intended to return to the Cape, where another frigate, the *Semillante*, would join him. It appeared that he had quarrelled with Decaen, the governor of Mauritius, and so Linois now intended to make the Cape his base.

Popham reported all this to the Admiralty, and added that Linois' ship *Marengo* had 86 guns, a crew of 800, and was healthy. He thought that two more sail of the line under Admiral Margeaux were expected to join him, when Linois would have a force of three line-of-battle ships, two frigates, and the brig he had taken. This was much the same force as Popham himself had, but *Marengo*'s 86 guns should tip the balance in the French favour if he came to a fight.

That was on 28 January. The day before an American ship came in with news of Nelson and death and Trafalgar and victory. The warships fired salutes in celebration, but this scarcely affected the picture in the South Atlantic.[15] Indeed, if Linois had heard of the defeat of Villeneuve, he might well feel it more prudent to remain away from European waters; his threat to arrive at the Cape was even more potent.

Popham got *Belliqueux*'s convoy, with the 59th Foot (except Captain Cuyler), on its way on 10 February, and sent off three of his transports as well, to bring back food supplies for the Cape from India, and five days later the cartel ships carrying the prisoners who had not been enlisted into the British army were dispatched to Europe. He and Baird had thus lightened the problem of supplies at the cost of one of Popham's line of battleships. Popham and Baird had kept Dutch flags flying on the castle and on the ships – which would deter any British vessel – in the harbour, so when another ship came blithely in on 21 February it was either an enemy or a neutral. Popham sent a boat out to the newcomer, with the men, as he put it, the 'dressed in French'; it proved to be the other of *Marengo*'s prizes, a brig called *Rollo*. The boat's crew captured it easily, and so quickly that the letters in the captain's cabin were taken intact.[16]

The *Rollo*'s captain, Enseigne de Vaisseau Vermet, did not know Linois' precise plans, not surprisingly, but one of the captured letters did suggest that Linois would be in need of supplies by early March. He would not go to Mauritius, so the Cape seemed to be his only supply base. One letter made it clear that he was short of water, and had been unable to get much at Principe, another Portuguese island in the Bay of Biafra. An early French return to the Cape was increasingly likely.[17]

Leda returned from St Helena with welcome supplies of flour, rice, sugar, and so on, for the Cape population, and was a useful increase in Popham's strength.[18] Then a Danish ship bound for Batavia from Copenhagen came in, and her master reported, when asked, that he had been boarded at one stage by men from another French ship, the frigate *Piemontaise*. He could only say it was 'a very large ship', pierced for fifteen guns on the main deck; it was bound, said the Danish captain, for Mauritius.[19]

Popham had complied with his original instructions regarding the disposition of his ships, had captured two enemy ships by intelligence and cunning rather than brute force, and the cartels had removed 804 enemy prisoners out of the Cape.[20] One of Baird's main headaches was thus removed. Popham cruised for several days several leagues to the west of the Cape Peninsula, hoping to intercept the French, but came back in on 3 March. Next morning – such was his luck – a signal from the Lion's Rump lookout reported the approach of an enemy force, at first one ship, then two more, one of them being a ship of the line. Popham assumed that this was Linois' *Marengo*, and that the French force he had been looking for had at last arrived.

There was a gale at the time, during which *Leda* had to cut her cable, and had then collided with *Diadem*. When the confusion was cleared away the foremost of the three approaching ships had hoisted French colours and was heading towards *Diadem* – all three of the ships in the Bay were flying Dutch colours still – and the two following ships were recognized to be *Raisonable* and *Narcissus* – so not following but chasing. *Diadem* waited until the French ship, a large frigate called *Volontaire*, was committed to the Bay and had come within hail, with the chasing ships blocking its retreat, and swiftly had the British colours hoisted. Popham fired once, directing *Volontaire* to strike. The surprise was complete, and *Volontaire* surrendered at once. As the doctor on the *Narcissus* pointed out in his diary, this was yet another capture made without bloodshed.[21]

Lieutenant Fernyhough of *Diadem's* marines was sent in charge of the party to take possession of the capture. As he came on deck, he was greeted by a small group of British officers, one of whom at once burst into tears. It transpired that the *Volontaire* had more British prisoners in the hold, most of them in a very sickly condition – and some of them died even as they were brought out. They were soldiers of the 2nd (Queen's) and 54th Regiments who had been captured in the Bay of Biscay on passage from

Gibraltar to England. All the prisoners were packed into *Volontaire*, a large 46-gun frigate, but scarcely large enough for such a number. Captain Brettel had failed to get into Tenerife to land them, and so headed for the Cape, believing it to be Dutch still. His prisoners were eating all his provisions and made his ship useless as a cruiser.[22]

The first priorities were to secure the new ship, extract the prisoners to the hospital and her crew to prison. Then the French officers were induced into conversation, and the British ex-prisoners were questioned. Popham found that one of the French officers, a lieutenant called Steetz, was a man he had known some years before in Germany; his inquisitive charm did the rest. Popham reported the results to the Admiralty on 7 March.

Volontaire was one ship of a fleet which had escaped from Brest in December. The others were eleven line-of-battle ships, four frigates and a corvette. They had split into two groups, under Admirals Lessiègues and Willaumez. *Volontaire* was with Willaumez, so Popham could report little on the other division. But Willaumez was frightening enough for a commander with only a few ships located a long way from help. Willaumez had only one frigate now, but he did have six sail of the line, every one more powerful than any of Popham's ships. Captain Brettel clearly considered the Cape as one of Willaumez' likely destinations. He even thought it possible that the fleet might come in two at a time to replenish. Baiting the hook rather obviously, one might think, he claimed that the *Veteran*, captained by Jerome Bonaparte, might be one of the first pair.[23]

Popham had to prepare to face attack. He conjured up the possibility of Willaumez reuniting with Lessiègues and both being joined by Linois for a grand assault on his three line-of-battle ships, twelve against three, very much in the way Baird had magnified the possible Dutch forces at the Cape in his preparation for the expedition. Already rumours were going round the fleet of the enemy force, six ships, said one story, eleven, said another.[24] Popham concerted his plans with Baird. There was no point in meeting such a force at sea, for Popham's ships would be quickly overwhelmed. So he used them as floating batteries: the three battleships, *Diomede*, *Raisonable*, and *Diadem*, were lined up, close inshore and anchored fore and aft. To either side of them were two shore batteries, the *Amsterdam* (not now needed as a prison camp) and the *Chavonnes*. The two frigates were stationed beyond the southernmost ship.[25] Popham had been at Copenhagen in 1801, when the Danish line of battleships had been used in that same way, most effectively. But, as at Copenhagen, he cannot have expected his ships to survive.

Baird issued a proclamation warning of a possible French attack and reminded all that aiding such an invasion was an offence punishable by death. A new battery was constructed at Green Point. Prisoners still in the colony, including the crew of the *Volontaire*, were swiftly dispatched to Europe in cartel ships; Popham got the paroles of the *Volontaire* officers by threatening to send them on to India.[26] Popham swiftly decided to buy in the *Volontaire*, and added *Rollo* shortly after, thus increasing his naval strength, though at the cost of spreading his manpower even thinner through the fleet.[27]

The tension had its effect in the colony, beyond the sailors and the army officers. Baird claimed the colony was 'tranquil' on 8 March, but this was mere soothing syrup. On the 10 March a man called Cornelis Maas claimed to have seen the French ships in Saldanha Bay. An alarm went out and thirty of the Light Dragoons were sent to have a look. This was particularly alarming since a Dutch fleet had arrived exactly there during the first British occupation; no doubt this was known to Maas. Then Maas confessed that it was all a joke. Baird reacted furiously; Maas was flogged around the town and expelled from the colony. It is clear that nerves stretched tight. On the night of the 18 March, a sentry was fired at and wounded, another sign of the general jitters, just as was Baird's savage reaction to Maas' ill-timed joke.[28] It was therefore doubly unnerving that on 15 March a report came in from Captain Arbuthnot, in charge of the cavalry picquet at Saldanha Bay, that an arriving whaler reported seeing a fleet of eight ships 1,000 miles due west of the Cape, exactly in a position to bear down on the Cape – along just the same route Popham's fleet had used. But the report was nearly three weeks old, and Popham thought they might be Indiamen.

Then next day a Hamburg brig reported being boarded by a French inspection crew on 25 February, the same day the whaler had seen the ships, though the position was not the same. The wind had been hard from the south-south-west at the time, and the French fleet lay to; the implication was that the wind was foul, and that it was trying to sail east, for the Cape. Another brig, spoken to by *Leda* at sea, also implied that the French were heading for the Cape.[29] But in fact, the news from the whaler and Hamburg brig was actually reassuring, for if the French fleet had been in the South Atlantic three weeks before, and had still not appeared at the Cape, it was probably not coming at all. Popham calculated that if it did not appear by the end of March it had almost certainly gone elsewhere.

All the alarms and excitements at the Cape, in fact, were unnecessary, for none of the projected attacks took place. But for three months, news dribbled in of the likelihood of attacks by fleets, all of which were more powerful than

Popham's. And if Popham's ships were sunk then Baird would be in serious trouble, short of supplies, blockaded and perhaps attacked by sea, and as the various incidents in Cape Town had shown, trying to control a population which was very jittery, if not still basically hostile.

By the end of March Popham had become convinced that no attack would occur. But that did not relax him. Far from it. He had already asked to be recalled, and at dinner on 12 March, he told Colonel Wilson that he would probably be home by August, and offered to take Wilson when he went.[30] Ferguson, suffering from a liver complaint, and perhaps not finding favour with Baird, had already gone.[31] But Popham's character was far too restless for the prospect of a peaceful winter in South Africa and a leisurely return to Britain to console him. Already he was contemplating further action.

Baird had kept control over the Cape Town area for the crucial early weeks after the conquest. He had parted with the 59th Foot, and had received the sickly survivors of French captivity from the *Volontaire*. His garrison was thus six battalions – 24th, 38th, 71st, 72nd, 83rd, and 93rd and the dragoons – and he had also recruited the Cape Regiment. Together with the men of the Queens and the 54th, reviving after their incarceration (about 100 men in each), and the recruits acquired from the Dutch army, Baird had quickly compensated for the 'loss' of the 59th. As a result all Baird's units, except the 93rd, were higher in numbers than they had been when they sailed from Cork, and he had in addition the refugees from the *Volontaire*.

No doubt Baird was happy to command such a substantial force, but its size was the result of his original over-estimate of the Dutch garrison, and with the effective ending of the threat of attack, he could no longer justify holding on to a garrison of so many troops. Popham, for one, realized this, and was contemplating the used to which the surplus soldiers could be put. (Neither man seems to have considered seriously the notion that the 'surplus' should be returned to Britain.) Popham's own naval force was also now bigger than it needed to be; with no serious French threat, he did not need three line-of-battle ships. Indeed, his instructions had included a requirement to send *Raisonable* to St Helena as escort for the East India convoy to England, but he seems never to have considered obeying this instruction. He had also been given a supplementary order to send a ship to cruise between Río de Janeiro and Buenos Aires, once his force had taken the Cape, in order to intercept, or at least interrupt, the Spanish trade along the coast.[32] He had not yet done so, principally because until late in March he had felt the Cape was still under threat from the French. But now the threat was not apparent, Popham was drawn to the idea of

South America, and of doing more than merely intercepting Spanish merchant ships.

He had already discussed the idea with Baird, who mentioned it in a semi-private letter to Colonel Gordon, the Duke of York's Military Secretary, a draft of which is dated 24 March, that Popham was urging on him 'a dash for Buenos Aires'.[33] This was a bigger project than a single ship cruising the coast, and Baird would only need to be consulted if he was being asked to send soldiers.

On 28 March an American merchantman came into Table Bay, and its captain, Thomas Waine, contacted Popham. He had come from Buenos Aires, sent by a group of merchants in the city, with information to the effect that Buenos Aires was defenceless, and that a British force would be welcomed.[34] The city had gone on the alert when the news of the approach of Popham's fleet had arrived from Brazil (the ships had watered at San Salvador). Waine's voyage cannot have been a deliberate search for the British expedition, though no doubt since Buenos Aires was not attacked it must have been quickly realized that his destination was the Cape. His arrival was certainly seized on by Popham, and his request and his news fitted his hopes. This fits in with Popham's discussion with Baird, but nothing was done about it immediately, though by the end of March rumours were spreading among the officers that some new venture was being planned; Captain Gillespie remembered that preparations began at the end of March, though this is unspecific and inexact; the author of an account published in 1836 mentioned rumours that something was going on, but again he is vague.[35] Both may, in fact, be using hindsight, for both were writing well after the events. Nevertheless it seems clear enough that some rumours about the discussions between Baird and Popham had got out. But there is no sign that anyone knew what was being contemplated.

On 4 April the frigate *Leda* was finally sent off to inaugurate the cruise along the American coast which Popham had been instructed to begin. The relatively slow passage which the ship made, and the apparent surprise of its captain when he found on his arrival that there was a British force there, are clear signs that Captain Honeyman knew nothing of Popham's scheme when he sailed from the Cape.[36] So it is clear that nothing had been decided by 4 April.

By 9 April, however, a decision had been reached. On that day Popham wrote to the Admiralty that he was leaving the Cape right away.[37] He said nothing of where he was going, nor did he actually go yet. (The letter would take months to reach London, and could not be sent until a suitable ship was available.) But by 12 April he had persuaded Baird, who on that day ordered the 71st Foot to embark. It is said by one source that Popham originally asked for a different regiment (probably the 38th), but Baird insisted on sending the 71st, his own old regiment.[38] This was presumably for the regiment's benefit, and would be regarded as an honour, at least by the officers, though it may also be because it was the strongest single unit he had, now that it had received nearly eighty of the new recruits added to its original numbers. It had a strength in the April return of 810 officers and men, which is eighty more men than the 83rd, and almost 300 more than the 24th. Seven of the 20th Light Dragoons were added, but without their horses, and thirty-five artillery men with four guns. Some extra officers joined, including Captain Arbuthnot of the Staff Corps and Baird's own nephew and aide-de-camp, Ensign Alexander Gordon, who no doubt went as Baird's informer. The total force was less than 1,000 men, and these were accompanied by the sixty women and forty children of the 71st. The command was given to Brigadier-General Beresford, the only brigadier Baird had left.

Colonel Wilson heard about the proposed expedition only when everyone else did, when it was announced on 12 April that the 71st was ordered to embark. He made his own investigations by interviewing a carpenter on *Diadem*, Popham's own ship, who had lived in Buenos Aires for some years, and whom Popham had already pumped for information. The carpenter gave Wilson a sketch of the place, which Wilson sent to Beresford, along with a note of the strength of Spanish forces in Buenos Aires, information which Wilson himself had acquired in England before he set out. This showed, he pointed out, the presence of a larger force than Popham had counted on. Thus the numbers game had been reversed. Popham's information was that the city was vulnerable. Hence he understated the forces available for its defence – just as Baird had deliberately over-estimated the garrison of the Cape. Popham wanted to go, so he was unduly optimistic; Baird, ever cautious, was prone to see enemies where they were not, and he took some convincing that Popham's force would not be lost.

Beresford sent the figures on to Baird, and Baird sent for Wilson. Popham was there too, 'very gloomy', according to Wilson. Popham accused Wilson of protesting at the despatch of the expedition, which, quite rightly, he denied doing, though the effect of his actions had amounted to that, as Popham pointed out. Wilson was clearly treading a delicate line. Baird wanted to know where Wilson had got the information. Wilson did not say, but replied that was his duty to provide it. This indirection could only imply to the three commanders that Wilson's figures were inventions – as they may well have been. Perhaps they thought he was angling for a place in the expedition; if so, they called his bluff. He was not asked to go (and in fact Baird let him return to England soon after). Wilson thought, after the meeting, when Baird and Beresford and Popham went on board the *Diadem*, that 'all is still in suspense'.[39] But it wasn't. The expedition sailed next day.

Chapter Four

The Consequences of the Cape Conquest

The Dutch colony was small, both in area and population, and so the British presence, which continued effectively for a century, had a correspondingly deep influence. Because of the successful conquest, the British military presence in the Cape was both large and continuous. A continuing control was seen as essential for the defence of the empire as a whole – meaning India above all – and when after 1815 this ceased to be a very persuasive argument, the defence of the Cape Colony itself became the main reason for the British military occupation. The size of that military presence, as compared with the resident population, made it obvious and pervasive. It was also quickly perceived that British control would be permanent, and the successful establishment of a British governor and his administration meant that British authority and culture, language and personnel, penetrated deeply into the Dutch society.

It was, however, not just a British presence, but a specifically Scottish presence, which had the major effect. The presence of the Scotsman Baird as governor for the first year was partly responsible for this, for he appointed fellow Scots to influential posts. The Cape Regiment, for example, was commanded by Colonel Graham, and it had many Scotsmen among its officers and NCOs. The British garrison all through the Napoleonic war included two Scottish regiments, the 72nd (Seaforth Highlanders) and the 93rd (Sutherland Highlanders). Admiral Stirling, though scarcely a Scot by this time, being domiciled in the South of England when at home, was also the naval commander-in-chief at the Cape Station from his arrival in September 1807 until late in 1808 – but the naval influence was small compared with the army's. The size of the garrison – about 5,000 strong during the wars, and only slightly reduced in the years following the peace – was a major market for local produce, and the soldiers' pay, meagre though it was, introduced more coin into the money-starved economy. And the most cohesive group in the garrison were the Scots.

It was one of the purposes of the governors, starting with Baird, to stimulate the local markets. This was, of course, less for the local than for the imperial benefit, but it was correctly seen as a measure which would work for both. The British takeover opened the port of Cape Town to British ships once again, despite the deterring effect there may have been of Popham and Baird continuing to fly the Dutch flag for some time after their conquest. In fact, there is no evidence that anyone was deterred. It would take some time for the news of the change of control to spread, so British ships in the area would not call for several months – by which time everyone would know.

The East India Company reactivated its agency in Cape Town by reappointing its former agent there, James Pringle, who arrived in mid-1808. He knew the colony already, having been the agent from 1794 to 1803, and one of his first acts was to open up his warehouse and sell the accumulated stores, which, he said, he realized the colony needed – it also made £2,000 for his company.[1] More important for the future was the continued presence all through the short Batavian Republic period, of several British merchants, such as John Murray from Aberdeen, who had arrived in 1797, and maintained his farm at Mossel Bay, and a coasting vessel which plied between his home and Cape Town. In the Batavian period he had simply stayed put.[2]

After 1806 others, merchants first, began to arrive and settle. A man called Carey was given permission to live in Cape Town in September 1806. He had also remained in South Africa during the Batavian time, but had taken the oath of loyalty to the Dutch government, which is why his case had to be dealt with by Baird – and also, no doubt, why he waited until September before applying.[3] Such men as Murray and Carey were reinforced after the reconquest by new arrivals, such as Alexander MacDonald, a merchant who had also settled there during the first British occupation, but had, unlike the other two, left when the Dutch returned in 1803. By March 1807 he was well enough established to ask to be granted the use of more land for warehousing; he 'is much in want of store room for his large importations from Great Britain', he claimed in his application.[4]

One constraint on new immigration was the uncertainty about the future status of the colony, but in London the War and Colonial Office was quite clear that the Cape would not be handed back to the Dutch again, but would become a British possession – though this depended, of course on a British victory, which did not seem likely until after Napoleon's Russian disaster in 1812. On the other hand, even Napoleon's power in Europe did not have much overseas reach, and the British overseas empire was hardly affected – except to grow to encompass all other European empires in one way or another – French Mauritius, for example, and Reunion Island were captured in 1810, Java and the other Dutch East Indian islands in 1811. This therefore became clear to others by that time, as the Napoleonic European Empire disintegrated. With the Orange family refugees in London and in hopes of British assistance to effect their restoration, there was little doubt that British wishes in the matter of the Cape would prevail.

So any British merchants who went to the Cape and who were alert to political matters could be reasonably certain, and increasingly so, that no political upset from Europe would disturb them, and also that the government of the colony would be generally welcoming. This was a far more certain situation than in the earlier British period between 1795 and 1803, when the occupation had clearly been seen to be temporary – yet even then several men from Britain had gone to the Cape and stayed. One element in the general confidence in the permanence of British control derived from Popham's insistence on revising the surrender terms to provide a more stable financial system.

As soon as the reconquest was evident, this trickle of emigration resumed. Henry Nourse, a London merchant, sent out an agent in 1806, Kenneth Duncan, who was from Edinburgh. John Ebden was shipwrecked on his way back from India and took a post as a clerk in the Naval Victualling Office at Cape Town. Thomas Doyle went out as a missionary, arriving as early as May 1806. Another clerk, James Howell, arrived in June 1807, and by 1813 he was in business as a ship's chandler. Philip Henderson, a carpenter from Fife, came out in 1809 and became a shipwright, to be joined by his brother Thomas in 1820. A recent survey of merchants lists thirty-eight men who moved to the Cape from Britain by about 1820, to become active merchants in the colony. Of these eleven were Scots, seven were English, and one Irish; the rest are not specified as to origin, but another five have Scots-type names.[5]

This is a strong Scots presence in such a small community of merchants, in a land where the white population was less than 30,000, at least three quarters of whom were concentrated in and about Cape Town; the black population of Cape Colony was only a little less.[6] The merchants' presence brought connections with Britain and India, and they also brought with them a spirit of enterprise and development which was new, for the old Dutch regime had been repressive in these matters. So Alexander MacDonald wanted to expand within a short time of his arrival, Philip Henderson went from being a carpenter to being a shipwright, John Murray expanded from whale fishing to coastal trading and farming, and so on.

These merchants settled mainly in Cape Town, naturally enough. Their business was essentially with the ships which called on voyages between

Europe and the east. That had been the original purpose of the Dutch East India Company in planting its station there, so in many ways the function of the place had not changed. For the present the Cape scarcely produced much more than fresh food and water to interest these men. But Baird was alert to the possibility of expansion, as also to the need for developing local revenue; he sent a consignment of Cape wine to several members of the government in London, and persuaded the prize agent to release government-owned Spanish sheep which had been brought in by the Batavian regime. Later in the year he inspected the harvest and found it promising, and the Secretary W.S. van Ryneveld encouraged the continuation of a programme of improving the quality of local cattle which the Batavians had begun.[7] Baird was constantly concerned with the supply of money in the colony, but the main influences there were the presence of the large garrison and the opening of Cape Town to trade when the blockade was lifted, the result of the British conquest.[8]

The Batavian regime had been concerned to promote 'improvement' – witness the sheep – though Janssens had less than three years in which to achieve anything, subject as he was in that time to a continual British blockade, so this had not got very far. The new British regime, despite some early nervousness, never seemed in any real danger of being overthrown, either from internal troubles or from external attack. Its gestures towards development were thus more convincing and backed by more resources. In May 1807, the new Governor-General of India, Lord Minto, called at Cape Town on his way east, and wrote a brief report to Windham in London – though as it happened Windham was already out of office by then. Minto considered the garrison, even in the absence of the soldiers who had been diverted to South America, to be quite adequate, and said that it was in 'the highest possible order and the British regiments are the finest body of men ever sent out of England', which seems a little extravagant – as well as geographically inaccurate in its assumption of their origin – a curious error for a Scot. He looked at the Cape Regiment, and commented: 'The Cape Corps is thought ... likely to be a more useful and serviceable corps ... Colonel Graham must have had the greatest merit in forming them.'

Of course Minto had his own agenda and hoped that any extra troops, which were not immediately needed at the Cape, would be sent on to India, and later he did gain the use of the 72nd Foot for his attack on Mauritius. But he also remarked that 'I am glad to think the colony capable of solid and intensive improvement ...', though this cannot have been more than a bland hope at the time. A subsidiary item on his agenda seems to have been to praise the Scots he met, even if he referred to their origin as 'England'. He himself was an Elliott from the Borders (hence 'Minto'), and was looking at the Cape soon after Baird had left. He praised not only Colonel Graham, but Captain Munro as well, who was on the local Staff.[9]

The garrison of the Cape seldom fell below 5,000 soldiers while the French wars were on. No attack was ever launched on the Cape from Europe – or from anywhere else – and so one might say that the deterring effect of the army stationed in the Cape was successful, though it was the sheer distance involved, and the constant vigilance of the Royal Navy in European waters, which formed the real deterrent. The Cape was also used as a base for the conquest of the French islands of Reunion and Mauritius. The 72nd Foot (Seaforth Highlanders) was used in that expedition, co-ordinated with forces from India under the overall command of Sir John Abercromby, Commander-in-Chief in India. The regiment remained in the island until 1814, then returned to the Cape for another eight years.[10]

Within the Cape Colony, however, there was the constant problem of the eastern frontier. The infiltration of the Xhosa, and Nldambe's people, into the Zuurveld since 1800 had left Uitenhage, Captain Cuyler's new command, almost as a beleaguered outpost, though the area was reinforced by a garrison after 1806. In 1809 Colonel Richard Collins toured the frontier areas and reported to Baird's successor as Governor, Lord Caledon, on the conditions there. The next Governor, Sir Francis Cradock, was a Protestant Irishman (as was Caledon, despite his title), and a professional soldier, and he finally took action. In 1812 Colonel Graham, with the Cape Regiment which he had recruited, developed, and trained, and a white militia from the frontier areas, systematically drove the black settlers out of the Zuurveld, then pushed them and others further east across the Great Fish River back into the lands they had originally come from.[11] In the newly emptied lands Graham established two new settlements called Cradock and Grahamstown, and planted a series of small forts designed to hold the new base and to prevent the return of the Blacks (Map 2).

Next year (1813) the Rev. John Campbell travelled through the area on an inspection trip for the London Missionary Society. On 1 April 'at 5.00 pm we came in sight of a beautiful valley between the mountains, of about four miles extent. The sides of the mountains were covered with Caffre Gardens among the trees, from whence they had lately been driven by the military. The skeletons of many of the houses remained, and some tobacco was still growing; but all their cornfields were destroyed.' In this desolate but fertile area, he found that the forts were more often than not manned by

Scots officers commanding the Hottentots of the Cape Regiment. Campbell carefully noted them: 'Messrs. Boyle and MacKenzie from Glasgow and Galloway,' 'Lieutenants Gore (from Fortross) and Laycock,' 'Lieutenant Leydenham from Edinburgh,' and so on, all under the overall command of Captain Fraser the deputy landdrost, whose centre was Grahamstown, which was already developing as a town in the year after the clearance.[12]

In 1819 Ndlambe – who had won the civil war which followed the expulsion of his people – tried to return to the lost lands west of the Great Fish River, so temptingly empty. His invasion was defeated and his people were then deprived of yet more land, and the territory between the Great Fish and Keiskama Rivers was cleared as a buffer zone.[13] There was now a substantial cleared area, roughly sixty miles along the coast and stretching eighty miles inland, populated by a few whites (and their slaves) and controlled by the soldiers in the forts. It was comparatively well-watered and fertile land – as the Blacks had shown – and it was not going to be left empty for long.

Away from the frontier the army's routine was as a garrison, which meant drill, moving to camp in the winter, military exercises, but for the individual soldiers probably considerable boredom, inspections, occasional postings to outposts, of which the eastern frontier forts may well have been the most congenial, since it offered activity, and possible action. This may be one explanation for the unusual conduct of the 93rd Regiment. This was a unit almost entirely recruited from the Countess of Sutherland's lands, and was thus unusually close knit, with very few of the men coming from outside the North of Scotland. This was perhaps the main explanation for the fact that no men were lost by desertion during 1806, a record which was maintained in 1807; the regiment also had a remarkably low incidence of courts-martial and punishments, though it did steadily lose men to disease, just like the other units.

A further sign of its internal cohesion is the fact that the regiment as a unit organized itself as a Church of Scotland presbytery, found and engaged a minister, a Scots missionary called George Thom, and appointed two Sergeants, two corporals, and two privates as their elders.[14] In 1812 John Campbell preached in the Great Meeting House in Cape Town to a congregation 'attended chiefly by soldiers of the 93rd and 83rd Regiments' (the 83rd was an Ulster unit and so largely Presbyterian, though not as fervent as the 93rd).[15] The loyalty of the Sutherlands was thus directed towards their homeland, their own people and their Church above all, and this is emphasized by the extraordinary fact that the men remitted much of their meagre pay to their relatives at home, and some also to the Church Missionary Society.

This was clearly a most unusual regiment. After the victory at Blaauwberg in 1806 they did no more fighting as a unit while in South Africa. There was a steady loss of men by sickness and accident: fifteen men died in 1806, apart from those killed in the landing and the battle, and nineteen in the next year, Scots leaving their bones in a strange land, but this was not a particularly lethal record and is quite comparable with other regiments.[16] Some of the men worked as teachers in local schools – 'dominies' – and when the regiment was ordered back to Britain, several men took their discharges locally.[17] So the influence of the 93rd in South Africa could be expected to be substantial, all the more since the Calvinism of the Church of Scotland was close to the religion of the Dutch at the Cape. This influence, however, produced unexpected results.

The British military presence in South Africa after 1806 meant that the colony was well protected, and the British governors were fully prepared to use their military power to defeat the Blacks in the east, as Governor Cradock showed. The increasing British familiarity with the area meant that it was only a matter of time before the emigration impulse which had developed in Britain, particularly after 1815, turned in that direction. The men of the 93rd Foot who took their discharges there were symptoms of this also, and it remained also when the regiment left in 1814, and this was also the case with the 21st Light Dragoons and the 83rd Foot, both of which were in the Cape even longer than the 93rd.[18] But it was from Scotland that the recent tradition of organized groups of emigrants transferred itself to South Africa.

The emigrant impulse in Scotland was, of course, not entirely voluntary, in this time of the 'clearances', but neither was it entirely forced, and those who went to South Africa were generally volunteers. It was in part the knowledge of the colony which the Scottish military presence had fostered, and the presence of Scots merchants there, which was one of the sources of the Scottish emigration.

After the peace treaty of 1814, which settled that for the foreseeable future the colony would remain under British control, it was Scotsmen who organized the first parties of emigrants from Britain to settle in South Africa. Benjamin Moodie, son of an Orkney laird, but himself from Leith, brought out a party of 200 men, mainly recruited in the Edinburgh area, in 1817; most of them settled in Cape Town, but Moodie himself moved on to Swellendam. Peter Tait brought out another small group of Scots next year, and organized a further group two years later. The Moodie group was composed mainly of labourers and skilled craftsmen, and their skills and labour were soon in such demand that they scattered throughout the colony. The Tait group went to George, close to the coast at Mossel Bay – John Murray's home – and so both were very largely reinforcing these older settlements.[19]

The British government in the Cape had also almost from the start looked to encourage settlers to come from Britain. Especially after 1815 the British were conscious that they were a small governing group amid a much larger non-British population. Also the emptiness of the cleared land in the east was a constant problem as both the local Boers and the local Blacks eyed its possibilities and encroached on it. As early as 1809 Colonel Collins, in his report on the conditions along the frontier, had suggested that the solution was to plant settlers there. From 1818, perhaps triggered by the arrival of the Moodie settlers, the Governor Lord Charles Somerset began to encourage emigrants to settle in the Zuurveld. In Britain, beset by the post-war depression, the home government began to subsidize emigration as a safety valve to avoid a feared revolution.

So the settlements led by Moodie and Tait were essentially the preliminaries to the more famous, and larger, but less successful, emigration parties of 1819–1820, who were intended to occupy the lands vacated by the Xhosa on the Eastern Frontier, and guarded until then by the Cape Regiment. In this settlement the most successful part was the Scottish group which settled in the Baviaans River area, though that success was due less to the nationality of the group than to the fact that the emigrants were granted much larger tracts of land than the rest. This in turn was because one part of the group did not set out, and another part died when their ship caught fire and sank. There was thus more land for those who actually arrived (see map 2).[20] The region became called Albany, in part in tribute to the heavy Scottish presence. The settlers, of course, had been enticed by government promises and deluded by inaccurate government propaganda. Nevertheless, the arrival of the 1820 settlers definitively led to the occupation of the cleared area between the Bushmans and the Great Fish Rivers, though this still left a further cleared area beyond on the Great Fish to separate them from the Blacks who were confined beyond the Keiskama.

The other aspect of the legacy of the 93rd Foot and their fellow Scots in South Africa is arguably much more profound, and certainly longer lasting, and is intimately linked with this 1820 settlement of Britons on the frontier. This extra factor was their religiosity, as shown by the men's assiduous attendance at church worship, their choice of elders, their contributions to the Missionary Society. This will have been all the more impressive to the Dutch at the Cape in that both they and the Scots were of the same Calvinist faith. The conduct of the 93rd was in its way revelatory, for the Dutch Reformed Church in the Cape was in a bad way. There were few parishes organized, and little piety; the few ministers were isolated from each other, and for most of the time after 1796, isolated also from the parent church in Amsterdam. The trekboers, the Dutch who had moved east into the veldt, had taken with them only the rudiments of their original faith, the Dutch bible and their self-designation as 'Christian' in contradistinction to the Blacks. Their contact with any organized church system was minimal; in many cases it came only once a year, and sometimes not even that, with a visit by a minister. Such a visit was always the occasion for the baptism of children, sometimes up to 4 or 5 years of age, which implies the long intervals between visits.

Attempts had been made to institute a sort of travelling ministry, but the two ministers involved, agents also of the unpopular British occupation regime, had been driven out by the rebels of 1799. The Batavian regime, in accordance with its passion for rules, had drawn up new regulations for the church in the Cape, and these continued in operation under the British, but there was no local impetus to develop the church, or any from outside while the wars in Europe absorbed all energies. And, of course, after 1815 the Dutch at home had little interest. Yet the presence of two Scots Regiments in the Cape brought to Scottish attention the situation there, and it was clearly Scotsmen who would be the best candidates for missionaries in a Calvinist land.[21]

The British regime responded at last, in 1818, the same year as the governor began to promote British settlement. Two Scots ministers were already in the colony, former missionaries of the London Missionary Society. One of them, George Thom, had been the 93rd's choice as its minister. These two were now appointed as ministers of the Dutch Reformed Church, a power of appointment which resided with the governor, according to the Batavian church regulations. This was, given their mutual Calvinism, the obvious thing to do. (Appointing a Dutchman from Europe might have excited Dutch patriotism both in Europe and Africa, and was clearly to be avoided.) These appointments began a process which produced a majority of Scots among the ministers of the Cape by the time the local church was recognized as a Synod in 1824 – another power of decision of the governor. The new ministers were vigorous and dedicated, and set about taking their ministry out to the isolated farms, baptizing, preaching where a congregation could be gathered, and establishing new parishes – to be manned, in many cases, by other Scots.

The Dutch Reformed Church thus became a Scottish ecclesiastical colony, yet it also reflected the society of which it was a part. The missionaries had extended their activities to the black population as well as the Dutch so that the older distinction in which 'Christian' equalled 'white' no longer applied. To the north the London Missionary Society had established a quasi-protectorate over Griqualand, a factor which illustrates the new influences emanating from Britain.

In the frontier area, the arrival of the 1820 settlers had restricted the area over which the Boer cattle farmers could move their animals. The land further east was fully occupied by the Xhosa, who were both militarily more than a match for the Boers and under a degree of British protection – the governors had no wish for a war on the frontier. This was, of course, regarded as unwarranted interference in their rights by the Boers, who wished to be able to settle in the empty lands, and to conduct raids into the black areas, but British protection was nevertheless effective.

The frontier was thus, with restless Boers, new British settlers, and Blacks confined in the land east of the Keiskama, a turbulent region. In 1834 a long drought drove many Blacks into moving west, and they had to be driven out by the army – this was another 'Kaffir War'. They were also, of course, under pressure from further east, where the Zulu explosion was driving refugees in all directions. In this situation the Boers of the frontier area, eyeing further deserted lands to the north, where the Zulu refugees had driven others out, decided they could no longer remain.

They were, of course, under pressure from the drought, though their large farms meant that they suffered less than did the Blacks. They were under pressure from the British settlers, whose arrival had restricted their grazing territories. They were damaged by the Black invasion. And they also found that their Black and Hottentot people were now classified as slaves by the British administration and were to be freed by the British Act of Slave Emancipation of 1833. The result, in very brief terms, was the Great Trek, where large numbers of Boers, overwhelmingly from the eastern frontier region, sold out and moved themselves, their families, their animals (and their slaves) north, out of the range of the British.[22]

They took with them their religion, recently revised, reorganized and revitalized by the Scots ministers. One of the motives for (and results of) the trek was to maintain Boer racial attitudes, and this gradually became formalized among those who trekked and those who remained in the Cape Colony. And so as early as 1851 separate services for blacks and whites were accepted by the Synod, a clear recognition that this was a requirement of the whites if they were to continue as church members. The rationale was that people were to be brought into the church first, and that obstacles to their attendance were to be removed. As usual the church took the easy way out, and accommodated itself to the local society, formalizing the local prejudices; texts from the Bible could always be found as justification.

The Scots ministers, who were always sent to the Netherlands to learn Dutch before going to South Africa, inevitably became fully absorbed into Boer society, identified with it, and in some cases became its vociferous advocates. Andrew Murray Junior became the most widely respected minister of the Dutch Church, and may be taken as an example, though possibly an extreme one. He was the son of one of the first recruits from Scotland who had been minister at Graaff Reinet for forty years. He repeatedly took the side of the Afrikaners in their disputes with the British imperial regime in the later nineteenth century. He established the church presence in the Orange Free State in the period following the Great Trek, he argued in pamphlets for the Boers at the time of the wars of 1879 and 1899, and he joined the Boer leaders in the dedication of their monument to the women who died in the British concentration camps during the Second Boer War (1899–1902), the memory of which was treasured by the Afrikaners as one of the main items in their determined insistence on maintaining their own national identity. In the conditions of defeat after 1902, the Dutch Church became the great vehicle, along with the Afrikaans language, for Afrikaner nationalism. And so the separation of whites and blacks, already institutionalized in the church for half a century before that, became normal in society as well. And this process led on inexorably to the formalization of apartheid by the new National Party after 1948, despite its illogicality, injustice and internal contradictions. The Scots in South Africa, beginning with the regiments of the conquest, had thus a profound effect on the local society.

Chapter Five

The 71st Regiment of Foot

Before considering exactly what happened when Popham's unauthorized expedition invaded South America, I want to go back to Britain for a chapter, to look at the troops which were to do the actual fighting. It is impractical to look at every man on the expedition, indeed it is impossible since not all are known even by name, but it is possible to make an investigation of the men of the particular regiment which Baird sent.

Before doing that, however, it is worth noting something else first, since it will only be referred to briefly later. Most of the British units travelled with a complement of women and children. There were 4,616 men and 633 officers and NCOs in the regiments on the original expedition, and 366 women and 272 children as well. Each regiment had the right to carry sixty women and forty children on its strength, and four of the regiments had the full allocation, including the 71st, which will be here looked at in some detail. One rather suspects that this was sometimes a statistical fudge, and that the numbers often varied from that apparent accuracy. But in the background these camp followers need to be remembered. When the men fought, some of them knew that they did so in immediate defence of their wives and children.

When Sir David Baird arrived at Dublin at the end of July 1805, he took command of an expedition which included regiments recruited, at least in theory, from all parts of the British Isles. Of course no single regiment was exclusively recruited from a particular locality – though the 93rd, as noted in the last chapter, came close to that, as did the 72nd. Most of them however, did develop, or retained, a strong connection with a particular area. Three of Baird's regiments were more or less from the English Midlands, the 24th Foot from the Warwickshire area, the 38th from Staffordshire, and the 59th, the regiment which was destined ultimately for India, from Nottinghamshire. One, the 83rd, was originally raised in Northern Ireland. The other three, the 71st, the 72nd, and the 93rd, were Scottish, and all three of them were originally based on clans of the Highlands.

The 93rd Foot, the most recently risen of the three, was still very much identified with its origin in the Sutherland estates in the county of that name.

It had been raised in the old way, in 1800, when the Countess of Sutherland had sent word into her lands that she required the young men to form a regiment, and they had supposedly turned out, almost 1,000 strong, more or less instantly. Almost all of the men, therefore, came from the Sutherland area, and of those who did not, most came from Ross-shire or Caithness next door.[1] This is the regiment which figures prominently in the South Africa story, and it will feature again in the last chapter; it kept its almost exclusive Scottishness very successfully throughout the wars, until the very end.

Particular clans had been the origin also of the 71st Foot, recruited in the Mackenzie lands of the Earls of Cromartie, and of the 72nd, which originated in the lands of the Earls of Seaforth, but these regiments had been raised twenty years earlier than the Sutherlands, and they were no longer almost purely Highland. For, as soon as a regiment had been recruited time and events began to wear away at it. Men were lost, by sickness, by death, by desertion, by transfer, in battle, by accident, and replacements did not always come from the old homeland – indeed, these replacements generally came from the area where the regiment happened to be stationed, at least if it was in Britain – but elsewhere there were no scruples about recruiting foreigners, as Baird demonstrated at Cape Town. But, despite such changes, the identification with the old homeland, increasingly tenuous as it often became in the personnel of the regiment, nevertheless remained, and would appear in such everyday matters as dress and music, and often the officers, and in such more important matters as military and battle honours.

This chapter concentrates particularly on the activities and fortunes of the 71st Foot, later to be the Highland Light Infantry, in South America in 1806–1807, and it may also stand as an illustration of the Scottish regiments of the time in these matters. The regiments had different experiences, particularly as will be seen, the 93rd, as did the 71st but in some respects it was very largely typical, and while in others it was wholly atypical.

The regiment originated in 1777, as a clan unit. In that year Lord MacLeod, the heir to the Earl of Cromartie, returned to Britain for the first time in thirty years. His father had taken part on the Jacobite side in the rebellion of 1745–1746, and had been duly attainted by the victors, though he was permitted to go into exile, rather than suffer execution. His son was also implicated, but was allowed to go into exile without the need for a reprieve. He eventually joined the Swedish army, rose to the rank of major-general, and was created 'Count Cromarty' in the Swedish nobility. In 1777 he took advantage of the passage of time since the Jacobite rebellion, and of the British government's new need for troops for its American war, and returned to Britain. He obtained a private audience with King George III, and promised to raise a regiment from among his own people. The unspoken threat which lurked behind his words was that he might be able to do the same in rebellion, of course – which is exactly what was happening across the Atlantic.

His offer was accepted, and within a very short time he managed to raise a new regiment, MacLeod's Highlanders, which later were numbered the 73rd Foot, and later still the 71st. Of the 1,100 men who were paraded in April 1778, 840 came from the old Cromartie estates, despite the absence for a generation of the earl and his son. Of the rest, 236 were Lowlanders from other parts of Scotland, and thirty-six were English or Irish, though these were actually recruited in Glasgow. One of those who worked in the Lowlands to recruit men for the regiment was Lieutenant David Baird, who then transferred to the new regiment in the rank of captain. Lord MacLeod was immediately commissioned to raise a second battalion, of the same size, which he did.[2]

The second battalion served at Gibraltar during the siege of 1779–1783, and was then returned to Britain and disbanded, though the officers were given the option of joining the first battalion, which had gone to India. From 1780, when it arrived in India, until 1797, the 71st, as it was by then numbered, marched and fought in South India, fighting first Hyder Ali of Mysore and then his son Tipu Sultan, in three successive wars. It was in the second of these wars that Captain Baird was captured and imprisoned for four years. When the battalion was due to be returned to Britain, those men who were still fit were drafted into other regiments which were to remain in India. Only the disabled, the non-commissioned officers, and the officers were returned to Britain. They were to become a cadre around which a new battalion could be recruited. Only ten of the original officers survived, of whom Baird was one, now a colonel (he had been a local Major-General for a time in India). The use the British government had out of MacLeod's Highlanders is notable: not only did the men fight Britain's wars, but 2,000 potential rebels, all young and fit men, were siphoned off and sent away from Scotland. Of the men who were recruited into the first battalion in 1777, it is doubtful if more than a handful ever saw Scotland again; India's wars and climate and diseases took a heavy toll.[3]

The regiment was to be reconstituted in Scotland, but not necessarily from the men of the Highlands. It was now quartered at Stirling, with the intention of attracting new recruits from the men of the more heavily populated Central Valley. Peace was in the air, however, and was actually agreed late in 1801, and so recruiting was slow, and the regiment had built up to only about 200 men by mid-1800. The solution was to gather volunteers from the Scottish fencible regiments (i.e. the militia), 600 of them, and at the same time to move the regiment to Ireland, so making it difficult for the homesick recruits to desert to their homes, and providing access to another pool of potential recruits. The renewal of war in 1803 led to the re-establishment of the second battalion, this time based in Glasgow, with the aim of feeding recruits across to the first, which in the meantime was also recruiting in Ireland. Until 1805 the regiment remained there.

After its return to Ireland from the South Atlantic in 1808, a 'Description Book' was compiled of the members of the regiment. It was to contain the details of each man, his age, appearance, his place of origin, his civilian occupation, and so on. It is incomplete. Some men are no more than names and others are certainly missing.[4] In addition to this book, there are the monthly pay lists, which list the men in each company, and indicate the money due to them each month.[5] Together therefore these documents give some idea of when new recruits joined, of their rank as they were promoted, if at all, their company, extra duties, illnesses, and so on. Combining these two sources produces a list of the men of the regiment, and considerable miscellaneous information about many of them. Over 1,100 men are listed in the various documents for the period studied here, and varying amounts of personal information are preserved concerning about half of them.

Their origins are stated for 429 men, either directly or by implication from their names. Of the 429 men who can be classified into their countries of origin, two thirds were Scots, one in twenty was English, and about thirty per cent were Irish. Those who cannot be classified either do not have their homes noted, or their names are not national-specific. It is, for example, reasonable to assume that a man called McKenzie or Fraser is a Scot, or a man called Byrne or McDevott is Irish, but where does a man called Brown come from, or Miller, or Smith? It seems likely that there were rather more Englishmen than are actually noted as such specifically in the documents of the regiment, but in all likelihood, given that the regiment was stationed in either Scotland or Ireland all the time after it returned from India, the proportion of Englishmen is probably no greater than the specific origins suggest – five per cent.

The Englishmen of the regiment came from a wide area (diagram 4). Six were from the London area, three from Staffordshire, three from Lancashire, with a certain bias towards the towns, which would be where the recruiting officers and sergeants set up their stalls, but only two Englishman had been recruited since the regiment was stationed in Ireland. All the others had been recruited in or before 1800 and only one since 1801.

The Irish came overwhelmingly from Ulster, that is, from the nine northern counties which were the province at the time (diagram 5). This was no doubt the result of the regiment being stationed for a time at Dundalk, where many of the men from the Scottish Fencibles were signed on. A number of the names of the men whose homes were stated to be in Ireland betray a Scottish or English ancestry, though two-thirds of the recruits whose Irish origin is given or implied have Irish names. These men were presumably Catholics, just as most of the others with names originating from Britain were no doubt in the main Protestant. We may thus suppose that a fifth or a sixth of the men of the regiment who sailed from Cork in August 1805 were Catholic. This is not a judgment which can be made concerning the Scots, though we know from later events that there were undoubtedly a number of Catholics among the Scots (and, for all we know, among the English as well). Without a clearer indication, such as that provided by the Irishness of the names, it is impossible to estimate numbers. Very few of the men came from the Western Isles (though several were from the Northern Isles) where the MacDonalds retained their Catholicism; one man whom we do know to be Catholic was called MacDonald.

The Scots did not originate too predominantly from any one part of the country, as did the Irish soldiers, but two areas did produce more than their share of the men (diagram 6). The Highlands, from Shetland to Argyll, was the origin of nearly half of the men whose home is stated. There was, as might be expected, a strong representation of Mackenzies, the family name of the Earls of Cromartie, with thirteen soldiers and no less than six officers bearing that name. There were ten MacLeods and ten Murrays, twenty Mackays and twenty Rosses, sixteen MacDonalds and twelve each of Campbells and Sutherlands. Of the other Scots almost fifty came from the Northeast (including Perthshire, and ninety from the south, though very few came from the furthest south. Out of this southern group the most significant number is forty-two from Lanarkshire, which means, of course, mainly Glasgow (noted as either Glasgow or 'Barrenry', and a few nearby villages such as Gorbals). The reformed second battalion was stationed in Glasgow from 1804, and it became a popular institution in the city (the Highland Light Infantry was later regarded as a 'class' regiment). By contrast only fourteen men came from Edinburgh or Leith.

The soldiers were in the main mature men (diagram 9). Some certainly were young, the youngest only 16, but the majority were in their twenties.

The average age of all those whose age was recorded was 28.7 years. This, in fact, was the average age in 1808, and in theory it should be reduced by three years to take account of the time elapsed, since I am discussing the regiment as it was in 1805. But this was a steadily changing population, as men died, or were killed, or were discharged, and as others were recruited or were transferred in from other units. The average age is thus unlikely to have changed very much during the war years. Certainly the ages of these men, the ones whose ages are recorded, were three years lower in 1805 than in 1808, but the average age of the whole battalion will have remained much the same.

There was, however, a significant difference in the average ages of the three national groups. None of the English was under 25 years of age in 1808, and the average age of the small English group was over 29 years; the much larger Scots group was a little older on average, but the spread of ages was much greater, from 18 to 48. These were men who had in many cases been in the Fencibles before joining the 71st, and so will have had several years of part-time soldiering before they joined – and they will have joined because they chose to do so, true volunteers, and the more valuable for that. The Irish, however, were on average two years younger than either the English or the Scots, at just under 27, although they also had the oldest men, one of 49, and one of 62.

The explanation for these differences in ages lies in the pattern of recruitment. No recruiting in England had been undertaken since 1801, though one man from Cheshire joined in 1805 – he must have done so in Ireland, perhaps at Dundalk. They were thus inevitably older, just as the Scots were who had been largely recruited before 1800. The Irish, on the other hand, were younger because many of them had been accepted into the regiment since 1800, when it moved to Ireland, and so were raw recruits when they joined, unlike many of the older Scots. The result would be to emphasize the Scottishness of the regiment even more, but one would expect Englishmen to have an influence out of proportion to their numbers, being older soldiers.

A further point may be made based on the ages of these men. Most of them had been in the army for many years (diagram 10). Two men had been recruited originally in 1787; thirteen had been in the army since before this bout of the French wars began in 1793. The vast majority of those whose date of recruitment is known had been in the army before the peace of Amiens went into effect in 1802: 287 out of 367 – over three-quarters. This was not merely a regiment of mature men and largely volunteers, it was one of long serving, experienced soldiers, men who knew their job well, men who were skilled survivors. The regiment, of course, had not been in any sort of action since 1797, but a third of the men had been in the army since before that date, and had been in other units from which they had transferred into the 71st. There was plenty of old-soldier experience and expertise to spread among the later recruits.

Further, the years 1798 to 1801 had seen the arrival of the over 150 men, recruited at Stirling after the regiment returned from India, and thus transferred from the Scottish fencible regiments as volunteers; these latter were already trained, and with some experience. They were men who had volunteered twice, first into their original fencible units, which were regiments recruited for home defence, and then into the 71st. They were thus men who had taken the decision quite deliberately, and in all likelihood for patriotic motives, or perhaps because they liked the military life. They were physically fit, trained, and keen: ideal soldierly material, and as a unit they had mostly been together for several years, during which their training will have been honed. This was a regiment of the very highest quality.

Physically, however, the men were not particularly intimidating (diagram 11). One man was 6′ 2″ in height, and four more were measured at 6ft, but the average height was about 5′ 5″, though none were less than 5′ 2″ – no doubt a minimum height requirement was operating. The English tended to be smaller than the overall average, but this is because none of them was over 5′ 10″. Between the Scots and the Irish there is no difference, though the tallest man was, in fact, a Scot.

The civilian occupations of these men were entirely working-class (diagrams 7, 8, 12). Not a single man came from what might be called a middle-class occupation. This is only to be expected. The middle classes did not normally go into the army, and if they did they became officers. Almost half of the men were classified as 'labourers', that is, unskilled, mainly no doubt agricultural workers – what on the continent would be called peasants. Another 100 men gave their occupation as 'weaver', which was little more than a semi-skilled job in the circumstances of the early Industrial Revolution, men who had perhaps been put out of work by the development of the new machinery – though that is no more than an assumption. The rest had a variety of skilled occupations, which it will have taken time and effort to learn. There was a gunsmith, and eight other smiths, several carpenters, more than a dozen shoemakers, three painters, and so on.

A more detailed classification of these men, considering their occupations alongside their homes, reveals more about them. The labourers and weavers formed a higher proportion of the intake from Ireland than from the other countries: four out of five Irishmen were in these categories. Almost all the weavers came from Ulster (the nine counties), whereas those with greater skills were recruited from across the whole island. The explanation is presumably that the textile industry was concentrated in the north. In the southern counties the recruitment of skilled men and labourers was roughly equal; indeed, if weavers can be put into the skilled category, there were more skilled men from the southern counties than labourers. From the north there were three times as many labourers as skilled men who joined.

From Scotland a different pattern emerges. The labourers were heavily recruited from the north, the weavers from the south. Indeed from Inverness, Sutherland, and Argyll, only labourers were recruited. From the Highland areas, only seven weavers and only sixteen skilled men joined the regiment, whereas over eighty were labourers. From the Northeast, however (Moray, Aberdeen, Angus, Perth) the proportions were more even. In the south, they were reversed. There the skilled men and the weavers were about equal in number, and the labourers only one in five. Indeed more weavers were recruited from Lanarkshire than from the whole of Scotland north of Stirling, whereas Ross and Cromarty and Inverness each produced more labourers that all Scotland south of Stirling. In the same way, from the two counties of Lanarkshire and Midlothian, holding Glasgow and Edinburgh–Leith respectively, there came more skilled recruits than from the whole of the north or northeast.

The pattern is thus geographically different in Scotland and Ireland, but socially it is, in fact, much the same. The economically more developed areas – the north of Ireland, the central belt of Scotland – sent men into the regiment who were at the lower end of the economic scale, labourers and weavers. In the less-developed areas – the Highlands in particular – the recruits were very largely unskilled. In the more developed areas, where the Industrial Revolution was beginning its transformation of the working practices and opportunities for the workers, there were more skilled men available to be recruited, and so the proportion of recruits with skills was higher. This is a reflection not of need, or of unemployment, or of starvation, but of the society as a whole. The chance of gaining a skill in the Highlands was minimal; in the central belt and in Northern Ireland, the most common occupation for a workman, apart from labouring, was weaving. Therefore, these occupations were the more heavily represented among the recruits. There is, therefore, no real indication here that men were driven into the army by economic deprivation.

The absence of any middle-class private soldiers is also a reflection of the society as a whole: the officers and men in the regiment were a military version of the class division in the country at large, and this was especially so in the clan society of northern Scotland. But there were other reflections of the society also. There were so many and variedly skilled workmen in the regiment, from a gunsmith to a bookbinder, from shoemakers to painters, that a man could be found who could do almost any task that was required. The regiment was thus, not merely a reflection of the society it came from and fought to preserve, but was actually a functioning microcosm of the society. As it moved about the world, it presented to that world a picture, distorted to be sure by the military mode of the regimental institution, but a picture of British society, its classes, its skills, its organization, and no doubt its maddening condescension. Even the proportion of men to women (say, twelve to one) was a reflection of the distribution of power.

The 71st Foot had been stationed at Baltinglass, in County Wicklow, until it was ordered to Bandon in County Cork in March 1805. This placed it close to the embarkation port of Cork, in readiness for its despatch overseas, no doubt originally with a view to being part of Sir Eyre Coote's proposed West Indies expedition, and the order to embark came in July. But then, of course, all was halted, and Coote's force was scaled down. Baird had arrived at Cork on 2 August, and was undoubtedly gratified to have his old regiment under his command, even if its personnel was totally different from those he had known in India. Despite his statements of instant readiness to be away, the next month saw several developments in the regiment and no doubt in the other embarked regiments as well. It may be taken as fairly typical, for instance, that eleven men deserted in the next month. With the men locked up in the transports, getting away was not easy, and took some determination and ingenuity, but because they went before the regimental records were systematized, we know little more than their names. One man, however, Private Edward Kelly, from County Monahan, is recorded as having deserted on 14 August, but he is also recorded as being appointed a corporal later, and then reduced to private again. Presumably, therefore, he did not actually desert – or, if he did, he returned fairly quickly. This is not the only detectable confusion in the records.

The deserters, in the nature of things, have few details recorded of them. They came from a variety of the regiment's companies, and went on a variety of dates between 24 July and 10 August, though two went on 4 August and three on 29 July, possibly together. Their names suggest that most of them were Scots – Christie, Craig, McAndrew, Mackay, McMaster, McVicar –

but since the great majority of men in the regiment was Scots anyway, this is not surprising. Only one – Patrick MacAulley – can be clearly categorized as Irish.

The date of Private Kelly's supposed desertion, 14 August, is significant, for it was on that day that a party of soldiers arrived at Cork from the second battalion in Glasgow. There were thirty-two men in the group, and they were conducted on the march by Sergeant Alexander Knowles. The party will have been sent for when the order to embark was given in mid-July, or perhaps a little earlier. Apart from Sergeant Knowles, eighteen of these men have some information about them recorded in the regimental sources. All but one were Scots, and eight of them were from Lanarkshire; the stationing of the second battalion in Glasgow was having its effect. Thirteen of the men had been recruited within the previous twelve months; seven (including the sergeant, no doubt), had been in the regiment much longer, one having joined as far back as 1790. These long-serving men had, no doubt, been involved in recruiting in Glasgow, and the whole group were presumably detailed for the move to bring the first battalion up to maximum strength. Nine of eighteen were very young, eight of them seventeen or eighteen. Seven of the whole group did not return from the expedition for one reason on another; these are mainly the men whose details are missing.

Little or nothing is known of these men's feelings or of their attitude to the expedition they were about to sail on. Most of them clearly expected to go, for the regiment had been in effect on notice to embark for months, and, with whatever feelings of resignation or enthusiasm, acquiesced. The officers, however, were more articulate, and several have left accounts, in the form of letters or diaries or memoirs and these have been and will be quoted as and when necessary and opportune. We have a single letter from this embarkation period, which gives an idea of the confusions, but also of the individual preparations required for heading into the unknown, and the downright practicalities as well. It is a letter by Major Robert Campbell of the 71st to his brother Archibald at Inverary, 'North Britain', dated from the *Majestic* transport, Cove of Cork, 7 August.[6] The first paragraph suggests that the major was not a very regular correspondent:

> The 71st regiment was suddenly marched from its quarters in the County of Limerick about three months since, with orders to embark at this place immediately for foreign service. Various circumstances attended with orders and counter-orders almost innumerable, and

abundantly perplexing to the troops assembled in this neighbourhood, have however protracted our embarkation until the present time.

On the first receipt of the order to embark and on the spur of the occasion I executed a trust deed certain friends whom want of time did not allow me to contact, empowering them to superintend and regulate my affairs during my absence, and among them I have taken upon me to include your name, a liberty for which I trust to find an excuse from your friendship, and further to hope that you will have the goodness to grant your aid as circumstances may arise to require it during my absence.

The troops assembled here for an expedition consisting of ten regiments were originally placed under Sir Eyre Coote – who is now with his whole staff it is said going to Jamaica – and Sir David Baird with the Brigadiers Beresford and Ferguson under him (the latter having the Highland Brigade) has been placed in command of the 24th, 38th, 71st, 72nd, 83rd and 93rd Regiments now embarked and ready to sail at the shortest notice. Their destination unknown, but said to be for the Cape of Good Hope, which opinion gains strength from the selection of the Staff, it being almost exclusively composed of officers who have been there. We were to be sailed two days since but a King's Messenger arrived just in time to detain us, and as we were to have proceeded under the escort of two frigates only, there can be little doubt that we form only a division of some large force to which it is intended to join us; probably the fleet of Indiamen now at Falmouth, which is known to have troops on board. It is impossible to give you an idea of the indecision which has marked the movements here during the last three months; some Regiments have been constantly on ship board in the harbour during that time – others have been three times embarked and debarked, and each time with preparations made for distant voyages, to the utter ruin of their finances, together with considerable loss in some corps from desertion. Blue Peter has been constantly flying I believe for the last six weeks, but I think it is now at last determined on to send us.

In the period of waiting, four men 'returned from desertion', apparently without serious punishment, perhaps even voluntarily (one was probably Kelly); but three other men were discharged by the general's order, presumably because of unfitness or ill-health. And one man, William Kerr, died, on 13 August. In the previous month, the battalion had thus had a net gain of nineteen men. And we know something about one more officer, Lt

William Dennis. He was intercepted at Cork for some civilian offence, no doubt an unpaid debt, and was prevented from embarking. Whether he was relieved at not being able to sail, or annoyed at having been caught, we have no way of knowing.

This is the regiment which was part of the expedition which reached the waters off the Cape on 4 January of the New Year, 1806. It, and its fellow regiments, was a highly trained force, and with only ten men noted as sick in the January monthly return, they had remained healthy during the long voyage. Eight hundred and thirty-three officers and men were available for the landing at the Cape. This is the first time since its reconstitution after the 'return' from India in 1799 that the regiment was going into battle. And it had at last fought a successful, if minor, battle, at Blaauwberg. The 71st was then selected by its old officer to go on this new expedition to South America. Baird clearly regarded this as an honour for the regiment; how the men saw it is unknown. It is odds-on that few of them had any idea of their destination, though no doubt rumours soon flew about, and at least some of them will have been accurate.

Chapter Six

Buenos Aires: the Conquest

The fleet sailed from Table Bay on 14 April. Popham took his three line-of-battle ships, *Diadem*, *Raisonable*, and *Diomede*, the remaining frigate, *Narcissus*, and the gun-brig, *Encounter*. He left no naval force at the Cape. The troops were spread among five small transports, *Walker*, *Willington*, *Melantho*, *Triton*, and *Ocean*, which were not capacious enough, so the warships had to accommodate some of the troops. *Diadem* carried eighty-five, *Raisonable* had eighty-eight, and the smaller *Diomede* over 100. *Narcissus* had fifty, but *Encounter* had none. She was to be used for another purpose.[1]

The fleet's course was set for St Helena, though this was not necessarily its actual destination. After a week one of the transports, *Ocean*, parted company. Ensign William Gavin of the 71st was on board and noted in his diary that the mizen mast was lost in a storm on the 20 April, and that it took two more days to replace it with jury rig. Lieutenant Walters on the *Raisonable* suspected that the separation was arranged – 'I think myself [it was] a planned thing that the *Ocean* should part company for a plea' – but a broken mast is a drastic way of doing this.[2] The fleet had altered course to the northward on the 22 April, but *Encounter* was sent off on a scouting mission, and the rest headed for St Helena.[3] *Ocean* found itself without direction, but the master had sealed orders which he now opened, and so he headed for the Plate. What he did not know was that Popham had a special scheme in view in heading for St Helena.

Popham went to St Helena to get more troops. He had already had some contact with the Governor, Robert Patten, for Captain Donnelly's *Narcissus* frigate had called in for the latest intelligence the year before, and *Leda* had collected provisions for the Cape in January. It will have been in Popham's mind as well that Patten's predecessor as Governor, Robert Brooke, had provided troops to the previous British expedition of conquest to the Cape in 1795.[4] Popham was always careful to find a colourable precedent for his most outrageous exploits.

Governor Patten was just his man. His contemporaries were not wholly certain of his sanity, but he had made some progress in reforming and disciplining the notoriously ill-behaved St Helena troops. The island was a refreshment station for East India Company ships, and was the point from which the homeward bound convoys collected a naval escort. While the Cape was in Dutch hands, it was the only British possession south of the equator, the only place at which Company ships could safely call for fresh food and water on the long voyage to and from India. It was often assumed by the British that the island was a prime target for French attack, and so it was well fortified and garrisoned. The French, perhaps realizing this, never did attack.

The garrison consisted of three groups of soldiers. The least useful from all points of view, was the militia, essentially civilians. From Popham's point of view though, their existence was helpful since it could free other troops for service elsewhere. These other troops consisted, at the end of 1805, of a regiment of infantry containing 639 soldiers, 151 NCOs, and twenty-six officers, and the St Helena Artillery, counting 335 'mattrosses', 120 NCOs and gunners and fifteen officers, a total of over 1,200 soldiers, and forty officers.[5] These were, of course, East India Company, not British government, troops; there is no sign that the distinction bothered either Popham or Patten.

Popham sent *Narcissus* on ahead with a letter to the governor, pointing out that plans to attack the River Plate area had been made earlier, and that Patten had expressed himself as keen to help Popham in an earlier letter. When the rest of the fleet arrived – having been fired on from the island, according to Captain Gillespie, for not sending in a boat – Popham and Beresford went on shore to exercise their persuasive skills on a willing subject. This took no more than a single meeting and after only a day at anchor 100 artillerymen with two howitzers, and 150 infantrymen were embarked. A ship waiting there, a merchantman called *Justina* from London, was persuaded to divert on a venture to go with the fleet and carry some of the troops from the island.

The exchange of letters on all this between Popham and Patten contained an odd discrepancy. Patten loaned the troops to the expedition on the understanding that they would be returned after 'the capture of Montevideo and Buenos Aires'; Popham replied by undertaking that they 'shall not be detained one day after they can be spared'.[6] Both men had covered themselves, or so they thought. Events did not permit either of these contingencies to be acted on.

The fleet, now with *Justina* in company, sailed again on 2 May. Three weeks later it was in the sea route along the South American coast (which Popham had been instructed to interrupt) and by early June the various captains began to worry about their precise positions, for the one thing that was known to all sailors about the River Plate was that it was shallow water; they began sounding. They were soon in intermittent fog as well; these were conditions guaranteed to try the nerves of all sailors.[7]

Popham was now investigating the possibilities presented by the situation in the River Plate (map 13). He seems to have had no clear plan when he left the Cape, and Buenos Aires and Montevideo crop up as alternative targets, or sometimes as successive targets; sometimes he just says the River Plate. On 27 May he went into *Narcissus* with the American Captain Waine and sailed off ahead of the fleet. They sighted land on 7 June, the north shore of the Plate estuary. Surgeon Thompson noted the noise made by the huge number of seals on the Isle of Lobos, a noise he likened to that at Smithfield market. Next day the ship was off Montevideo, and Thompson noted that it seemed a large town and that there were several ships in the harbour.[8]

At times one is compelled to believe that there was a guardian angel hovering over Sir Home Popham. At the Cape Captain Waine arrived with news of the vulnerability of Buenos Aires; the arrival of the *Volontaire* and its prisoners replenished the British force at the Cape, so allowing Baird to release the 71st; before they reached St Helena he had lost a ship and the troops therein (*Ocean*), and he was able to recoup that manpower loss from Governor Patten; at St Helena he heard of the approach of the line-of-battle ship *Tremendous* and he used that as an excuse to keep *Raisonable*, rather than detach that ship to the homeward bound convoy as he had been instructed to do; he had left the Cape just before orders arrived to send back his transports to Britain. And now his luck – for none of this was planned – continued. On 9 June, *Narcissus* intercepted a Portuguese brig which was bound from Buenos Aires to Rio de Janeiro, which had on board no less a person than 'a Spanish governor', several other important passengers, and a river pilot, who turned out to be a Scotsman called Russel. That is, Popham found a pilot for one of the most difficult waterways who turned out not only to speak English, but actually to be British. Russel had lived for nearly a quarter of a century in the River Plate area and he told Popham that Buenos Aires was, as surgeon Thompson put it, 'full of money and treasure.'[9]

And Popham's good fortune continued. Next day *Narcissus* met the lost transport *Ocean*, whose master had opened his sealed orders and obeyed them. Then Popham fell in with *Encounter*, which he had sent on ahead, and on 14 June all these ships met up once more with the fleet.[10] In the meantime, and probably ever since the first conversation with Russel the pilot, Popham had decided what to do. With a regiment and a half he would attack the city of Buenos Aires, population 45,000. But he still had to persuade his naval and military colleagues to do as he wished.

On 13 June Popham called a conference. Who attended it is not clear. General Beresford was certainly there, and presumably the captains from the other naval ships, Colonel Pack of the 71st, and Colonel Lane of the St Helena troops were also present; Captain Gillespie of the marines is our main source for what happened, but it seems unlikely that he was present. He reports that Beresford wanted to attack Montevideo, but that Popham argued for an attack on Buenos Aires.[11] Beresford's views had to be taken seriously. He was one of the few professionally trained soldiers on the British side, having attended the military school at Strasbourg before the French Revolution. He had a high reputation in Britain, had fought in Corsica, the West Indies, and, by special request of Marquess Wellesley, in India. He had commanded the march from the Red Sea to the Nile across the Egyptian desert in the campaign of 1801; which was of course, where both Popham and Baird had also shone. Beresford's career had, in fact, been an almost effortless rise, from an ensign in 1790 to local major-general now, assisted in no small measure, no doubt, by the support of his father, the Marquis of Waterford, who acknowledged parentage of this illegitimate son.[12] Beresford's opinion, therefore, was weighty, and his choice of Montevideo as the preferred target of his attack presupposed an intention to stay in the estuary. He was advocating the capture of the strongest point in the estuary as a preliminary to the intimidation of the rest, and the securing of an adequate base, which was, of course, the correct military method.

Popham's argument in favour of attacking Buenos Aires, however, was based on a different premise. He could quote Russel's information that troops were few in the city, and of poor quality. He may also have pointed to the formidable fortifications of Montevideo by contrast with the open condition of Buenos Aires, and that the expeditionary force had no siege materials. More likely, all he had to mention was silver; all the officers were attracted to the expedition above all by the prospect of acquiring loot, and of gaining prize money, and they had talked of it right from the start, and Popham's reputation is of a man more than usually anxious to win prize money.[13] Not only that, but the size of the expedition – or rather, its smallness – does argue that a raid was intended rather than a conquest, for what could a mere 1,500 men hope to conquer and hold? At all events Gillespie reports that Beresford was voted down, and Popham's plan to launch an attack on Buenos Aires was agreed. However, what was intended beyond that is not known, and was probably not even discussed beyond getting hold of the silver.

On 16 June, therefore, the dispositions were made. All the troops, the marines, and the companies of sailors (the 'Blues'), were transferred into the smaller ships – *Leda*, *Narcissus*, *Encounter*, and the five transports. Of the line-of-battle ships, *Diadem* was posted to blockade Montevideo, and *Diomede* and *Raisonable* went to cruise off Maldonado at the northern entrance to the estuary; these larger ships were unable to get further upriver than Montevideo because of their greater draught.[14] Popham went in front of the main attacking force in *Encounter*, navigating the invasion force through the shoals and banks, no doubt helped by the pilot Russel. *Narcissus*, carrying Beresford and his staff, grounded on the Ortiz Bank and could only be refloated by shifting some of its guns into *Encounter*, and then it grounded again the next day, but got off quickly. Often the wind was adverse, or there was fog. It took nine days for the small fleet to thread a way to within sight of Buenos Aires. Next day, 26 June, the ships moved eastwards a few miles to Quilmes, and began landing the troops.[15]

The landing turned out to be a difficult and most laborious exercise. *Narcissus* and *Leda* drew too much water to approach the coast, so *Encounter* was run in as close as possible to provide cover for the landing soldiers, and even that was no nearer than a mile from the shore (map 14). Surgeon Thompson in *Narcissus* had clearly been talking to knowledgeable men, probably Russel:

June 26. The whole face of the country is quite flat. The river here is twenty-one miles broad (most excellent water [presumably meaning fresh]). The *Narcissus* is the largest ship of war that ever went so far up the river, except two Spanish frigates; they were obliged to take their guns out at Montevideo.[16]

The process was similar to the successful landing at Losperd's Bay, but the distances were much greater, though there was no danger from surf. The troops were taken towards the shore in the boats of all the ships, but even then they had to wade the final part. Popham gained Gillespie's admiration during this fraught time, for he showed 'a great equanimity of temper and unruffled genius which uniformly marked and directed his words and actions'.[17] Ensign Gavin recorded the experience of the soldiers:

[June] 25th. The boats were launched, the troops got on board and proceeded to the shore, but being too shoal we were forced to get into the water and proceed knee deep about a quarter of a mile. Captain King [of the *Diadem*, one of Popham's protégés], of the Royal Navy, remained the whole time in the water as a mark for the troops to be guided by. We were under arms for the whole of the night; it rained incessantly.[18]

Once ashore, there was no relief for the troops. Their landing had been observed – it could hardly have been missed – and they camped that night (the landing went on till midnight) within sight of the Spanish campfires, disturbed by alarms and occasional musket shots. And, as Gavin noted, it rained all night. It is heavy enough to render some of the muskets unusable. Beresford was informed by a guide he had found, that the land between the landing place and the village of Reduction, where the Spaniards had gathered, was swampy in winter, but even for guns it was supposed to be practicable now. Perhaps the night-time rain prevented the Spanish advance by causing the swamp to liquefy, or the guide told Beresford only what he wanted to hear.[19]

The Spanish response had been very quick. Next morning Beresford reckoned that he was opposed by a force comprising 2,000 horse, eight guns, and some infantry; Popham estimated double that. The presence of this force, however, was not so much due to care and speed as to last minute improvisation. The Viceroy Rafael de Sobremonte had been told of the presence of the British ships in the estuary by 16 June – over a week after their arrival, but the very day the fleet began to move up the river.[20] The year before, the news of Popham's watering-call at Sao Salvador on his way to the Cape had provoked a spasm of alarm in Buenos Aires, and the militia had been mobilized in anticipation of the British attack.[21] The alarm had passed, of course, when the fleet had not turned up, but the mobilization had revealed that the army and the militia were hopelessly undermanned, badly armed, and disorganized. Further, to embody them again would be both alarmist and useless. British ships had been seen in the estuary before and no landing had taken place, though there had been a British attack on Colonia, on the north bank, back in 1763. Furthermore the small size of this British fleet, and the fact that at least one report had said they were merchant ships, did nothing to alarm the government. 'The little squadron was a trifling affair, unworthy of any concern', reported Colonel Santiago Liniers y Bremond, the commander at Ensenada, which was one of the possible landing places.[22]

It seems that no one even thought the British would land and attack the main city. Hence, despite the fact that its presence was known, Popham's force to a degree retained the element of surprise; and, of course, his judgment was justified, at least for a time.

Nevertheless, next day (17 July), the viceroy considered whether the British troops might really land at Montevideo, or perhaps at Maldonado or Colonia. Just in case, the Volunteers battalion was called up, though very few of the men appeared at the barracks. The strength of the British fleet varied with the report, one saying it was one ship of the line, eight '*fregatas*' and two '*bergantines*', which was clearly the result of mistaking the transports for more heavily armed ships.[23] Despite the appearance off Buenos Aires of Popham's landing force on 24 June, there was still no expectation of a landing on the Buenos Aires side of the estuary.

Sobremonte had gone ahead with a planned reception and a visit to the theatre. This is, of course, emphasized in a derogatory spirit, suggesting that he was putting personal pleasure ahead of public duty. Yet although the presence of the British fleet in the estuary had been known for two weeks, it had done little to show hostility, its composition was not known, it was not known that it carried a substantial military force, and the difficulty of large ships approaching the shore was fully appreciated. So it was only on 24 June, as he sat in the royal box at the theatre that Sobremonte was informed that the fleet was hostile. Colonel Liniers at Ensenada claimed that his post had been fired on (though none of the British say this).[24]

Without a serious naval force to hand Sobremonte could have done little or nothing to this point. It was only when the landing began on 25 June that he could take measures of defence. The landing was taking place only a dozen miles from the city, at Quilmes, so the viceroy's time was very limited. Those troops, mainly cavalry and a few guns, which could be sent were collected and ordered out, so that next morning Beresford faced more than equal numbers. Other troops, the available infantry, followed on behind the swifter moving cavalry, aiming to block the easiest route into the city.[25]

Most accounts simply say the viceroy fled.[26] This is not true. He was surprised by the invasion, of course, as was everyone else. But he was, by early training, a soldier, and he had worked his way up from Cadet to Captain in the Spanish army before switching to administration. In this crisis, the orders he gave were sensible. He sent the treasure away westwards, away from the invaders. He sent a force out of Buenos Aires to defend the obvious approach by land, at Puerte Chico, a force which included artillery; next day he went out himself, to be with the troops in the third action of the day.[27] These are not the actions of a man in a panic and about to flee.

Beresford, meanwhile, drew up his weary and soaked men in two columns in order to negotiate the 'morass' between their landing place and the Spanish forces which had gathered in and around the village of Reduction, which was two miles or so inland from the landing place, and on dry land. The army at his disposal was an odd mixture. The core of the force was the 71st Foot, which formed half of his men; he made that regiment his right hand column. The left column was composed mainly of the marines from the ships, along with the corps of seamen (the 'Blues'), altogether 440 strong, half the size of the column of the 71st. The artillery, which seems to have moved between the columns, consisted of two howitzers from St Helena, four six-pounders of the British artillery, and two three-pounders with the seamen. The whole force advanced fairly cautiously, with a reserve, the men of the St Helena Regiment, 100 yards or so in the rear, to act as a reinforcement for either column if necessary.[28] To the enemy the whole force must have looked rather like a square. The enemy was the force sent out by the viceroy in his first reaction to the landing. The commander was Don Pedro de Arce, who had originally been sent to block the Puerte Chico pass, at the head of the Rio Chuelo, a small river that flowed across the route between the landing place and the city; the pass was the easiest way to get to the city, and it was used next year by the second British invasion. Colonel Arce had moved forward from the pass to Reduction once it was clear that the British landing was taking a long time, but he was unable to interfere with the landing itself, which was protected by the swamp. He drew up his force in two groups. To the left, from the British angle, was a mass of cavalry, called by Gillespie 'a dense column'. He is the only witness to remark on this group, but since he was in the marine column whose purpose was especially to watch that force, his recollection looks acceptable. The other Spanish force was drawn up in a line between the village of Reduction and the cavalry column. This was partly cavalry, partly infantry, and was flanked by two small batteries of guns, four in each. It was also a good disposition of his forces.[29] The plan was presumably for the infantry to hold the British attack, and then the cavalry would charge into their flank.

It is worth noting that, despite the surprise landing, within twelve hours the Spaniards had gathered a force larger than the British and had moved it, in the dark and the rain, twelve miles, so as to oppose the landing force as close to the beach as possible. Only the viceroy could have given the impetus and authority for all that.

Beresford's account of the attack, sent to Baird a week later, is a formalization of what actually happened:

It was eleven o'clock in the morning of the 26th before I could move off my ground, and the enemy could from his position have counted every man I had … He was drawn up along the brow of a hill on which was the village of Reduction which covered his right flank and his force consisted principally of cavalry (I have been since informed 2,000) with eight field pieces. The nature of the ground was such that I was under the necessity of going directly to his front, and to make my line as much as I could equal to his, I formed all the troops into one line except St Helena Corps one hundred and fifty, which I formed one hundred and twenty yards in the rear with two field pieces; with orders to make face to the right and left as either of our flanks should be threatened by his cavalry. I had two six-pounders on each flank, and two howitzers in the centre of the first line; in this order I advanced against the enemy and after we had got within range of his guns a tongue of swamp across our front obliged me to halt whilst the guns took a small circuit to cross, and which was scarcely performed before the enemy opened their field pieces on us, at first well pointed, but as we advanced at a very quick rate, in spite of the boggy ground, that very soon obliged us to leave all our guns behind, his fire did us but little injury; the 71st Regiment reaching the bottom of the heights in a pretty good line, seconded by the marine battalion. The enemy would not wait their nearer approach, but retired from the brow of the hill which our troops gaining and commencing a fire of small arms, he fled with precipitation leaving to a four field pieces and one tumbril, and we saw nothing of him that day.[30]

From his point of view, and with the benefit of writing a dozen years later, Captain Gillespie remembered matters a little differently:

Our troops formed into two columns: and after a forward movement of 800 yards they deployed into line. The 71st Regiment formed the right; and the marine battalion a little to the rear of it, the left; and the St Helena Corps 200 paces behind the reserve. An instantaneous advance brought us to the bog, and the enemy noticing one of our guns entangled and our men irretrievably committed to it, they opened their fire with an oblique direction to the right. The 71st, however, undismayed by obstacles, rattled through, and soon came down to the charge, while the marines doubled rapidly onto its rear, and somewhat to the right, in order to cover that flank from any impression attempted by the stationary body described, which seemingly waited for the chance of such an advantage. Having surmounted the marsh and gained the summit beyond it, a close fire was thrown in by the grenadiers of the 71st, which put their army to flight in every direction, leaving behind their cannon and the mules that drew them.[31]

It seems clear that the fight was effectively out of either general's control from the moment the Spaniards opened fire. To this, the British troops reacted almost instinctively. Lieutenant Fernyhough in the marine column says Beresford ordered the advance, but no one else seems to have heard him and he does not claim the distinction himself; it is perhaps what he expected should have happened. The instinct of the troops was to attack at once, and that was what they did. The guns were left behind, stuck in the swamp, as the whole line doubled forward. The swamp scarcely delayed them, but the distance was so great that the line seems to have stopped momentarily at the foot of this slope below the Spanish line. Perhaps the officers did this deliberately to dress the line. By this time the 71st, more used to this sort of movement, was in advance of the marine line. The Spaniards were still shooting, and several men had been killed or wounded in the advance. But now the British infantry climbed the slope and came close enough to fire effectively, and 'two or three volleys', according to Fernyhough, or simply firing by the grenadiers of the 71st, according to Gillespie, was enough for the Spaniards, who broke up and retreated, a movement Colonel Arce could not prevent. The marine battalion faced the great cavalry mass on the 71st's left flank. But cavalry will not face steady infantry, and they scattered as well.

Then there is a much more personal account by Captain Henry Le Blanc of the 71st, complete with prescience:

[T]he 71st was ordered to Buenos Aires, and the ship that I was on board of, a transport, having rolled away her masts, was separated from the fleet [i.e., *Ocean*]. While we were making the best of our way to South America, some of my brother offices were lamenting our situation, and regretting that we should be too late to share in the conquest. I replied, 'You need to be under no apprehensions, you will be in time enough, for I shall lose my leg there.' I said this, fully assured in my own mind that it would be so; but if you ask me from whence that assurance arose, I am unable to answer. Some days afterwards the surgeon said his instruments had contracted a little rust and asked me who could best put them in order. To which I replied – as they would first be used on me, I was the best person to get it done, and gave them to a man of my company to do. The assistant surgeon was a friend of mine, and I prevailed on him to teach me how to apply the tourniquet to my leg. I selected one with great care, and by its application (humanly speaking) I saved my life – without it I should have bled to death. We landed next evening at Pointa da Quilmes, under the village of Reduction. My brother officers appointed me prize agent, when I begged another officer might be nominated, as I was assured I should not be able to act.

The next morning when the drums beat to arms I saw the surgeon, ran to him and said, 'Look out for me, I shall be the first that falls.' The third shot the enemy fired from the first gun thus opened struck me on the calf of my leg, and nearly took it off – as I lay on the ground I successfully applied the tourniquet. I had been speaking to Colonel P[ack] as we were advancing, who was just about to order my company to the front as sharpshooters, when the first shot was fired – the second took away the musket of the man on my right (i.e.), the left hand man of the company on my right, passing between his head and mine – the third struck me. I saw it coming all away from the gun, a Spanish six-pounder, about six or seven hundred yards distant, but I think not so much. So accurately did I see it that my covering sergeant called out 'Stoop.' I said, 'Stand up, it's coming low.' I asked myself when on the ground why I did not attempt, by stepping right to left, to avoid it, but could never give any reason. I state these things to show it was not a transient thought I uttered at random, but that it took root in my mind, and governed my conduct.[32]

(This of course is a similar story to that of the corporal of the 71st before and at Blaauwberg, though he is said to have died; but one does wonder.)

Captain Le Blanc was the only officer wounded, though Assistant Surgeon Halliday of the St Helena Corps is listed as missing. Otherwise only one seaman was killed, one sergeant of the 71st wounded, and ten men, out of all units, wounded.[33] The speed of the advance had clearly been responsible for the small casualty list since the Spaniards had scarcely had time to fire, and those who did, having to aim downhill, generally fired too high. The 71st could justifiably be proud of itself. This was a much more professional action than that at Blaauwberg. One might be inclined to point to a different commander as the responsible agent, but Beresford had actually done very little but organize the troops and set them in motion. The actual attack from then on was as much instinctive as anything. The 71st, in its second action, was clearly a professional force.

The Spaniards had scattered after the fight, and Beresford did not bother to pursue. The British infantry could not hope to outrun the Spanish horse, and for them to scatter in turn meant to be cut down piecemeal. Captain Donnelly of *Narcissus* organized some of the seamen to extricate the bogged-down guns. A two hour halt then allowed the further advance to be organized, and made it clear that the Spanish force was definitely dispersed.

Then the advance on the city began. Beresford knew – he had local guides with him – that the Rio Chuela had to be crossed, but it was eight miles to the river, and he can have had little hope of capturing the bridge at the village of Barrancas before it was destroyed. Sure enough, when the British were still a mile away flames could be seen. Three companies of the 71st under Colonel Pack, with two howitzers, were rushed forward, but the bridge had been destroyed. It was clear that there were Spanish forces across the river, and, since it was now about 6.00 pm, Beresford withdrew Pack's force and camped for the night about a mile from the remains of the bridge.[34]

The viceroy Sobremonte was with the soldiers at the burned bridge. His headquarters were in a large house belonging to the Videla family, about a mile from the river. The bridge had not been burnt until absolutely necessary, but then Colonel Yumin had performed efficiently. Since the British were camped nearby – and some soldiers came down to the river for water about 9.00 pm, to be fired on by the Spaniards – it seemed clear that next morning would see a fight at the river. The viceroy had about 3,000 troops with him, about double the British force.[35]

In the morning Beresford sent Captain Kennett, his senior engineer officer, to reconnoitre. He found that the two sides of the river were very different. On the British side the land was grassy and open, with little or no cover: on the Spanish side, by contrast, it was hedged and farmed, and provided plenty of cover. The river itself was thirty yards wide, and all the boats had been taken across to the Spanish side, where they provided further cover for Spanish troops. Not unreasonably the Spaniards clearly thought they had a strong position.[36] It may be added that the viceroy had clearly positioned his men correctly, or had efficient officers who did so on his behalf – but Sobremonte was there and was clearly responsible. Ensign Gavin describes the situation from his own experience at the bridge:

27th June. This morning observed the enemy drawn up on the other side of the River Chuelo, and occupying small ships at anchor in it, between which and our line was an extensive plain. General Beresford ordered a company to proceed and get under cover of the bank, and annoy those in possession of the ships. Lieutenant Lestrange, who commanded this party, accomplished it in defiance of the fire of the enemy, without loss. The general, fearful that the lieutenant was expending his ammunition too freely, and having none nearer than our own ships, ordered the writer down to desire he would be more frugal of his fire. Of course, orders should be obeyed; with this not really pleasing duty, I had to proceed through a plain of 300 yards, exposed to the musketry and two pieces of cannon of the Spaniards, who peppered away at me with the same eagerness as if they had the whole British force before them. I ran in desperation towards my destination, but the bullets whistled so thick about my ears that I thought diverging a little towards the right might be safer. When I got into a dyke and proceeded towards my destination, there a six-pounder shot came by me (en ricochet). I resumed my old situation on the plain and arrived under the bank of the river a great deal more frightened than hurt.[37]

Beresford determined to attack at once after hearing from Captain Kennett:

As soon as it was light I sent Captain Kennett of the Royal Engineers to reconnoitre the sides of the river and finding that on our side we had little or no cover to protect us whilst the enemy were drawn up behind hedges, houses, and in the shipping on the opposite bank, and the river not thirty yards wide; yet as our situation and circumstances could not admit the least delay I determined to force the passage and for that purpose ordered down the field pieces; which with the addition of those taken from the enemy the day before were eleven (one I had spiked and left, not being able to bring it off) to the water's edge, and ordered the infantry to remain in the rear under cover except the light company and grenadiers of the 71st; at our guns approach the enemy opened a very ill-directed fire from great guns and musketry. The former soon ceased after our fire opened; the latter was kept up for more than half an hour, but though close to us did but little or no injury, so ill was it directed. We then found means by boats and rafts to cross a few men over the Rio Chuelo; and on ordering all fire to cease what little of theirs that remained ceased also.[38]

The better training of the 71st clearly told, and their more accurate firing was decisive in silencing the Spanish guns. But Beresford rather glosses over the acquisition of the boats. Captain Gillespie also took part in the attack and makes clear what happened:

> Before daylight we were formed, and after it, put in motion; preceded by a strong detachment of artillery, upon which the enemy commenced a heavy fire from their recesses among the ditches, hedges and houses about one hundred yards from the Chuelo, but after an interchange of an hour it was silenced, when their troops disappeared. Several seamen swam across the river about forty yards broad, and bringing over some vessels that were fastened to the side, a bridge was made which soon passed our whole force with their equipage. This accomplished, we took possession of the little village of Barrachas, with its dockyard and a large flotilla of small craft.[39]

And Gavin gives more details of the crossing and what followed:

> The army now advanced and drove the enemy from their position on the river. We set to and lashed three or four of the small craft together, and procured planks to make a gangway. All passed over and advanced towards Buenos Ayres. On our way we were met by the alcalde and the chief civil officers of the city, who came out in their official robes with an offer to deliver up the city to the English. We marched into town and took possession of the castle and the barracks called Rangaris.[40]

Captain Gillespie remembered the entry more colourfully, but perhaps he was also remembering other Spanish cities conquered by British arms later:

> We entered the capital in the afternoon, in a wide order of column, to give a more imposing show to our little band, and amidst a downpour of water, and a very slippery ascent to it. The balconies of the houses were lined with the fair sex, who smiled a welcome, and seemed by no means displeased with the change.[41]

These accounts, from the viewpoint of relatively junior officers, are accurate so far as they go, but the matter was actually a good deal more complicated. Viceroy Sobremonte retreated into the city along with his soldiers. Two defeats in two days had convinced him and them that further resistance was pointless, at least for the moment. He still had no clear idea of the strength of the British force, or more importantly, of its intentions. The viceroy quite reasonably concluded that the city, unfortified, unarmed, and with its soldiers defeated and demoralized, was now indefensible. He had already sent off the public treasure – thereby stating his opinion of the British motives – and now he sent off his own family. He gave orders to Colonel Quintana, the commander of the fort in the city, who was his own uncle, to surrender when the British appeared, and set off himself for the interior.[42]

There was little else he could do. His responsibilities extended well beyond the city of Buenos Aires. He was the king's governor of the Viceroyalty of Buenos Aires, which extended as far as the Andes and into Upper Peru, and he had to protect the royal property – hence his rapid dispatch inland of the public treasure. Above all he would not be able to control the rest of the viceroyalty if he remained in the undefended city to be captured. The lack of troops in Buenos Aires could be remedied by calling up his forces from the interior, though this would take time to accomplish. It might be that the British were merely on a raid, and would leave without any more fighting. Perhaps equally persuasive was the knowledge that he had friends in the interior. He did not, in fact, go very far away, remaining with the public treasure at Lujan, waiting to see if the British force would be withdrawn fairly quickly. In effect, by leaving the city for the interior he was acting in a very similar manner to that of Governor Janssens across the ocean six months before, when he abandoned Cape Town and brought his troops to Hottentots Holland Pass. Both were, in effect, attempting to use the vast interior spaces of their territories to defeat the invasion of a small enemy force. The crucial differences were twofold: there was more public spirit – and a large population – in Spanish America than at the Cape, and Beresford's invasion force was very much smaller than Baird's.

So when the British marched into the city in the early afternoon of 28 June, they faced no resistance. As soon as the whole British force was across the Rio Chuelo, about noon, a Spanish officer appeared with a flag of truce. Beresford replied by demanding the instant surrender of the city and sent Ensign Alexander Gordon into the city to bear this message to 'the governor', though this was in fact Colonel Quintana. Gordon was just the man for such a task. He was Baird's nephew, and the son of Lord Haddo, and grandson of the Earl of Aberdeen, an ensign in the Guards, who had been Baird's *aide-de-camp* at the Cape. (He was also the younger brother of the fourth earl, later Prime Minister in another war.) This ancestry and position guaranteed the arrogance and youthful confidence which would push these negotiations to a rapid conclusion.[43] Quintana's reply was that the Spaniards wanted to delay the surrender by, according to Beresford, 'some hours'. According to Fernyhough, Beresford threatened to storm the city unless capitulation was immediate, but he must have been relieved when his bluff worked. He had sweetened the pill by promising in advance to respect the religion, the property, and the persons of the citizens. He had set his troops to marching on the city, after his threat, and when they were almost there 'the governor' replied by offering to capitulate on the conditions offered by Beresford.[44]

So the city of 45,000 inhabitants surrendered to an 'army' of 1,500 men. The Spanish troops were to surrender with the honours of war, but were to become prisoners; officers were to give their paroles. The people, their property, their archives, and their religion were to be protected, and none would be compelled to serve the British against Spain. Public property, on the other hand, was to be given up, and that meant the treasure. Civic government was to continue 'for the moment', as were taxes and duties, and the Ecclesiastical Court could also continue.[45] These assurances meant that, when the British forces marched into the city to receive the surrender of the fort, it was met by the bishop and his clergy, by the civic authorities, and by Colonel Quintana. The British marched in wide column order to exaggerate their numbers, though Captain Gillespie's recollection that the *senoritas* on the balconies were smiling at the victorious warriors is not noted by anyone else.[46] On the other hand one lady, Mariquita Sanchaz, later an actress, took close note of the Scottish dress and in particular the bare legs below the kilt, and described them as 'the loveliest troops I have ever seen', a sentiment the Scots no doubt fully agreed with.[47]

The fort was occupied, the British colours run up, and a royal salute was fired. In the estuary the sailors on the British ships, which were moored some distance off shore because of the shallow waters, had followed all these events imperfectly since the landing. Popham recorded that they could see the Spaniards fleeing from the first fight at Reduction, though he exaggerated their numbers. Gunfire was heard next day from the Rio Chuelo, but Beresford does not seem to have been able to let Popham know what was happening, nor perhaps did he try. So the royal salute from the fort, and the British colours flying there was the signal for celebration in the fleet, which at once returned to salute.[48] Without really willing it, it seemed that Britain had acquired another colony.

Chapter Seven

Buenos Aires: the Reconquest

H aving captured the city, Popham and Beresford had to decide what to do with it. The first priority was to gather and count the loot. Popham sent Lieutenant Groves and a detachment to the city's outport at Ensenada de Barragon, to seize both the place itself and the ships – two gunboats and two merchant ships – which he found there.[1] The loot was counted and was correspondingly gratifying. In the fort were found ninety guns, 550 barrels of powder, nearly 3,000 muskets and carbines and over 4,000 pistols.[2] In a way this emphasized just how fortunate the invaders had been. Those muskets in Spanish hands would have doubled the forces to be defeated, quite apart from the use all that artillery could have been put to – though much of it was, of course, fixed in the Fort. But there was apparently no silver, which was what the British really wanted.

The purpose of the expedition had never been made clear. Was it a raid, to collect silver, capture ships, humiliate the Spaniards, demonstrate the length of the Royal Navy's reach? Or was it the beginning of a conquest? None of Popham's letters explain what he was doing to resolve this problem. He had scarcely taken a big enough force to conquer Spanish South America, yet to have taken 1,500 troops to the River Plate suggested that he may well have had more in mind than a naval raid.

Popham was something of an expert on Spanish America, and he was one of several men who had sent testimonials to members of the government in London recommending various policies towards that land. He was also a friend of Francisco Miranda, '*el precursor*', who had been agitating for years for British support for liberating South America from Spanish rule. Miranda, in fact, at the very time that Popham's expedition was approaching Buenos Aires, was also mounting his own invasion of his homeland, Venezuela. Popham did not know of this, and wrote to Miranda at London with the news of the capture of Buenos Aires. This suggests another source of confusion; for Miranda obviously thought in terms of the independence of his homeland, while Popham was promoting either a conquest or a raid, but certainly not a revolution.

Popham was a busy and prolific correspondent. Writing letters seems to have been one of his methods of releasing tension, and when he was set on a course he sprayed letters in all directions. He had already written to various people from St Helena, more or less explaining what he was about – though his ultimate intentions are carefully left unstated – and now that Buenos Aires had been captured, he set about writing again. Apart from his official reports to the Admiralty, letters were sent to Baird, to Miranda, to Lord Melville, his old patron, to Sir John Sinclair the Scottish developer and statistician, and to many of the developing industrial cities of Britain.[3] His aim, of course, was to spread the news, the good news, of a conquest, and, for the industrial cities, of a new market for their goods, and so generate support for his action. He aimed also for political support at home, for he had broken so many Admiralty rules that he had become very vulnerable.

So when the news was released in London, it is not surprising that *The Times* headlined the story 'Buenos Aires is a part of the British Empire'.[4] The story revealed a further source of British misapprehension, for 'Buenos Aires' was a term which had two applications. One was the city which Beresford's troops had now occupied; the other was the Viceroyalty of Buenos Aires, which comprised about half of Spanish South America, from the River Plate to Upper Peru (modern Bolivia), and included the modern states of Argentina, Chile, Uruguay, Paraguay, and Bolivia, an enormous territory. There is no doubt that some in Britain assumed that the conquest had been the viceroyalty, not just the city.

The ease with which the city had been occupied fostered the belief that further conquest would be equally easy. It was assumed that the people of Spanish America were eager to throw off the yoke of Spanish rule, which was believed to be obscurantist, repressive, and mercantilist: in short, all the things which British rule was supposed not to be. And many went further. The unpopularity of Spanish rule being taken as a given, it was assumed that its replacement by that of Britain would be welcome. All that needed to be done was to loosen the restrictions, import British freedom, and the people of Spanish America would voluntarily join the British Empire. The only obstacle was the Spanish occupying forces.

This was the background to the work of Popham and Beresford in Buenos Aires city. Beresford worked hard to establish his rule over the city. He had been appointed lieutenant-governor on a contingency basis by Baird, who had also authorized him to assume the local rank of major-general.[5] Now he issued proclamations assuring the population of justice, security of property and religion, and he promised to reduce the customs duties, and eventually to establish a free port, such as the British operated at Trinidad.[6] Beresford's original simple guarantees were thus elaborated into the full-blown Articles of Capitulation, signed by Beresford, Popham, and Quintana on 2 July.[7] All this implied that Beresford, or Baird, who had given him his commission, were clear that it was a conquest they were undertaking.

Such agreements provided a legal basis for the British occupation, but the real sanction was the presence in the city of the garrison. Popham reclaimed his sailors, of course, but the marines remained on shore. The officers were billeted in inns and in private houses – Gillespie was in the Tres Reyes Inn – and the men were housed in the barracks of the defeated or absent Spanish forces; Gavin called the barracks 'Rangaris', but this cannot be located.[8] This spread the officers about the town but concentrated the men; the officers could thus sample opinion insofar as they could communicate.

The British were surprised to discover a number of their compatriots in the city. Ensign Gavin recalled:

> To our surprise we found a number of English men and women; they were part of the crew and convicts of the transport *Sarah* [actually, it was the *Jane Shore*], who rose on the captain and those who were faithful to him on their passage to Botany Bay. They murdered the captain and mate, and carried the ship into Buenos Ayres, where they sold her. Some of the female convicts were well married, and the male working at their different trades. One we found very useful, named Patrick Carey, and another, Smith, that General Beresford brought to England … The fellow that killed the captain by a blow of a hatchet as he came up the companion steps, and two females, were the only persons of the whole that followed the dissolute lives they were accustomed to lead in England.[9]

Popham had gone ashore as soon as he could after the mutual salutes. He interviewed a group of British merchants who had turned out to be living in the city in neutral guise, but he was not so gullible as to be prepared to accept their estimate of the local situation.[10] After all, he knew Miranda, and he had composed memos on the subject of South America, which implies considerable research. He approached the situation with two basic ideas. The first was that there was enmity between those born in Spain, the *peninsulares*, assumed to be the oppressors, and those born in South America, the *criollos*; a second idea was that relief from the economic depression of the recent past, caused in large part by the British naval domination of the Atlantic and the blockade, was generally desired. He was right on both, but he thereby ignored the real problem, for it seems not to have occurred to him that to be a Spanish patriot, whether a man was born in Spain or in Spanish America, was a tenable intellectual position.

Beresford, as governor, was more concerned with events in the city than Popham, but the latter was never reluctant to provide advice and to interfere. In the city, in the absence of the viceroy, there were three sources of power: the Fort, which was now occupied by the British, the Church, and the Cabildo. The Church could exercise considerable influence, but it was the Cabildo, the city council, which was the real repository of local political power now that the Viceroy was away. It was the Cabildo which could co-ordinate any movements of resistance, and gather together the fragments of Spanish military power.

During the negotiation of the terms of capitulation, Popham – of course – learned that the evacuated treasure was at Lujan, 80km away to the west of the city. Popham's explanation is that the Cabildo were angry at the viceroy's conduct in abandoning them, and proposed to Popham a joint expedition to recover the treasure.[11] The Argentine explanation is that Beresford threatened to extract the equivalent from the merchants of the city unless the royal treasure's location was revealed. Threats may well have been made, and it is certain that the merchants were condemned for their attitude, but it is more likely that Popham's manner elicited information quite easily. It was, after all, well known in the city that Sobremonte was where the treasure was; in a gossiping community it would not be difficult to find out.

At the same time, it may be that the Cabildo gained the impression that the treasure was Popham's real objective, and that once he had captured it, he would go away; this view implies that the Cabildo was in effect buying him off with the king's silver. And since the silver was destined for Spain, it mattered little that the British would get it; it was lost to Buenos Aires in any case. It is thus likely that this reflected Popham's original aim, namely, that the expedition was little more than a raid. But the ease of the conquest clearly persuaded him to bid for permanence; and so, of course, had Beresford, who was now his senior officer, thanks to Baird. By 30 June agreement had been reached on the final capitulation terms, for Beresford issued a proclamation that day, saying that ships captured in the estuary would be returned.[12] This was part of Popham's agreement with the Cabildo, and it is a clear sign that he and Beresford had decided to hold onto Buenos Aires. The ship owners were now British subjects, so their property could be returned.

The treasure was collected by a small force of three officers and thirty men commanded by Captain Arbuthnot, formerly of the Staff at the Cape, and Lieutenant Charles Graham of the 71st. They rode to Lujan, apparently leaving on 3 July, secured the treasure wagons without opposition, and returned to the city by 10 July. It was claimed locally that they damaged the prison and the school, which is quite likely.[13] Meanwhile the city was combed for other elements of the public treasure, perhaps with the memory of how Janssens had tried to hide the treasury at the Cape. In the report which Beresford made to account for the money, he reported having seized cash from the Philippine Company, the Post Office, the Tobacco Administration, and the Customs House, as well as the treasure collected by Captain Arbuthnot's detachment. Arbuthnot's treasure was boxed, partly held in skins or as ingot. The precise returns assessed it all at a little more than $1 million, half being Arbuthnot's treasure and half from sources in the city. A priest was found to be holding a box with nearly $3,000 as well, which was reckoned to be public.[14]

Popham's priority, once the treasure was gathered, was to get it on board a ship and off to Britain; this was his ultimate justification for bending his orders to breaking point. *Narcissus* was chosen, and loading began on 15 July. A committee was organized to see to this. It included Captain Pococke of the 71st, the cantankerous character who had survived a court-martial at the Cape. He wanted the treasure distributed over several ships and agitated for a proper accounting. The first idea was nonsensical, since several ships could not be spared. The second suggests that all was not well in the accounting department. This fits with a suggestion made by Richard Waite in his doctoral thesis on Popham, that Popham stole some of the silver. Waite puts the quantity at almost $52,000.[15]

This accusation is based on a comparison of the return by Beresford which was sent to London with the treasure, with a Spanish statement which was published sixty years later in a French account.[16] The problem is that the figures given by Beresford are, in several cases, approximations, and in one case no more than a valuation of ingot. The comparison is thus not one of like with like, and Waite's accusation must be rendered unproven. On the other hand, Popham's money-hunger is well attested and one would not be at all surprised if his fingers were sticky. He was, of course, entitled to prize money, but this would be allocated much later.[17]

With the silver on board ship, Popham's report and letters could also be sent. *Narcissus* carried nineteen letters from Popham to the Admiralty when she sailed and others from Beresford to the War Office. The Scottish connection – Melville, Sir John Sinclair – was not forgotten, not, at least, by Popham. One of the several industrial cities in Britain he wrote to was Glasgow, a city with extensive American connections, and host to the second battalion of the 71st. Also Sinclair was locally powerful in Caithness, whence a substantial fraction of the 71st was recruited – there were six men called Sinclair in the regiment. No similar letters from Beresford are known, but, unlike Popham, he could always claim to have been acting under orders.

The letter Popham sent to Baird at the Cape, however, which was one of the first he wrote, probably on 6 July, addressed more immediate concerns. By then he and Beresford had decided to hold on to Buenos Aires, but they knew full well that Beresford did not have enough soldiers to hold the city against a serious counter-attack, and both were sensible enough to appreciate that such a riposte was inevitable in the long, if not in the short, run. So his letter to Baird was an appeal for help and reinforcements. He compared his virtually bloodless conquest with that of Wellesley in India, a sly comment since he knew Baird detested Wellesley. He also clearly thought that the capture of the capital implied the capture of the whole viceroyalty. This was a mistake others would make. He promised that Baird would be the richer by £650,000 in prize money, a ludicrous over-estimate, though Baird as commander-in-chief of Beresford's force was certainly entitled to a large sum. And he asked three times for more troops, in the end even going so far as to specify the colonel of the 38th, Vassall. And he further indicated that he aimed to attack Montevideo, possession of which would be necessary if the region was to be held.[18]

Beresford also wrote to Baird, on 2 July, also asking for assistance, but he knew it would take some time for anything to arrive, and he must have known that Baird would be reluctant to part with more men.[19] Popham meanwhile also wrote to the senior naval officer at the Cape – he wanted more ships as well as soldiers – Popham said that Buenos Aires was 'perfectly quiet'.[20] This may well have been Popham's perception of the situation, but he was in the process of being disproved even as he collected the silver and wrote his many letters. Perhaps it was the fate of the treasure which brought the men of the Cabildo to the realization of the fate in store for them. They had surely not co-operated in the capture of the viceroy's silver in order to see it shipped to Britain, and then to be subject to a continued British occupation. It was a clear indication that British intentions towards Buenos Aires were essentially the same as those of Spain; control and exploitation. They could not know that Popham's expedition was unauthorized, but the smallness of the British force will have quickly become obvious, and as soon as it did Spanish prospects of a reconquest became brighter. Ensign Gavin remembered:

> I was accosted one day by an inhabitant, who inquired as to our numbers, which I exaggerated some hundreds, when he very pertinently asked, 'How were they fed, as rations were only issued for such a number?' I accounted for it as men in hospital, servants, etc., but it would not do, they knew to a man our strength.[21]

The Cabildo members, however, had been trapped. Beresford had insisted that they take an oath of loyalty as soon as they surrendered. The same oath was administered to the officers of the armed forces. This oath, which all concerned took very seriously, prevented the men concerned from organizing or taking part in any form of armed resistance. Nevertheless resistance developed. As early as 7 July Beresford had ordered the collection of all weapons, though it was not until the third week in July that the British gained a clear impression of the enmity with which they were regarded.[22]

The resistance was organized from four separate directions. On the first Sunday in July, that is, 6 July, Colonel Santiago Liniers, the former commander at Ensenada de Barragon, attended mass at the Confraternity of the Rosary in the city, where he told the prior that he was going to Montevideo to begin organizing an attempt to reconquer Buenos Aires.[23] Liniers was a Frenchman by birth who had been in the Spanish service for his whole adult life. He had started his military career as a cadet of the Knights of St John of Malta (of which Popham was a knight, of course), and he had joined the Spanish service in 1774. He had been in the Plate estuary on and off since 1776. In the war against Britain which lasted from 1796 to 1802 he had been in command of the naval forces in the estuary, whose task was to operate against the British blockade. In 1802 he was made Governor of Misiones, the area precariously poised on the Portuguese Brazilian border, laced by the great rivers of the Uruguay and the Parana. His brother-in-law, Lazara de Rivera y Espinola, was intendant of neighbouring Paraguay. The command at Ensenada which Liniers held now was no demotion, but one which came to an able loyal soldier-administrator with naval experience, for the place was the normal landing place for Buenos Aires, one of the most important naval stations on the estuary. His rank of colonel in the army was the same as that of many intendants.[24]

Liniers reached Montevideo by 16 July, travelling by way of Colonia de Sacramento, a place captured by the Spaniards from the Brazilian Portuguese back in 1776, an action he had taken part in. He seems to have had little or no trouble getting out of Buenos Aires, or in getting a boat to take him across the estuary, a sign of the lax British supervision on land and sea, though he had to travel to Las Conchas, 40km upriver, to get a boat to get across. He found that the news of the capture of Buenos Aires had preceded him, but not by very long. Liniers offered his services to the governor of Montevideo, Pascual Ruiz Huidobro, and was put in command of a force of 500 regular soldiers, comprising a company of artillery, a small force of grenadiers of the El Fijo Regiment which had been detached from Buenos Aires some time before, three companies of dragoons, and two companies of Blandengues, the volunteer militia.

The Montevideo Cabildo was enthusiastic about supporting the reconquest. If Montevideo was to rescue Buenos Aires, then Montevideo would receive a major psychological boost in its rivalry with the bigger city, and might reasonably expect some serious rewards. The Cabildo of the city backed the governor's plan and the city's militia was embodied and expanded by more volunteers. There were almost 350 men from Montevideo, two companies of infantry, the Catalan company made up of regular soldiers, and a company of French volunteer sailors under a privateer captain called Hippolyte Mordeille. All told, Liniers began his reconquest with 871 troops. They took a little time to collect arms and to become organized, but the force was able to march out of Montevideo on 23 July.[25]

Liniers' action was much criticized later by Popham and Beresford. They claimed that he had given his parole, along with the other Spanish officers. Liniers pointed out that he had been at Ensenada when the city was captured, and thus was not included in the parole arrangements. He did admit, however, that he had visited Buenos Aires (presumably around 6 July when he attended the mass), under a safe conduct. It is possible that there was confusion in British or Spanish minds over this. Popham claimed that Liniers had 'frequently' called on him to complain of the treatment of the Spaniards, or to ask for Popham's assistance in merchant ventures. Popham suggested, in effect, that Liniers would not have been able to do this unless he was on parole. He adds that almost all the Spanish officers were on parole. Thus he does admit that some were not. The best reconstruction is perhaps that Liniers really was overlooked in the paroling, and the British assumed that all Spanish officers had been neutralized by the parole. Liniers, when he realized this, must have used the immunity it provided to spy out the British strength, and their weaknesses. Then he left for Colonia and Montevideo.[26]

While Liniers was busy in Montevideo, the Marquis of Sobremonte was equally active in Córdoba. In terms of distance by land, Córdoba is only a little further from Buenos Aires than Montevideo – from Montevideo the road leads some way up the lower course of the Paraguay River to the nearest crossing; Córdoba is about 400 miles in a straight line, Montevideo about 300 round about the estuary. Sobremonte reached Córdoba on 12 July, having delayed at Lujan until his treasure was captured. At once he set about establishing the town as the new viceregal capital, with a full administrative system, and gathering troops for the reconquest of his lost capital. He ordered up the local forces of Córdoba, 600 of whom were placed under the command of Colonel Allende. Almost the same number of men from Paraguay were under the command of Colonel Espinola. A thousand of the local militia came from a variety of places, but they were almost entirely untrained. And there were about 400 Blandengues and dragoons. He collected there a total of about 2,500 troops.[27]

These men took time to assemble. Sobremonte also sent word to his colleagues in Peru and Chile. One group, from Penco in Chile, took three months to reach Buenos Aires.[28] It is likely that Sobremonte had an exaggerated idea of the strengths of the invaders. He had after all been beaten by them twice – three times if the loss of the treasure at Lujan is included – and he is unlikely to have diminished their numbers in his mind. He could gather 2,500 men or so at Córdoba, perhaps in a month, but it must have looked an impossible task to use these men, mainly untrained as they were, against the British forces, all professionals. He heard of Liniers' expedition, and wrote to him to wait until all the forces of the viceroyalty were gathered.[29]

This was sensible, and Sobremonte deserves a better press than he has received. He was doing just what one would expect a professional soldier-administrator to do. The problem was that the situation was itself not sensible. It was not sensible that 1,500 British troops should have captured a city of 45,000 people; it was not sensible that a French colonel should lead 800 men against the 1,500 British and hope to win. The senselessness of the situation, however, called for nonsensical measures. The soldier-administrator Sobremonte did not see that; the sailor-administrator Liniers did. The difference probably lay in the fact that Liniers had accurate information about the situation in Buenos Aires, from his own observations, but Sobremonte did not.

The third source of resistance was in the countryside around Buenos Aires. The leader here was Juan Martin de Pueyrredon, who gathered support from fellow ranchers in the area west of the city. He had been across to Montevideo, but seems to have disapproved of the slow pace of Liniers' preparations, just as Liniers was impatient of the viceroy's deliberation, and Sobremonte of Liniers' precipitation. Pueyrredon's movements back and forth across the estuary consumed time, but by 28 July he had gathered a force of about 800 men in the country near the city. These were untrained horsemen, the predecessors of the gauchos, brought out to fight by their chiefs. In the city Beresford knew all about the gathering.[30]

Beresford was perhaps rather less informed about what was going on under his nose. There the resistance had begun the day after the surrender, among the workers and shopkeepers of the city. The British did get to know something of what was going on, but only by accident and indirectly. For some time the shock of the conquest paralyzed most of the citizens, but the resisters were encouraged when the smallness of the British force became obvious. It was also discovered that not all of the invaders were actually British, and not all of them were loyal. The Germans who were recruited at the Cape where an obvious target and three of them deserted on 17 July, though this only meant that they were expected to fight on the Spanish side. The knowledge of what the British would do to them if they were recaptured no doubt increased their zeal. But the problem was recognized on the British side as well. Captain Pococke commented in his diary that 'this looks like a cloud hanging over our heads which one day or other will burst'.[31]

Beresford was doing his best to institute a system of government which was a clear improvement over the Spanish Imperial regime. He had promised to respect the Catholic religion, he reduced the customs duties, and began to establish a free port. He appointed local men to administrative positions. But it was a regime which would need to cease to be British if it was to be accepted locally, and any displaced Spanish functionaries – such as Sobremonte and Liniers – automatically became resisters, all the more effectively for being persons of authority, to whom the inhabitants were habitually obedient.

Within the city, therefore, the tide of resentment rose against the occupiers. By the middle of July the sentiment was obvious to the British themselves. Captain Gillespie, at the Tres Reyes Inn, was the officer in charge of registering the paroles of Spanish officers. He was also involved in discovering who in the city was willing to become a British citizen, and eventually claimed to have a list of fifty-eight men.[32] This contact with the local population may have made him more sensitive to local opinion, and it should they have made him a prime intelligence source for Popham and Beresford. He remembered:

In the middle of July a circumstance developed that a plot existed for the overthrow of our power, and that the Cabildo were chief actors in it. Intelligence was received that a large magazine of gunpowder had been formed at Fleuris, about three miles from the city ... [T]heir levies in the country ... were collecting from afar with the ultimate view of its reconquest, and supplies from it had already been pushed on to an army in a state of forwardness under the command of Pueyrredon. Captain Ogilvie was ordered thither to complete our tumbrils and his orders were to explode the remainder ... [W]e had two killed and several badly wounded upon that service, from accidents. In so very wide a city it were impossible to observe or to check the workings of the people. Nightly meetings took place among them to be trained to arms, and several instances occurred of our advanced sentries being forcibly carried off, mounted and instantly driven into the interior ... [M]any of the friars tried to seduce our men from their duty but all withstand them except a few of the Roman Catholic persuasion.[33]

Gillespie's marine colleague Lieutenant Fernyhough remembered that 'assassinations were very frequent', which, even if exaggerated in retrospect, suggests something of the atmosphere.[34] Ensign Gavin recorded the discovery of some bizarre preparations:

After some time in peaceable possession of the town a man cleaning his firelock in one of the barrack rooms happened to stick his ramrod in the ground floor which instantly disappeared. When searching for it we found that the whole range of the barracks was undermined from the other side of the street where there was a convent of friars.

On examination we found that they had been at work many days and had mined under the main street, and had actually placed some barrels of gunpowder and would if not so fortunately discovered have blown us to atoms.[35]

The city's opposition to the British involved the Church as well. No matter how vociferously the British claimed to protect the Catholic Church, no matter how often they could point to the toleration of the Catholic community in Canada, the fact remained that the British were overwhelmingly Protestant. Under Spain the Church was powerful and rich, under Britain it would be tolerated, probably less rich, and certainly with much less power and influence. The bishop was actively hostile, in Gillespie's judgment, by mid-

July, and friars in the city were found to be attempting to subvert the loyalty of the British soldiers. The British administration was now trapped in its own toleration, for any move against these ecclesiastical plotters would only convince even more of the citizens that the toleration was a sham.

The British occupiers behaved in ways that could only confirm the enmity of the general population. A group who were with Gillespie at Los Tres Reyes formed a Masonic lodge, an action which could only inflame opposition from the Church. One had already existed among the foreign merchants living in the city, and had been discovered and broken up in 1804. Now there was another, or perhaps the old one was simply revived and enlarged. The re-emergence of this atheist organization could only encourage the Catholic hierarchy to stimulate the public to resistance all the more.[36] A more direct hostility will have been felt by the lady who came home on the day the British marched in, to discover a British officer (not named, but the odds are that he was a Scot) billeted on her, who had fallen asleep on the sofa, still wearing his mud-caked boots; the sofa's covering was a quilt, one of the family heirlooms.[37] But then conquerors always become boors, and British conquerors are no better behaved than any others.

By mid-July the signs of approaching trouble were all present. Beresford appealed to Popham for more men, but Popham's marines were all ashore already, and his sailors were now stretched very thin. The squadron was reduced and scattered: *Narcissus* and *Melantho* had been sent away to Britain and the Cape respectively, with the treasure and with letters. The big ships were watching Montevideo, since they could not get higher up the estuary; *Raisonable* had been detached to Brazil to try to get another anchor after losing two. Popham used the remaining transports as warships, and had also added a few small ships by capture. He was able to send a small force to Ensenada in a captured schooner, but he was grievously short of the most suitable vessels. Only *Encounter*, the gun brig which had covered the landing at Quilmes, was able to navigate with any freedom amid the shoals and banks of the estuary.[38]

The northern side of the estuary, off Montevideo, had to be guarded, both to warn of a foreign attack and to intercept enemy ships, and Montevideo had to be blockaded, preferably by more than one ship. Popham himself needed to be near Buenos Aires so as to be able to consult with Beresford. It soon became clear that the harbour at Colonia (where Liniers had landed) had to be watched as well, as small ships gathered there. It was also necessary to keep a watch even further up the river, usually off San Isidro, 25km or so from Buenos Aires. Popham was concerned that enemy forces were gathering on the north coast and he named in particular San Lucia and Colonia as rendezvous. He sent the *Walker* transport to reconnoitre the whole coast, and *Encounter* was sent further up the river to Las Conchas, the ferry point. In fact *Encounter* went to San Isidro, where it remained, often and for long periods aground, 10km from the coast. Despite all this activity it was clear that he did not have enough ships and what he had were rarely suitable for the work.

Inexorably the British position decayed, partly because of the erosion imposed by the lapse of time, partly due to the recovery staged by the Spaniards. On 19 July, Popham reported that he had 249 seamen and marines on shore with Beresford, but that Beresford had asked for more, which Popham said he could not spare. Beresford was clearly nervous, and Popham had much the same information about the gathering problems of Liniers, Pueyrredon, the viceroy, and the unrest in the city.[39]

Four days after Popham's reports, on 23 July, Liniers and his force left Montevideo for Colonia. In the harbour a number of boats were gathered, and it may be that it was hoped to make an attempt at a crossing from there, for Colonia was directly across the estuary from Buenos Aires. But Popham's ships, few though they were, did cover the ports and harbours well, and a crossing was impossible. In Buenos Aires itself, however, the more immediate threat came from inland, where Pueyrredon's force was growing. Pococke was told that there was an army of 8,000 or 10,000 men at Montevideo. He says he did not believe it, but that such a rumour was spread is a sign of returning Spanish confidence. By 24 July Pococke heard that a rising was planned for that night. He heard the same next day and, 'lay in my clothes last night to be in readiness to turn out ... I am inclined to think that the reports will come true in the end, and perhaps when we least expect it.'[40]

The British tried simultaneously to carry on as normal and yet to be extra vigilant as well. On 29 July the whole of the garrison marched about in various directions, greatly alarming the few people remaining in the city – many had left to be out of the city, assuming an approaching conflict, or had gone to join the various groups preparing to make that attack. On the evening of 31 July Beresford went to the theatre, despite a threat to capture him there. While there – in a curious repetition of Sobremonte in the same theatre five weeks earlier – he heard from a Spaniard that Pueyrredon's force was at Perdriel, about 25km from the city. It had grown to over 1,000 men, partly the original gauchos, and partly men who had gone out from the city to join him.[41]

At 1.30 am that night 500 men of the 71st and fifty of the St Helena infantry were alerted and paraded. They marched at once, through the night, and at dawn came up on the force at Perdriel. There was no surprise, for Pueyrredon had drawn up his men in battle formation, with guns on either flank and in the centre. Gavin described the fight:

> August 1st … [W]e advance with the weak garrison (leaving Lieutenant-Colonel Campbell and one company 71st in the castle) to attack upwards of 1,500 Spaniards assembled about five leagues from the town, under the command of Pueyrredon. We came in sight of them about 12 o'clock, drawn up on an extensive plain, with a six-pounder on each flank and one in the centre. Order was given to the column to form line; the late Lieutenant John Graham (killed afterwards at Fuentes de Onoro), and the writer were ordered six paces to the front to give the line, and advance in slow time, till we came within a few yards of the them, and then opened a brisk fire from right to left and immediately charged, the enemy giving way in all directions, leaving their guns and many prisoners. Five or six gentlemen were so sanguine in the cause and so sure of victory that they galloped round our right flank, where the general was stationed, with the intention of making him prisoner, and actually attempted it, but were cut down and made prisoners. In the evening we marched into the town in triumph.[42]

Pueyrredon's force had been only a half of that dispersed at Quilmes, and it had been similarly scattered. The British had lost only a few men in casualties, and just as few Spaniards had died, though a number were captured. But it had taken half of Beresford's armed force to drive Pueyrredon off, and his men had mainly survived. Furthermore, Beresford had been presented with the problem which gave the affair a distinctly unpleasant aftertaste. Gavin continues:

> A few days previous to this the Dutch recruits we received at the Cape deserted to the enemy, and one of them was actually taken with a lighted match in his hands at one of their guns. He was sentenced to be shot by decree of a court-martial. The Bishop of Buenos Ayres waited on General Beresford and offered $2,000 to save his life, but was refused, and he was accordingly shot next day.

The officers of the 71st had had to stop the enraged man from killing the recaptured deserter, Private Jacob Eckarts, a German and a Catholic, outright. By 11 a.m. the British were marching back to the city, having, so they thought, scotched the attack they had been hearing about. They brought with them other prisoners, among them men of the city. Pococke remarked that 'consequently the articles of capitulation are infringed upon and broken', though it suited everyone to ignore this inconvenient fact.[43]

This all presented Beresford with the sort of judgment Solomon had faced. If he acceded to the bishop's request to reprieve Eckarts – whether it was accompanied by a cash offer or not – he would dismay his troops who were clearly enraged; if he went ahead with the execution he would alienate the *portenos*, even more than they were already. Probably he did not hesitate, using the soldierly instincts, and went ahead with the execution. But this would not bring the deserters back, and would surely make them fight the harder. The ex-Waldeckers might not be very good soldiers, but they were trained and could pass on that training, and faced with the prospect of virtually automatic execution if captured, their determination would surely grow. So Beresford had, in fact, merely ensured that the attack, when it came, would be all the stronger.

Liniers had reached Colonia, on the north shore, three days before Beresford went to the theatre: the *Walker* transport was patrolling the north coast and effectively prevented the troops Liniers had collected at Montevideo from crossing the river. An attempt was made to drive *Walker* away on the day after Liniers' arrival. A flock of gunboats came out of Colonia to attack the transport – Liniers thought it was a gun brig – but none of the shots hit, and *Walker* was able to escape its tormentors and returned to its post.[44] So Liniers had to wait. Meanwhile Popham rearranged his forces. *Diomede* was brought over to Ensenada, and *Leda* stationed off Buenos Aires. *Dolores*, a captured schooner, was sent to San Isidro, a little downriver from Las Conchas.[45] Thus he had a line of ships blocking the landing places which Liniers was likely to use to get Buenos Aires. But none of these ships could get close inshore, so all the ships' boats were brought into use and Popham began to arm as many Spanish ships as he could find. He came ashore in Buenos Aires from *Leda* on 1 August, partly to help with the Pueyrredon affair and partly to organize more gunboats.

On 3 August a heavy gale – all the British sources call it a hurricane – cut communications between ship and shore for a time. Captain King of *Leda* had started for the shore with a reinforcement of 200 seamen when the gale blew up, and he and his men had to take refuge in *Justina*, the British merchantman which joined at St Helena, and which was anchored off Buenos Aires. King and his men finally got ashore on the afternoon of 4

August, and began arming as many ships and large boats as they could man. They worked through 5 August, by which time the wind had died down sufficiently to allow Popham to reach *Leda*, but next day the gale increased once more. King had managed to arm and man six gunboats, but the second gale destroyed five of them – two were driven ashore and three were sunk – and it also sank four of the ship's boats he had gathered as well.[46]

While the British were thus immobilized by the weather, Liniers was released by it. It seems likely that the local sailors at Colonia successfully predicted the storm – a *pampero*, a powerful gale blowing from inland to be expected at that time of year – and that the British were taken by surprise. It was certainly the decisive event of the campaign, for it was Liniers' possession of small boats and Popham's loss of them which permitted Liniers' force to cross the river unmolested during the lull in the gale. During the storm, while all the British were preoccupied with survival in the shoals and banks, Liniers' flotilla crossed over from Colonia to land at Las Conchas. The captured schooner *Dolores* was guarding San Isidro, but the Spanish boats were able to evade her by landing at Las Conchas. It scarcely mattered where they reached the southern shore: any landing was disastrous for the British. Pueyrredon's troops, smarting from their defeat, had only been scattered, and they re-assembled and joined with Liniers' force. Liniers thus now had 2,000 or so troops, and the good half of them were of professional quality, or nearly so.[47] Liniers had decided to go ahead without waiting for Sobremonte, who was still at Córdoba.

In the city Colonel Pack of the 71st announced at a parade on the afternoon of 5 August, the day after Liniers' landing, that the enemy's attack was expected that night. The regiment slept to arms. Captain Pococke remembered:

> About 10 p.m. four Spaniards surrounded one of our sentries at the tobacco store, and took his firelock from him. There was no great courage in doing so, as he was only a boy of sixteen years of age – a marine.[48]

The captured deserter, Jacob Eckarts, was to be shot on 6 August. The man's agony was prolonged by the weather since it rained heavily that day and the next. Then it was prolonged by the bishop, who requested a day's delay so as to administer the sacraments. He was finally shot on 9 August.[49] The bishop was regarded by the British as an active enemy, and his request for a delay may be a sign that he was hoping for Liniers to assault the city and so save Eckarts' life in the confusion. The relentlessness of the British determination on executing Eckarts is peculiarly unpleasant.

It was the weather which also prevented the British from interfering with Liniers' approach. The rain continued for most of the time between his landing on 4 and 9 August, reducing the city streets to lanes of liquid mud and the country roads to swamp, in which the British infantry was effectively immobilized. The Spaniards, on the other hand, were often on horseback, and seem to have been able to ignore such roads as there were as necessary. At all events, while the British remained weather-bound in the city, Liniers' force rested at San Isidro from 6 to 9 August, and then advanced in two stages to the edge of the city. There they were joined by many of the citizens, who made up in numbers and enthusiasm what they lacked in skill and weaponry.[50]

Captain Gillespie recalled the advance in some detail:

[H]e made good his landing with 2,000 men and ten pieces of cannon upon the 6th of August. Heavy rain ... retarded the junction of Pueyrredon's army, again rallied, until the 9th, and [he] brought with him not only his own original strength, but great accession to it of Catalans from Montevideo ... A small schooner under Lieutenant Herrick riding close to the beach opened his fire upon their encampment so successfully as to compel Liniers to take up a new one out of sight and at some distance. At that time the garrison of Buenos Aires was prevented from meeting him in the field by the rugged roads, not in a condition to admit the transportation of artillery without a powerful drawing train.[51]

On 10 August the beginning of the fighting was signalled by Liniers' formal demand to Beresford to surrender, sent by the hand of Captain Hilarion de la Quintana, the son of the man who had surrendered the city to him in the first place. Beresford had received Quintana in the Fort, where he had assembled the city notables, the bishop, the Cabildo, and the senior merchants. In the presence of these men, and by implication with their consent and approval, Beresford gave Captain Quintana an equally formal rejection of the demand for surrender. The British troops had dumped their knapsacks in the castle, and now prepared to fight for the city.[52]

Liniers began his attack as soon as Beresford's refusal to surrender was received. An isolated British guard post at the Retiro, commanded by Sergeant Kennedy of the 71st, was surrounded and captured.[53] Beresford sent a force to relieve or rescue his men, but now discovered that the Spanish forces were not only large in numbers, but were sensibly organized. The unarmed townspeople were enlisted to move the guns; sheer numbers overcame the ruts and puddles of the roads, and Beresford's relieving force was driven back by volleys of grape shot. Then the Spanish guns were turned seaward and were fired at the *Justina*, which was bombarding the shore. She was hit and a mast brought down. The Spaniards captured the artillery stores near the Retiro on the north edge of the city and armed themselves with still more guns. Only broken gun carriages were available, so the craftsmen in the crowd repaired them.[54]

Popham came ashore during the day to confer with Beresford. It was clear to both that the end was nigh. They decided to evacuate the wounded and the women and children to the ships. No one actually says so, but it is clear that the decision was made, if only implicitly, to evacuate all the forces as well. But, once more, the lack of small craft was crippling, and a worsening of the weather delayed the evacuation still further. However, thirteen wounded and sick men of the 71st were taken off, along with the assistant surgeon Benjamin Radford; whether, or how many, women and children were taken off is not known, but some were certainly captured later.[55]

Beresford described his dispositions in a later letter to the Secretary of State:

As already mentioned, I had taken position in the two squares in front of the fort, into them to openings came by the rear, one each side of the fort, but protected by it, two streets led in upon each flank and two met at each of the front angles of the front square. These last I directed to be left open to invite the enemy to enter. The square was about 100 yards across. Two squares are separated by a public building having a colonnade quite round it, under which was posted the 71st Regiment, looking to and having charge both of the front and flanks; the St Helena Infantry being placed to flank and rear entrances and the corps of marines and seamen placed in the fort. I had besides protected the flank entrance with guns, and occupied the most commanding houses in the squares.[56]

The fighting was recalled by the participants. Ensign Gavin was brief:

They ... advanced by all the streets leading to the great square (where our small force to draw up). Our position was commanded by the enemy, who occupied the tops of the houses and the great church, being completely secured by the parapets that surrounded the flat roofs. We were picked off at pleasure. At a gun near the church three reliefs in a short time were killed or wounded, Lieutenant Mitchell and Ensign Lucas, 71st, were killed here with Captain Kennett, Royal Engineers.[57]

Captain Gillespie remembered it at greater length:

Having approached the city on the 10th Liniers advanced his whole force against a sergeant and seventeen men which was most imprudently our total number then posted at the Retiro. These brave men occasioned some loss to the assailants and covered with dead bodies the ground that they occupied, saving two who escaped to us badly wounded. Along with this hostile step he also pushed on a flag to the gate of the castle demanding its immediate surrender.

Throughout Sunday afternoon and the whole of Monday the 11th of August much fighting took place in the streets attended with heavy loss on both sides.

During the whole of the night of the 11th the constant barking of dogs was heard from the Retiro and its vicinity, which indicated some extraordinary movements. The dawn of the 12th showed us the churches and houses crowded with people who only wanted for the approach of Liniers to co-operate in the general onset. Most of the former and all the latter commanded our bastions in the fort, and they likewise regulated all the motions of the columns in the streets below them. Our orders were to spare the sanctuaries, but they became so troublesome from the fire of small guns and musketry that we could not refrain from indulging them with similar favours, which always produced a momentary pause ... The battle raged in every adjoining avenue to the castle, but whenever an enemy or a gun dared openly to combat with us, they were successively beaten or captured; such glories however but dearly bought, or they were finally unavailing. A last stand was made at 11 in the marketplace, where the gallant 71st Regiment was formed with guns on each flank and one in the centre. Every outpost had been previously withdrawn upon their respective bodies. At this hour our dispositions besides were as follows: the marines and seamen were attached to the batteries within the castle, and the St Helena Corps were a little thrown out in two divisions under the east and west bastions of it, which commanded the approaches from the streets of St Domingo and Three Kings that run parallel with the Plata. A communication was maintained between them all.

As a feint to draw the enemy from his fortresses, the 71st fell back, but without the desired consequences. Nothing could tempt him to the open fight with all his numbers … Several officers had fallen, some were wounded, and the drawbridge was crowded by those who were borne upon the shoulders of their brother soldiers into the fortress. An immediate retreat into it became expedient, after which the gate was shut, and two cannon were planted within to defend it.[58]

Lieutenant Fernyhough recalled events also, again somewhat differently:

Soon afterwards the Spanish general sent in his aide-de-camp (Quintana) with a flag of truce. He had a great drum beating before him; this unusual mode of procession made some of us smile. He brought us a summons to surrender; demanding an immediate answer and saying that General Liniers was ready to enter the town, at the head of a numerous army, and that he should only allow fifteen minutes. Our general returned for answer, that he should not surrender, but would meet him at the point of the bayonet.

The enemy advanced that night as far as the park, where we had a guard consisting of a sergeant, corporal, and twenty privates (this park is situated at the northwest end of the town), who, all excepting two were put to death in a shocking manner, their bodies being cut and mangled and afterwards thrown naked on the beach. We had several skirmishes during the night, in which Captain Ogilvie of the artillery and several of the men were wounded.

August 11th. Early this morning the enemy had taken possession of a number of houses from which he commenced a brisk fire of musketry, which galled our men severely. This kind of warfare was kept up the whole day without intermission. We had many killed and wounded.

August 12th. Soon after daylight a heavy fire commenced on both sides, which was continued for some hours, when the Spaniards attempted to make a charge up one of the streets, but we gave them such a reception with our guns, loading with grape and canister shot, as compelled them to make a hasty retreat, with considerable loss.

Towards the middle of the day our men began to fall very fast, particularly those at the guns. They were picked off from the tops of the houses, which were occupied by the enemy, who kept up such an incessant fire of musketry that it became impossible for the men to stand to their guns. We lost three officers almost at the same time. One was Captain Kennett of the Royal Engineers; he was shot dead by the general's side.

At intervals the enemy's cavalry made several attempts to charge, but they were always repulsed with loss. However, about two o'clock the retreat was sounded, and our general ordered a flag of truce to be hoisted. His motive was that he saw it would be only sacrificing the remainder of his men to hold out longer against an enemy six times his own number; the hospitals at this time being so full of wounded that no more could be received; and, ultimately, the Spaniards were sure to gain victory over us by dint of numbers.[59]

These accounts obviously vary in detail, not surprisingly. Gavin's is the closest to the actual events, for both the marine officers wrote some years later. In compensation the officers inevitably had a much wider view of what happened. Captain Pococke of the 71st recalled events very similarly. Just occasionally a particular event is remembered, as by Fernyhough:

A grenadier of the 71st, during the attack observed a Spaniard, with a long red feather, every now and then popping his head out of a window and firing upon the English, then withdrawing himself till again ready to fire. One of this man's shots fell very near the grenadier, who picked it up, put it in his own musket in addition to the charge, and when the Spaniard appeared again from his hiding place, fired, and shot him dead.[60]

General Beresford was clinical in his recollection, written several months later:

It was about half past nine o'clock when the enemy showed his whole force, considerable bodies advancing against our right flank, others passing our front to get to the left, whilst the front was also attacked. His principal effort was for a considerable time directed against our right, but he constantly beat back with very great loss, and at length he appeared to threaten the front, against which he kept up a heavy fire from his guns, three of which he had advanced near to the square, but which were abandoned at the approach of Lieutenant Graham, 71st Regiment, with a party and they fell into our hands. But never during the day would he be induced to attempt to enter any body of men by the streets left open to our front. The enemy had during the whole of their attacks kept up a galling fire from the tops of churches and convents that commanded at a short distance the fort and squares and in proportion as he was beat out of the streets the firing from those houses increased and on his finally desisting from all direct, or open attack he bent his whole attention to that from the houses, which was not only more destructive to us but almost without danger to him, and at length he possessed himself of those that, close to him, commanded both the fort and the squares, and even many of the houses in the latter. So circumstanced our men were falling very fast, and not only without being able to get to the enemy, but without even seeing him, and as now all further resistance would only serve to add to our killed and wounded, and as even had a retreat been possible I could not think of leaving the number of wounded to be slaughtered, I determined to hoist a flag of truce, which was done on the fort, and in a short time aide-de-camp from the enemy's commander came to me.[61]

It is clear that Liniers had thought through the problem of attacking a well-disciplined force with an undisciplined and excitable, if numerous, army. He did well to avoid Beresford's traps, and to utilize his own strengths – his numbers, the buildings, his army's enthusiasm – very well. Above all, he had kept his people at a distance from the British, for in a close fight the 71st would overwhelm his numbers with discipline and firepower – as it had already at Quilmes and Perdriel.[62] But the amateur soldiers of Buenos Aires, whose city had been so suddenly occupied, were unaware of the conventions and niceties of European warfare. For many of them the flag of truce put out by Beresford meant surrender. In this, of course, they were not wrong, but they were ignorant of the accepted military procedure. The British soldiers took refuge from their defeat in contempt for the victims. Pococke described the scene in the Plaza Mayor:

> … the whole square from the Cabildo to the castle was crowded with their soldiers etc., etc., of all descriptions and such a rabble I have never seen before and I hope never to see again.[63]

His distaste was shared by other diarists and chroniclers. Lieutenant Fernyhough remembered at greater length:

> Never shall I forget the scene which followed the hoisting of the flag of truce, and the advantage gained over us; about 4,000 ragamuffins

rushed into the square, brandishing their knives, threatening us with destruction. The savages paid no regard to our flag of truce, and were firing in all directions.

The whole of our little army was arranged within the square of the castle, and all our guns double-shotted, expecting every moment to come to close quarters with bayonets and knives (most of the Spaniards being armed with the latter, which they use with great dexterity). Previously to this the general had ordered us not to allow the men to fire a shot without his express orders, but it was with the utmost difficulty that the general himself could prevent it; the officers being obliged to use force to remove the men from the guns. The poor fellows lamented not being allowed to continue the action. Some of them with tears in the eyes, requested most earnestly to be permitted to die with arms in their hands, I believe the set of men were never more ready to sacrifice their lives for their king and country, than the brave men who composed our little army on that day.[64]

It was some time before Liniers and the professionals on the Spanish side could stop the firing and fighting. Liniers sent his adjutant Captain Quintana once again into the fort see what terms Beresford wanted. Beresford described what happened:

It was however impossible, situated as the two contending parties were, to prevent the continuation of the firing, our troops being at this period in the precise situation I had taken up previous to the action, but to have the flag of truce respected I directed them to return to the fort, expecting the enemy would remain in his then position, but in this idea I was deceived (as I had been in every one I had framed of honourable conduct on the part of our enemies), for on the British retiring the Spaniards seeing no longer danger or dread, advanced into the squares, and thence finding they were not fired at from the fort advanced to it (I had previously sent my men off the ramparts to prevent any breach of the flag of truce in our part), and in spite of the efforts of some of their officers and particularly those of the aide-de-camp then with me on the walls, they proceeded to act in a manner the most repugnant to every law of war and of honour. This conduct kept me on the ramparts using every effort to prevent being under the necessity of firing, which under a flag of truce I was resolved but under the last extremity and having no other alternative not to be forced to.[65]

Why Beresford expected the civilian population of the city to have any knowledge of 'every law of war and of honour' he does not explain, but at least he retained enough sense not to fire into the crowd. Captain Gillespie, who, as the senior marine officer present, was presumably involved in the discussion of terms, described the negotiations:

> A tedious discussion ensued upon the parade in the force, in which ... Frenchmen took the leading share, and pledged their protection to us against the popular fury. Accordingly verbal terms were stipulated upon the spot, to be afterwards ratified, the leading articles of which consisted in 'security to our persons and properties, a speedy embarkation for Europe, not to serve until regularly exchanged, and that the expenses of the voyage would be defrayed by the Spanish government. These conditions with others of a minor import was signed by Liniers four days after the 12th of August, but the deed was basely denied by him, from a servile compliance with the wishes of the ruling authorities ...[66]

Liniers, as Gillespie noted, claimed afterwards that he had not agreed to allow the evacuation of the British forces, but Beresford believed he had *de facto* agreed through his adjutant. The British, said Liniers, said they could have recommenced fighting, but Captain Pococke knew that there was little or no artillery ammunition left.[67] Further fighting would only have resulted in an even more comprehensive British defeat. As it was, about fifty of the British were dead and over 100 wounded. They believed that the Spaniards had suffered about 700 casualties, but a modern count suggests that the Spanish casualties were much the same as the British: fifty dead and 136 wounded. There was clearly much more noise and fury than coolness or accuracy in the fighting.[68]

Chapter Eight

The Prisoners

The surrender of Beresford's force, including almost the whole of the 71st Regiment, was a confused affair, which resulted in an unpleasant dispute between the Spaniards and their prisoners. The British thought they had been given permission, once they had surrendered, to evacuate their troops. The Spaniards, or rather it would be best now to call them the *portenos*, the people of Buenos Aires, did not agree. Instead, once they had disarmed the prisoners, they claimed, through Colonel Liniers, that no decision of that sort had been made. The surrendered troops were then soon dispersed out of the city and throughout the interior of the country.

This is a crucial event in the developing story. Had the British been allowed to leave, events would have taken a very different course, for it was the British perception that Liniers and the *portenos* had broken their word which was part of the fuel which drove the British on; another part was their determination to rescue the prisoners; only a long way behind became a wish to conquer, to ensure that, as *The Times* had said, 'Buenos Aires is a part of the British Empire.' It is unlikely in other words that a series of major British expeditions would have been mounted had it not been for the imprisonment of the 71st Foot.

As it happens, the *portenos* were probably mistaken in their fears. Had the troops been released, they would have been without arms, and would then have sailed off. The sting would have been drawn from British anger. Popham's and Beresford's expedition, after all, was quite unauthorized, and blame for its defeat could, and would, have been put squarely on him and Baird. But the *portenos* did not know that. By continuing to hold the prisoners of war, they in effect legitimized the original expedition, at least to the extent of submerging its lack of official authority under the British outrage.

It is possible to go further. The repeated British assaults over the next year hammered especially severely on the authority and prestige of the viceroy, and thus, through him, on that of the Spanish monarchy, which he represented. If the prisoners had been released, there would have been no more fighting, and the viceroy would have been able, without too much difficulty, to re-establish his authority in Buenos Aires. But his failure to prevent or defeat the successive British invasions, first at Buenos Aires, then at Maldonado, at Montevideo, at Colonia, and again in Buenos Aires, fatally undermined his authority. The success of the *portenos*, first in recovering the city, and then in resisting the second attack, gave the Cabildo and the *criollos* the self-confidence to take matters into their own hands. This they would not have had but for the defeat of the British attacks. And that self-confidence was the foundation for the assumption of independence by Buenos Aires in 1810, a political development which would not have taken place without it. The independence of Buenos Aires was the first decisive break in the unity of the Spanish empire in America, and the failure of Spain to recover control of the city and its viceroyalty was a standing example to all the rest of those in Spanish America who were actively seeking independence.

The imprisonment of the 71st Foot, therefore, triggered major developments in the history of Spanish South America, though the officers and men could be forgiven for not seeing that at the time. They had much more personal concerns. Each man was now faced with an individual decision, for the opportunity was presented to all of them to settle in the new country. The dilemma was particularly acute for those who were Catholic. The Germans forcibly recruited at the Cape had almost all made the decision even before the surrender of the regiment, and had either deserted then, or took the opportunity to do so after capture. Now the British also had that choice.

General Beresford had time to brood on his wrongs, and in May of the next year, on his way home, he wrote an account of what had happened after the surrender. It is not necessarily to be accepted as wholly accurate, and it is certainly not to be accepted as the only possible explanation, but his recollection was as follows:

> I will proceed to state the facts, which are, that the terms were agreed to on the 12th, by Señor Liniers without the least hesitation, and he desired from the great confusion that reigned to postpone till the morning putting them to paper. The next morning I met him for that purpose, and they were put in writing in rough English and French copies, the latter was left with him, and he requested I would have the terms put into English and Spanish for our respective signatures, immediately on which he dispatched a vessel with a Spanish officer having a letter from me to Sir Home Popham, to send back the transports (which the previous

evening he had taken down the river), to receive the troops. This officer sailed I think about 12:00 p.m. on the 13th and the transports returned and were received as cartels in consequence, which perfectly contradicts his assertion that it was some days after the 12th that at my entreaties he agreed to the capitulation. A few days after he came to me, when I had not been able to get the translation of the terms; I had a fair English copy which was read over and translated to him paragraph by paragraph, and in presence of Lt. Col. Pack and a friend of his, a Señor Casamajor, first officer of the royal treasury at Buenos Aires. Señor Liniers was extremely anxious with me to make some alterations in our original agreement, but which except in one case I refused, and he finally on signing this paper took it and gave it to his friend Don Felix Casamajor, desiring him to get it translated and to see that it was such as they understood it, making the alteration I had agreed to. This he did, and the fair copies afterward signed by Señor Liniers were wrote, the English by my aide-de-camp, the Spanish part by the said Señor Don Felix Casamajor. This I believe occurred on the 16th and about the 20th or the 21st the transports having some time before arrived. I thought it right to remonstrate against any for this delay in the completion of the treaty, to which no other answer was at the time made, but verbal assurances to my aide-de-camp that the treaty would be strictly complied with, that the delay was occasioned by forms only, and that I need not have any anxiety on the subject. Señor Liniers promising daily to call upon me to make the final arrangements, then assurances daily given to my aide-de-camp, lasted till the 26th, when I saw Señor Liniers by appointment at his own house. I had with me Major Tolley, 71st Regiment, and my aide-de-camp Captain Arbuthnot, 20th Light Dragoons, and as soon as we were seated, with a great deal of a sensibility, and declared regret, Señor Liniers for the first time communicated to me that the British troops were to be detained ...[1]

What Beresford does not do is make any pretence of explaining, or understanding, Liniers' position. It seems likely that Liniers intended to get rid of his British prisoners quickly by exchanging them for any Spanish prisoners who were being held by the fleet. This was certainly the impression gained by several of the prisoners. Captain Pococke was told by Beresford that they would be exchanged as soon as the ships appeared. Captain Gillespie understood the prisoners would be evacuated. The ordinary soldiers and some of the officers, on the other hand, such as Private Balfour Kennach and Ensign Gavin, do not seem to have heard this. The difference is probably due to their differing treatment. The officers were quickly released from their prisons on parole into the care of Spanish civilians, probably in many cases those on whom they had been billeted before the surrender. Lieutenant Fernyhough, for instance, was put up by the merchant with whom he had lodged before the Spanish reconquest. Pococke got a billet with three other officers on the 16th. The soldiers however were kept in prisons, and according to Pococke, were not fed for two days.[2]

The basic problem was that the lines of authority on the Spanish side were thoroughly entangled. There was widespread popular disgust at the viceroy's perceived failure either to resist the British assault in the first place or to remove them later. That this feeling was unjust to Sobremonte is beside the point. The hero of the hour was Liniers, and political authority in the city lay with him, with his army, and with the Cabildo, which was under the presidency of Martin de Alzaga, a merchant. Alzaga and Liniers quickly formed an alliance, and eventually the viceroy recognized Liniers as the official military commander in the city. But by failing to retain control of his viceregal capital and remaining in Córdoba, Sobremonte had effectively half abdicated.[3]

The Liniers–Alzaga alliance was necessary because there was a partial collapse of order in the city after the British surrender (which is probably the explanation for the failure to provide food for the imprisoned soldiers). Some of this was sheer celebration, but partly there was an uglier revengeful side as well. Captain Gillespie's servant was murdered on 14 August; Pococke reported that the British were being robbed if they ventured out. The soldiers' knapsacks had been left in the Fort during the fighting.

> Some days after the surrender of the place our packs were delivered to us, plundered of their contents by the enemy, no useful article of any description being left.[4]

Fernyhough, because of his brown complexion, was often mistaken for a Spaniard in a British uniform and was several times threatened with death. Pococke resisted an attempt to steal his baggage only by appealing directly to Liniers.[5] Gavin was rescued by his host:

> I was taken to a Spaniard's house whose inmates treated me most kindly, and during the frenzy of the mob in search of the English officers concealed me under a bed.[6]

The *portenos* desire for revenge was fuelled by rumours, such as that the British had fired poisoned bullets – which was presumably the result of wounds festering. Clearly the atmosphere became more hostile as time passed. On the other hand, Gavin having been treated 'most kindly', remembered other kindness:

> 18th [August]. I ventured out, protected by a worthy priest, and was met by a contractor who supplied us with bread during the time we occupied the town. He, with the most unfeigned joy, clasped me in his arms and informed me he had searched among the dead, the hospitals, and prisons in vain for me and gave me up for lost. This good man's kindness continued during our stay in Buenos Aires. He visited me daily, and the night previous to our being sent up the country brought me as much excellent biscuit as a huge black could carry ... After we were made prisoners, the Spaniards formed a corps of volunteer light horse, and copied the uniform of our 20th Light Dragoons. They were composed of gentlemen. One of them, Don Pedro Gasper, took a great fancy to me, and offered to send me to a friend's house some miles in the country, but I preferred sharing the fate of my countrymen ...[7]

Similarly, Captain Gillespie remembered that:

> After we were prisoners many of the families in the city shewed a particular desire to have English soldiers for their domestics, far more from a liberal wish to alleviate their captivity than to benefit from their services ... an evident partiality existed on the part of the females to English officers over that shewn to that class of their friends. The only bar to the closest connexion was the difference in their creed which only sacrificed, the ladies would have viewed the military rank of their admirers as a minor consideration, one of them was married to a cadet in the St Helena Corps, who was a voluntary convert, and who soon after received a captain's commission in the Buenos Ayres army.[8]

There was widespread conviction among the British, but it is only manifested in accounts written after, sometimes a long time after, these events. There are, though the sources are poor, no documented cases of marriages. (Note that Gillespie's example provides no names.) There are a number of romanticized stories. But there were other attractions in Buenos Aires besides the women. It is clear that there was a serious shortage of artisanal skills in the city. Any of the captured men who had such skills could have used it as the basis for a prosperous life. This had been the main reason, no doubt, why the mutinous prisoner-criminals on the *Jane Shore* had been permitted to remain in the city. As was seen in Chapter 5, many of the private soldiers in the 71st also had such skills; all it would have taken would be conversion to Catholicism, or perhaps not even that, since a number of them were already Catholics. This is a subject to be returned to when considering the effects of the British invasions in more detail (see Chapter 14).

For the *portenos* the most nerve-racking part of the situation was the uncertainty about future British intentions. This meant, in the short term, Popham's intentions, for he was now in sole control, though with very little military, as opposed to naval, strength. But he could, and did, institute a formal blockade of the ports of the estuary. Popham had written as early as the day of the British surrender to the 'General Commanding the Spanish Forces in Buenos Aires', suggesting a prisoner exchange.[9] But he did not promise to go away, nor did he promise that there would be no more attacks.

Having failed to get a satisfactory reply to his letter, Popham then decided that the authority on the Spanish side lay with Liniers' superior, the governor of Montevideo, Ruiz Huidobro, and addressed a barrage of letters to him.[10] Popham had gone into letter-writing mode. The problem was that Ruiz Huidobro no longer had any real authority over Liniers, even though Montevidean soldiers had taken part in the reconquest. The *portenos* were never inclined to accept either the authority of or opinions from Montevideo, or vice versa. Thus Popham's decision to negotiate with Huidobro made him seem even more devious than ever to the *portenos*. Huidobro could promise nothing, since he could not deliver anything, but he clearly could not admit it, and this in turn simply made Popham intensely suspicious. Eventually Huidobro deflected him onto the viceroy, but Popham swiftly realized that Sobremonte had no authority.[11]

This was immensely frustrating to Popham, who seems to have felt personally responsible for extracting the prisoners – as indeed he was. Apart from the soldiers, over 300 of those captured were marines or sailors from his ships, which left some of his ships badly shorthanded. On the Spanish side it was no doubt just as frustrating; with the added ingredient of the possibility of mob violence in Buenos Aires if the provisional government of the city did anything that was too unpopular. There were rumours, picked up assiduously by Pococke, that Sobremonte was on his way back to his capital, but even to Pococke it was clear that there were internal disputes among the victorious Spaniards.[12]

In these circumstances of mutual suspicion the exchange of prisoners proved to be impossible to arrange. The two sides were too far apart. Popham could not promise not to go on fighting, because, after all, Britain and Spain were at war; on the Spanish side no single man had the authority to release the prisoners, Sobremonte was discredited, Ruiz Huidobro did not have the formal authority, Liniers had no official position, at least for a time. And anyone in Buenos Aires who proposed a concession to the British would find himself attacked, certainly verbally and possibly physically. Colonel Pack of the 71st gave an account of the crucial meeting between Liniers and Beresford, in a letter he wrote in February explaining his own conduct:

Immediately after the surrender of the fort of Buenos Aires on the 12th of August last, I understood from Brigdr-General Beresford, that the conditions verbally agreed to between him and Colonel Liniers were that the British troops were to be considered prisoners of War, but to be immediately embarked for England or the Cape, and to be exchanged for those Spanish prisoners made on the British possessing themselves of Buenos Ayres. On the 13th in the morning Colonel Liniers despatched a Spanish Officer to Sir Home Popham with a letter from General Beresford to send the British Transports back for the purpose of immediately carrying the treaty into execution and a few days afterwards I was present when Colonel Liniers unequivocally affixed his name to the capitulation containing the above conditions.

After the return of the transports, various delays took place, and I believe it was on the 26th that Colonel Liniers informed General Beresford in the presence of Major Tolley 71st Regiment, and Captain Arbuthnot, the General's Aide-de-Camp (from all of whom I learned it), that he regretted to inform him of his having been resolved in spite of his efforts, not to embark the British troops and at the same time declaring his (Colonel Liniers') abhorrence of such a breach of faith, and offered to second General Beresford's remonstrance on the occasion. On the 27th in the evening I heard that Colonel Liniers' Aide-de-Camp waited on General Beresford and stated it to be the Colonel's intention to carry the treaty into execution, by privately embarking the men, and requested that the General would for that purpose order the British transports to a particular place.[13]

Liniers' problem, of course, was that he was not a free agent, and had to pay attention both to the Cabildo and to the state of feeling in the city, where few people appreciated the delicate nuances of military honour and the 'laws of war' which were involved for Beresford and Liniers. Liniers, prompted no doubt by complaints in the city, claimed that a British ship carrying despatches from Baird at the Cape had been driven aground at Maldonado, and that the despatches showed that Baird had ordered the expedition to return to the Cape. This was clearly either a rumour from the Banda Oriental, or wishful thinking, for no such ship existed. A rumour spread of a sea battle between a British and Spanish fleet somewhere between St Helena and Rio de Janeiro which the Spaniards had won – only for it to be denied next day. Three days later the rumour was of a French fleet having arrived at Maldonado at the mouth of the estuary. And it was said that Popham had fired on an American ship, and had been fired on himself by a shore battery.[14] All this was pure imagination and rumour, but it is also clear evidence of the state of extreme nervousness in the city. One is reminded of the tension in Cape Town after the British capture, when anticipating the arrival of a French fleet.

One cause of this nervousness was the presence of the British prisoners. After all, a number of *portenos* had been persuaded by the British to support the British conquest. They had not done so publicly, but they were now concerned not to have this preference revealed. A number of the *porteno* merchants had directed Beresford onto the royal treasure at Lujan, or so it was thought. At the same time the fact that some had been friendly to the British was not unknown, and while the people involved were rarely identified, their existence as a group created further uncertainty. Some *portenos* might, it was clearly thought, be prepared to welcome the British back again to the city.

So if the British soldiers could be removed out of Buenos Aires there would be one less irritant in the body politic. Their presence as prisoners immobilized British power, but the Spanish populace did not trust Popham to sail away even if the soldiers were released. Liniers, Beresford, and Popham all wanted the prisoners to leave, but it became clear that this could only be arranged if it was organized clandestinely. So Liniers plotted to release them, and this was to be put into operation on 28 August.

The intermediary seems to have been Major Tolley, who visited Huidobro in Montevideo on 24 August.[15] Tolley was one of the prisoners, and so he was evidently Beresford's emissary, and he went on from Montevideo to see Popham, no doubt to make the arrangements for the men to be evacuated. On that same day Beresford protested bitterly to Liniers that his men's health was suffering by their close confinement, and he demanded to be allowed to embark, a letter which might be seen as providing Liniers with later justification.[16] By 28 August the arrangements for the embarkation of the prisoners had been completed, and the four transports in the British fleet, *Walker, Willington, Triton*, and *Ocean*, were sent to lie off Ensenada, which had been Liniers' official post before the invasion and where his authority was, no doubt, rather clearer than it was in the city.[17] In the city Pococke understood that the Cabildo had decided to move the British out under the pretence of sending them up-country, but actually it was intended to put them on the transports. Gillespie thought they would be released.[18]

At Ensenada the commandant, Juan Gutierrez de la Concha, who had been the organizer of Liniers' crossing from Colonia to Las Conchas, accused Popham of breaking the agreement by attacking a Spanish felucca. Popham investigated the incident and denied that it ever took place.[19] He may have been right, but it is certain that something happened which upset the arrangements. Possibly it was Spanish suspicions of British intentions, possibly the whole thing was torpedoed by de la Concha, or maybe by Liniers, or perhaps Alzaga. All these men had reason to fear a mob reaction if it became known that they were involved in such a conspiracy. Any of them could have had their own reasons for upsetting such delicate arrangements. The fact that these had been clandestine would, of course, bring blame on their heads when they were found out – as they certainly would be when the soldiers disappeared.

One of the major difficulties in reaching an agreement was that there were rifts within the *portenos*' ranks. Liniers, as a Frenchman, at least originally, was suspected to the Spanish, and as a Spanish government officer was subject to the *criollos. Criollos* and *peninsulares*, of course, were at odds, as ever. The Cabildo, under the leadership of Martin de Alzaga, were suspicious of royal officials. None of these groups or individuals had developed a specific policy as yet, but the absence of Spanish authority with the eclipse of the viceroy meant that those with power in Buenos Aires had greater freedom to exercise it. They would not be pleased to surrender this new power, and the fate of the British prisoners was therefore one of the aspects of that new authority. Whoever controlled the prisoners had the power of diplomacy and access to the British presence, and negotiating with the British commander would enhance their power in the city.

Whatever had happened to block the prisoners' release on 28 August, if anything – and the men themselves ascribed it to the sudden arrival of British reinforcements from the Cape – the Spanish decision was now to send their prisoners into the interior of the viceroyalty (map 15).[20] This would, of course, mean that no Spanish groups could easily use them as a source of power. Pococke recorded that it was only a rainstorm which prevented their journey from starting on 1 September. On 3 September 400 men were marched off inland, and on 5 September the officers gave their parole. The situation in the city is vividly illustrated by the fact that any tradesmen or married men (presumably those whose wives were also captured), were allowed to remain, the former no doubt being expected to ply their trades, while the single men were now to be safely removed from the gaze of the Spanish girls. Pococke thought about 150 men had joined the Spaniards, mainly from among the Germans who had been picked up at the Cape. By 24 September he recorded that there were only sixty-five of the prisoners left in the city. These figures are not to be taken as precise, of course, but they give some idea of the situation.[21]

The comments of the ordinary soldiers suggest they knew little or nothing of the real political reasons, and felt themselves only at the mercy of forces totally outside their control. Private Kennach remembered:

After remaining in prison two or three weeks we were ordered to be distributed in small parties through the different towns in the Province of La Plata.[22]

And Gavin recalled:

Notwithstanding this capitulation, on the Spaniards hearing of a reinforcement arriving in the river from England, under the command of Lieutenant-Colonel Backhouse, orders were issued to send the prisoners into the interior of the country.[23]

As it happened, however, the reinforcements did not arrive until mid-October. Gavin's explanation is thus a later rationalization, which only emphasizes how little he and his comrades knew of what was going on. But Lieutenant Fernyhough records their apprehensions:

We frequently visited our poor men in prison, who were on the eve of being removed up the country. When they were informed of it, the only reply they made was, 'They hoped their country would not forget them.' They hung about us and were much distressed and parted from us in despair.[24]

The men's reaction is interesting for more than one reason. They were clearly aghast at the prospect of being separated from their officers, and left in a condition of helplessness. It is clear that individual initiative was not encouraged in the regiment. But beyond that was the clear assumption that it was very likely that they would be forgotten, and that they could be left to rot for the rest of their lives in a distant foreign land. In fact, the need to rescue these men was one of the main motives for continued British presence in the River Plate. This comes through in correspondence of all the commanders, and among the government ministers in London. Their concern was clearly not something in which the soldiers believed, however.

The prisoners were marched, if that is the word, to numerous destinations, with the intention of breaking them into small groups, but also with the aim of removing them well away from Buenos Aires. Not only were they a political irritant in the city, but some at least were in danger of their lives. Not that this danger lessened at a distance. Private Kennach, for instance, was sent on a journey which he thought was 1,000 miles (actually not much over half that), to San Juan at the foot of the Andes:

It fell to the lot of the party I belonged to go to Saint Juan, a town on the frontier of La Plata, situated at the foot of the Andes and distant from Buenos Ayres one thousand miles. On this long and painful march I felt nothing but misery; my life was a burden to me. Having nothing to subsist on but beef our living was wretched in the extreme. We had no cooking utensils, no knives, no salt; our walking staff served for a spit, and on pampas plains, where neither wood nor water can be found, the dried excrements of animals served for fuel; there were neither towns nor villages, not a single house; we had nothing to shelter us from the inclemency of the weather but the canopy of heaven. How disagreeable the word prison sounds in the ear of a soldier; captivity in a palace is but misery when compared with sweet Liberty. How often did I think of my native country on these trying occasions, and would cheerfully have given the gold mines of Mexico to be free.

Although our course of living was filthy we were perfectly healthy, none having died, nor any sick. When a person is exposed to misery such as I have described it is easy to conceive the state the body must be in; we had nothing to wear and were only midway upon our journey, having still five hundred miles to travel, and having not once changed our body clothes they had almost worn out. My shoes had long fallen to pieces, and what remained of my red coat was turned parson grey;

nothing of the trousers remained but the waistband; of the shirt nothing but the seams; and the plumed bonnet, the Highlander's pride, with all its gaudy ornaments totally disappeared on the barren plains of La Plata.

After a period of twenty-eight days' travel we arrived at St Juan, the place of our destination, and were once more committed to prison. Our situation for sometime was truly miserable, nothing but the bare walls of a ruined convent, damp floors without bedding or any other comfort. Seven weeks had not elapsed since I was a prisoner, during which time I had not shaved; and with some prospect of being permitted to rest, at least for a time, I pulled up courage, the spirits rose, and I commenced cleaning. It absolutely became necessary to extirpate a certain bosom enemy. I accordingly commenced shaving, washing and scrubbing and in a short time I got rid of my troublesome neighbours.[25]

Two hundred of the men were sent to Mendoza, to San Juan and to Tucuman, a hundred to Santiago del Estero and fifty to La Certola and to San Luis. Cordoba received about three hundred. They were further split up by being billeted on local people.[26] Like Kennach they will have reached their places of detention by the end of October, give or take a couple of weeks. As will be seen some were moved on fairly regularly. This they regarded as a deliberate annoyance; in fact, it was probably more to relieve the pressure on the local communities. The sudden arrival of several hundred foreign soldiers will have strained the resources of these interior towns; none of the British, of course, thought of this. At the same time, several of them do express their gratitude at the consideration of the hosts.

The officers remained in the city for a time after the men had gone, and were then sent mostly to San Antonio, perhaps 100 miles away. Lieutenant Fernyhough remembered the journey:

October 11th. This morning we were employed in packing up for our march into the country, which was to commence in the course of the day. About three o'clock p.m., we were summoned into the square before the Cabildo, where we found a guard of soldiers, and horses ready saddled for us. We took leave of Buenos Ayres with heavy heart, not expecting to see it again for some time, if ever. About dusk we arrived at the ruins of an old college, where we halted for the night, having no other bedding than bullocks' hides.

October 12th. At daylight we set out again, and arrived in the evening at the village of Lujan, about seventeen leagues from Buenos Ayres. General Beresford and eight officers were to remain here till further orders. The remainder were to be distributed in two small villages some leagues further on.

As soon as the waggons came up with our baggage we proceeded, and arrived on the evening of the 14th at Capillo del Senor, a much smaller village than Lujan, but more pleasantly situated. We left here Major Tolley and twelve more officers.

October 15th. We arrived at St Antonio de Araco, a much better and neater village than either of the two former we had passed through. Here is a very handsome church. Some large groves of peach trees, which covered several acres of ground, afforded very pleasant walks. Colonel Campbell, of the seventy-first, and the remaining officers, except four, viz., Captain Mackenzie, Mr Lethbridge, late secretary to Sir Home Popham, one of the assistant commissaries-general, and myself, were to be left here.

We had a letter of recommendation to Don Felipe Ortorala, en sa Estancia, rivero Araco, who lived upon his estate, five leagues from St Antonio de Araco, where we proceeded on the 16th of October.

He received us with great hospitality, and informed us that every thing in his house was perfectly at our service, and his horses, whenever we wished to ride out.[27]

Similarly, Captain Gillespie recalled what happened, noting particularly the gratifying Spanish recognition of the endemic class distinctions of the British army. He was also much less sanguine about a whole business than Fernyhough, seemingly determined to complain for much of the journey:

After a long indulgence betwixt hope and fear, it was generally circulated on the morning of the 9th of October that our doom was inevitably fixed for the Upper Country, and that waggons were about enter the city to convey us ... In the same spirit of duplicity that had hitherto actuated the conduct of the public authorities towards us they now strove to palliate their dishonour by representing the cruel alternative as essential to preserve us from a disorderly populace.

Waggons also were allotted to us in the proportion of one to two officers, to serve as depots for our provender, the wretched remnants of our baggage and as retreats through the nights ... General Beresford with his staff proceeded in a coach at the same hour, and the waggons having set off early in the morning they had gone beyond the resting place that had been appointed for us until the ensuing day. This was an old college, formerly belonging to the Jesuits, and not unlike to an eastern caravansary, about two leagues from Buenos Ayres where we arrived about six o'clock but owing to the forward movement of our carriages we were without food or accommodation ... All were again on horseback by dawn, upon the 12th of October ... We reached a first house about ten, four leagues from Buenos Ayres ... Six leagues from Buenos Ayres we crossed the River Conchas, which falls into the Plata. General Beresford and those officers who were well mounted reached Lujan about four p.m., others at seven o'clock in the most woeful appearance from dust and fatigue, and as for myself it was eleven at night before I arrived ... At daylight of the 16th we renewed our labours and after crossing an arm of the river passing close to it we reached the village of St Antonio de Araco. After great trouble another officer and myself procured a small hut at the rent of three dollars a month behind the house of an inhabitant. Our abode had been recently devoted to a flour granary, and our contract was that it should continue so, but for form's sake that it should be entitled our house. We however were contented with our lot ... This village became our resting-place for three months, and yielded the pastimes of fishing, cricket, hunting, and riding.[28]

By the time that the great majority of the prisoners had been removed from the city, a new danger had developed with the arrival of extra British forces. The prisoners were now scattered from Buenos Aires to the Andes, and a substantial number had already decided to stay in their new land. Others were to be tempted in various ways to stay. One of the objectives of the British all along was to recover these soldiers, so that, by keeping them, the portenos thought they had been guaranteed further attacks.

Chapter Nine

Reinforcements

The reinforcements which arrived at the River Plate, and whose arrival seemed to some of the prisoners in retrospect to be the signal for the *portenos* to send them all into the interior, had been sent from the Cape by General Baird in response to the pleas of both Popham and Beresford. Ironically, Baird had received the letters, sent with the transport *Melantho*, on 12 August, the very day Beresford had surrendered.

As it happened, just six days earlier, a convoy had arrived at the Cape from England. The 64-gun line-of-battle ship *Lancaster* and the frigate *Medusa* arrived escorting a convoy of transports and Indiamen carrying the 47th Foot, which was to go to India, the fourth battalion of the 60th Foot, which was intended to become the formation which the recruits from the former Dutch soldiers at the Cape were to join, a party of recruits for regiments which were already in India, two squadrons of the 21st Light Dragoons, and some new recruits for the regiments which were already supposed to be at the Cape, including some for the 71st.[1] One of these recruits was a man, name unknown, whose memoirs have been several times printed; he is known just as 'a soldier of the 71st'.[2]

These dragoons of the 21st were replacements for the 20th, Colonel Wilson's men. Sergeant Landsheit remembered the excitement among his fellows at the thought that they were to return to England. No time was wasted. The orders to prepare were issued. 'Then a large black ship came into the Bay.'[3] This was the *Melantho*, from Buenos Aires. (Was it really black? Or was the good sergeant endowing it with that colour of foreboding only in retrospect? Or was it the name? Or his ghost-writer's imagination? Many of the historian's problems are encapsulated in that one sentence.) Baird certainly decided almost at once that he would send reinforcements to Buenos Aires.

The military force now at his disposal was substantial, thanks to the coincident arrival of the India fleet and the *Melantho*. He had his own garrison, of five British regiments and the Cape Regiment, the replacements for his British units, and the India bound soldiers. He quickly decided that all these were available for as he chose. He seems not to have hesitated in changing the orders and destinations of any of the units. Of cavalry he still had most of the original men of the 20th Light Dragoons, less those few who were sent with Popham and those officers, like Wilson, who had already seeped back to Europe. He now also had the two newly arrived squadrons of the 21st as well: 220 soldiers of the 20th and 158 of the 21st.[4] The foot regiments of the Cape garrison numbered five: the 24th, 38th, 72nd, 83rd and 93rd, a total of about 3,500 troops. Of these the usual ten per cent were sick or absent at the muster in August. The 47th, in the transports, were also present, with 784 men.[5]

To add to these Baird had the contingents of the 2nd and the 54th who had been rescued from the *Volontaire* when that ship was captured. They had been very sickly when released, and were slowly recovering – or, in many cases, dying. They numbered somewhat over 200 when rescued, but there were fewer of them now.[6] They could not be considered a useful reinforcement to the garrison since Baird could not be sure they were not going to be ordered away by the next post from Britain. Yet they were soldiers, and the longer they stayed at the Cape, the longer they would be thought of as resident troops, and thus available for use. At the same time, the Cape Regiment, the force recruited from the Hottentots, was becoming a useful force. It suffered from a high rate of both sickness and desertion (often only temporary), but these problems were being overcome under Lieutenant-Colonel Graham's intelligent training. The regiment had some 500 men usually available.[7] Now that the India fleet was at anchor in Simon's Bay, there were also the cadre of the fourth battalion of the 60th Foot and the recruits for India, though neither of these could be sent to South America. But if they could not be sent there, they, and the Cape Regiment, were on hand and available to release others to go, at least in Baird's mind.

Baird therefore had, temporarily at least, well over 5,000 troops under his hand. He determined to send almost half of this force to reinforce Beresford. This was a much bolder decision than the one he had made back in April when he sent just the 71st and a few others off with Popham and Beresford. At that time he was parting with only one sixth of his force and he had already sent on one regiment (the 59th) to India. Now he was detaining and diverting a regiment he had been ordered to send to India, diverting a force of dragoons he should be sending back to Britain and reducing the garrison of his colony to its lowest level during the present round of French wars. It all suggests that the original intention of Popham's expedition, at least in Baird's mind, was not conquest, but loot. Had conquest been in Baird's mind he would presumably have been more generous with soldiers in the first place – after all, he was the man who had argued strongly for extra forces for the assault on the Cape. Beresford's contingent appointment as a local major-general and lieutenant-governor, however, shows Baird covering all possibilities; yet the smallness of the original expedition implies likely failure if conquest was intended.

He now sent over 2,000 men to reinforce Beresford: two foot regiments, the 38th from the Cape garrison, and the 47th, destined for India, almost 400 dragoons (both of the detachments which he had available), and nearly 130 other troops, including those of the 54th who were available and fit to travel. These men were attached to the 38th since 100 or so of the 38th were at Algoa Bay and could not be brought up rapidly enough.

The letter Popham sent to the 'Senior Naval Officer' also produced results; *Lancaster's* convoy escorts, now not needed for India, were also diverted to South America. The troops were sent off in batches, as transports and supplies permitted. A first contingent was loaded and dispatched on 16 August with the frigate *Medusa* and the *Howe* transport. The *Melantho* transport was ready almost as quickly, and sailed with *Rolla* (the captured and bought-in prize) on 21 August with 140 men and two mortars and some medical stores. At first, Baird had decided to keep the 47th at the Cape and send another regiment with the 38th, but since the 47th were already in transports, he decided that they should go. A third contingent sailed on 28 August, convoyed by *Lancaster*. Baird also sent some Staff officers, particularly Lieutenant-Colonel Brownrigg and Major Tucker, but the senior officer of the expedition turned out to be the colonel of the 47th, Colonel Thomas Backhouse. Popham had requested Lieutenant-Colonel Vassall, commander of the 38th, by name. He went with the last division, sailing on 29 August.[8]

Meanwhile the news of Popham's original expedition was reaching Britain, but there, political changes had occurred since he had left. The Prime Minister who had favoured Popham, William Pitt, had died in January, and a new government, largely made up of his political opponents, had taken office under Lord Grenville. The first news of the expedition reached London in late June, in the form of the letters sent from St Helena from both Baird and Popham, but the news did not become public until mid-September, when Popham's rather more public letters reached their destinations in the several cities, and his private ones to various politicians. In the intervening time the government of Lord Grenville thrashed about gathering reinforcements, and devising schemes, but without any real sense of urgency. By the end of

August, one set of reinforcements for Buenos Aires had been dispatched from Britain.

The ministers had, of course, some excuse for delay and perplexity. Neither Baird nor Popham had given any clear idea of what the expedition was intended to achieve; both men had been appointees of their predecessors and political opponents, and their independent actions were regarded with suspicion. Within the Admiralty there was something close to consternation that Popham had taken all his ships away from the Cape, while within the War Office, in direct contrast, wild schemes of conquest were promoted. The Cabinet made a collective decision on 27 June to recall both Popham and Baird for exceeding their instructions, but also decided to send 2,000 troops to reinforce whatever success had been achieved in the Plate.[9]

It took a month for these somewhat contradictory decisions to be translated into actual appointments and actual troops and ships. Late in July Major-General Sir George Grey was appointed as the new commander-in-chief at the Cape, to go out as early as possible. His superior, the new governor, the Earl of Caledon, had already been appointed, but it seems there was no haste about his journey.[10] Popham's replacement as commander of naval forces at the Cape was Rear-Admiral Charles Stirling, the former commander of the squadron blockading Rochfort, who had taken part in the action off Finisterre the year before. He was to take out a convoy of reinforcements, whose commander was Brigadier-General Sir Samuel Auchmuty, who was intended to serve under Beresford's overall command. The reinforcing force was eventually settled to be two regiments of foot, the 45th and the 87th, three companies of the 95th Rifle Regiment, and a company of artillery under Captain Augustus Frazer.[11]

The delay in organizing and despatching these forces was partly due to the slowness of communications, but a large part must be ascribed to the person of the Secretary of state for War, William Windham. He had a high reputation as a parliamentary orator, but on paper he was verbose, and as an administrator he was woolly-minded and indecisive. He spent a good deal of time trying to have a favourite of his, Colonel Robert Craufurd, appointed to command the reinforcements, but he came up against the resistance of the Duke of York, the Commander-in-Chief of the army, who refused to give such a command to such a comparatively junior officer.[12] So Auchmuty was appointed.

But almost as soon as these decisions were finalized, they were cancelled. A rumour arrived that the French were about to invade Portugal, and Auchmuty's troops were taken to form part of an expedition to protect the threatened country.[13] The rumour was soon seen to be just that, but by then the expedition had sailed for Lisbon. By that time also the naval part of the original force for South America, under Stirling, had sailed without troops – the Admiralty was very keen to have Popham replaced as soon as possible. Stirling commanded the 64-gun *Sampson*, and the gun brig *Staunch*, with a storeship, four victuallers, and two Indiamen. General Grey sailed with him. They were to go to the River Plate first, and then on to the Cape.[14]

Then, before a new reinforcement could be organized, there arrived the news that Beresford's force had captured Buenos Aires and this had to be assimilated.[15] The death of the Foreign Secretary, Charles James Fox, one of the key men of the government, brought a Cabinet shuffle. Lord Grenville transferred the First Lord, Lord Howick, to the Foreign Office, replacing him at the Admiralty by his own younger brother, Tom Grenville. Tom was a nice enough chap, but thoroughly under the control of his brother and of his officials. Lord Howick was a stronger character, and eventually became the reforming Prime Minister, Lord Grey. (General Sir George Grey was his brother.)

The arrival of the news from Buenos Aires in government circles was closely followed by its wider dissemination, partly thanks to the letters Popham had sent to many men and to the industrial cities. These soon reached the newspapers, and stimulated some to make representations to the ministers, and a good deal of new commercial activity. Grenville saw the capture of Buenos Aires almost exclusively in the light of the situation in Europe, as a piece on the diplomatic chessboard, but others had different perspectives. Some considered that conquest was actually unnecessary, since what was really required, from Britain's point of view, was a severing of the connection between Spain and the colonies; that is, Britain should promote the 'emancipation' of the colonies. As early as 20 September, the leading article in a Manchester newspaper pointed out that it was not necessary to retain Buenos Aires, and that independence should be the aim.[16] Windham had been sent a long memo by Lord Selkirk in June, in which a detailed policy was laid out: imprison the office-holders, who could be assumed to be loyal to Spain, put the government in the hands of the *criollos*, proclaim the liberation of the land and provide protection. 'Antigallican', a correspondent of Lord Grenville's, also thought that the South Americans would require protection from Spain.[17]

Members of the government were very wary of a policy of advocating independence. There was no internal disagreement on this in the governing group, and all the pressure for it seems to have been external. Possession of the new conquest was accepted, though no undertaking could be made about keeping it at a future peace. This meant, however, not the possibility of independence, but that it could be handed back to Spain in a peace settlement. This was Lord Grenville's attitude, that the events in the South Atlantic had to be seen in the context of the European conflict. Not everyone agreed.

The real interest, in government and outside, lay not so much in the political future as in the economic present. Lord Auckland at the Board of Trade reacted with commendable speed to Popham's news and, as the news spread from Whitehall, others reacted to the apparent opportunity as well. Captain Donnelly of *Narcissus* had not merely delivered his dispatches and the silver, but Popham's letters too. By 20 September *The Times* reported that some had been received in provincial towns, and reprinted the Birmingham one, and the *British Volunteer and Manchester Weekly Express* printed that sent to the 'Mayor and Corporation'.[18] In them Popham variously referred to Buenos Aires as 'an extensive channel for the manufactures of Great Britain', as a 'rich province', and claimed that the population of the city was 70,000, who were 'wanting all sorts of European manufactures'. He listed the products of Buenos Aires, rather letting his imagination go, but including the essentials such as gold, silver, cotton, and indigo.

The treasure which *Narcissus* brought was landed at Portsmouth and was paraded through the streets of the town escorted by 30 of the frigate's sailors dressed as 'Blues', as they had been at the capture. The eight waggons which carried the metal were decorated with captured Spanish colours and British colours above.[19] Whoever organized the show – surely Captain Donnelly – was deliberately using contemporary means of publicity to drum up support. It also had a marvellously galvanizing effect on the mercantile interests. There was nothing like a large quantity of gold or silver to excite trading interests.

Further north, the Edinburgh *Evening Courant*'s comment on the capture of Buenos Aires was that it was 'likely to prove beneficial, incalculably beneficial' to British trade. In Leeds the great woollen firm of Benjamin Gott reacted to Popham's letter, which was printed in the *Leeds Intelligencer* of 22 September, by writing to Still, May and Co., of Greenock, to ask about the market at Buenos Aires; Gott's traveller in Liverpool, a man called Starforth, was inquiring about commercial houses exporting to Buenos Aires; Lord Lowther, the Lord of Westmorland, a man with several MPs in his pocket, wrote to Lord Camden that 'the trade of Lancashire, Glasgow, and Carlisle is become very brisk in consequence of the capture of Buenos

Aires', and he was saying this by 28 September, only a fortnight after the news had arrived.[20]

Other people actually set out to sample the reported wealth of the south. Ships were advertising Buenos Aires as their destination in newspapers by late in September.[21] Individual voyages seem to have taken rather longer to organize. Merchant Captain Robert Eastwicke, for example, was approached by Holloway and Davison, merchants of London, who had been alerted by a private letter from Popham. (Holloway seems to have been Popham's brother-in-law, and Alexander Davison was Lord Melville's agent.) Holloway suggested a partnership with Eastwicke, who was to go out to be the Buenos Aires end of the business. This was in October, but the voyage did not begin until early in November. Eastwicke captained the ship *Anna*, carrying merchandise (wine, brandy, and painted cottons), worth £100,000.[22] At about a same time the young James Paroissien boarded the *Gallant Schemer* at Gravesend, but the ship did not get away down channel until the end of December. Paroissien went with very few possessions, merely on the chance of making his fortune.[23] Also in December the Glaswegian James P. Robertson, aged 14, sailed from Greenock with his father in the *Enterprise*, again on a venture to make his fortune in the newly opened land.[24] The careers of all these men were to be very much more adventurous than their initial intentions.

Others had less mercenary motives. The London Missionary Society, already of course active in South Africa, had also received one of Popham's letters. They decided to send a missionary to promote 'the salvation of souls in heathen and other unenlightened centres'. A letter dated 6 October appointed the Reverend Creighton to the task. He was given £20 in Spanish dollars, some Spanish New Testaments, and the earnest good wishes of the society, but he was expected to find his earliest audience among the British troops. He sailed in the *Spring Grove*, on a passage which cost fifty guineas, which was to include the provision of 'wine, tea, and all other articles for your comfort'.[25]

On 22 September, meanwhile, the threat to Portugal having evaporated, Secretary of State Windham had reinstated the original reinforcing expedition to the River Plate under General Auchmuty. By instructions of that date he was to take two foot regiments, the 40th and 87th, the 17th Light Dragoons, three companies of the 95th Rifle Brigade, and a company of artillery, altogether about 3,000 men, to reinforce Beresford.[26] A letter was also sent to Beresford, more or less approving all he had done and telling him that reinforcements were on their way. Windham gave general guidance as to Beresford's government in a fair sample of the style:

> In truth every measure that can be adopted, consistent with prudence, to show the inhabitants of Buenos Ayres and all the adjoining provinces the wide difference there is between the oppressive rule under which they have hitherto lived and the benign and protecting government of His Majesty, must be an infinite importance in securing to this country in a manner at once efficacious and satisfactory, those brilliant prospects which the success of His Majesty's arms has at present opened to our view.[27]

But Windham reserved to the London authorities the question of customs duties, which would be Beresford's main weapon in bringing the merchant class to his side. Meanwhile a royal proclamation announced that Buenos Aires was now part of His Majesty's dominions – though there was still no definition of the term, town or viceroyalty, but one could by now assume the latter. Then he was worried about the danger of insurrection, for anyone fighting against British forces were now rebels, even if they had not heard of the proclamation – and Beresford was authorized to try to raise forces locally. Windham suggested that the local Indians or free blacks would be likely sources of recruitment – scarcely an idea calculated to win the hearts and minds of either *peninsulares* or *criollos*, though it was in line with normal British colonial practice, as with the Hottentots at the Cape. (But then this was exactly the source Pueyrredon had tapped for his band defeated at Perdriel.) Windham, however, did not provide any guarantee that British rule would continue after a peace, and this omission could only hamstring any real local initiative by the British.

The War Office, having reinstated Auchmuty's reinforcing expedition, now made new calculations as to its size, and the earlier and more extensive ideas of conquest were revived, with the result that a new and completely separate expedition was now concocted for Colonel Robert Craufurd. The Duke of York's objections to employing him were overridden, and Craufurd was promoted to brigadier-general so as to justify his command. The expedition was, in fact, bigger than Auchmuty's, and was designed for a different and more spectacular purpose, one which reveals much about the government, and the Secretary of State in particular. So the Admiralty now had to find escorts for both of these forces and the Transport Office had to provide ships to carry them. It all took time and scarce resources.

Auchmuty's total force was now over 3,000 men, and he finally got away on 9 October, escorted by the 64-gun *Ardent* – Captain Ross Donnelly's new command as a reward for bringing home the good news – together with the frigate *Unicorn*, the *Pheasant* brig, and two sloops.[28] By this time fifteen weeks had elapsed since the Cabinet had originally decided to send these reinforcements to Buenos Aires.

Craufurd had long been talking of a much more adventurous expedition than one which merely traversed the length of the Atlantic Ocean. Back in June, soon after the news of Beresford's destination reached London, he had written to the Prime Minister advocating 'subverting the authority of the Spanish viceroy in the province of Buenos Aires, Chili and Peru'.[29] But Beresford's new instructions, taken out by Auchmuty, envisaged him doing no more than holding the city of Buenos Aires. Like the Cape, the city could, it was thought, be used as a naval refreshment station and as a base for trade – clearly no one at the War Office had any idea of the navigational problems of the estuary. So all this took no account of the geography of the area, and this was a basic fault also with the instructions given to Craufurd.

He was given a force of 4,000 men, four regiments of Foot, the 5th, 36th, 40th, and 88th, five companies of the Rifle Regiment, five troops of the 6th Dragoon Guards, and two companies of artillery. This was a force almost as large as that which had been sent to take the Cape under Baird, and was larger than the combined forces of Beresford and Auchmuty – the reinforcement sent by Baird was not yet known about in London.

Windham's instructions to Craufurd were verbose, and a fairly extensive quotation is needed to give an idea of the sheer breathtaking scope of the expedition:

From the success which has attended His Majesty's arms on the east coast of South America and the experience which the inhabitants of that country have of the difference between the oppressive dominion of Spain and the benign protecting government of His Majesty, the knowledge of which must ere this have extended across the continent of South America, it is hoped that an attempt to gain a footing on the west coast of the continent may prove successful.

A competent naval force has also been ordered to proceed with this armament under the command of Admiral Murray with whom you are to co-operate and I am persuaded it is superfluous to point out to you how much the success of the enterprise may depend on your preserving the most perfect harmony and good understanding with that Officer, and on a like conduct being enforced on all the branches of both services.

The choice of the course to steer, whether to the eastward by the way of New South Wales or to the westward round Cape Horn is left to Admiral Murray to determine, and on your arrival at the west coast of South America, much must be left to your joint discretion in respect of the precise plan of operations which you shall pursue.

The object of your expedition is the capture of the seaports and fortresses and the reduction of the province of Chili, to which it is conceived both from positive information received, and also from a just inference drawn from the success at Buenos Ayres that your force is probably adequate.

It is, however, necessary to apprise you that it is not intended that your operations should pass beyond the limits of Chili, as by extending them to Peru and attempting the capture of Lima even under circumstances apparently favourable, you might engage in an enterprise disproportionate to your means, and by failure might even risk the loss of what may previously have been obtained in Chili, an event which would materially counteract the further views of government as to the future operations on a more extended scale in which the force under your command may be destined to cooperate.

Valparaiso being the seaport of St Iago as well as the port from which Lima is chiefly supplied with grain, and being represented by the most recent accounts as by no means formidable in point of defence, seems to afford the most favourable object for your first attack. Your determination upon this point must be taken in full concert with Admiral Murray as the question involves so many points of naval science with respect to the means of approaching the land and disembarking the troops with the least possible loss.

You will bear in mind that establishing and retaining a strong military position on the west coast of South America from which future operations may be carried on is the main object of your enterprise.

There were a dozen more paragraphs of varying exhortations and instructions, and ending with a most extraordinary instruction of all:

If you should succeed in obtaining possession of Valparaiso and St Iago, or establishing any other sufficient footing in Chili, you are to take the earliest possible means of apprising Brigadier-General

Beresford thereof, and of concerting with him the means of securing by a chain of posts or in any other adequate manner an uninterrupted communication both military and commercial between the provinces of Chili and Buenos Ayres.[30]

Craufurd was expected to sail east from the Cape, calling at Botany Bay to refresh the men after a voyage across the Indian Ocean of, at a minimum, 10,000 km, and there to collect reinforcements from its garrison. Then he was to sail on across the Pacific, a voyage of another 10,000 km. Apart from the soldiers, the convoy represented also a very large investment of ships: thirty-three transports, victuallers, and storeships were required, escorted at first by four line-of-battle ships, two frigates, three sloops and gun brigs, and two schooners, under the command the Rear Admiral George Murray. Governor William Bligh at Botany Bay was warned to expect the expedition.[31]

This is, of course, one of the most extraordinary sets of instructions to be given to a British commander. One cannot help speculating on what would have happened. For a start, the arrival of 4,000 British troops at Botany Bay could have seriously affected the history of relations between the settlers and Governor Bligh, who was not far from his 'second mutiny' – the first had been when he captained the *Bounty*. Then the condition of the troops when they reached Chile (if they did) after they had sailed the length of the Atlantic, and across both the Indian and Pacific Oceans, does not bear thinking about. But, suppose they survived and remained healthy, their arrival in Chili would have brought them into a country which was virtually demilitarized, but by no means willing to be thought of as part of someone else's empire. Craufurd, like Beresford, would have been faced, after initial successes, by a strong local reaction and probable defeat. He was, for example, expected to take Valparaiso, then Santiago, yet the two were 100 km apart, and separated by a mountain range. Nobody in London was bothering about geography.

The regiments detailed in these two expeditions, and in that commanded by Colonel Backhouse, were English or Irish, the 88th and the 87th, were in Craufurd's and Auchmuty's expeditions respectively. They had been recruited especially from the Catholic areas (and this would have been a source of weakness in Catholic Chile). The rest were English, recruited from the north, the Midlands, and the west – Northumberland and Lancashire, Nottingham and Stafford, Hereford and Somerset – in so far as any English regiment had a particular home location. Unlike Baird's original force, there was no attempt to choose a particular group of regiments in these cases; the commanders were given what was available at the time.

Those commanders seem from their names to have been overwhelmingly Scottish: Craufurd, Auchmuty, Murray, and Stirling. These names, however, deceive somewhat. Although all were of Scots descent, only one of them was in fact immediately of Scots origin. This was Robert Craufurd, from Newark in Ayrshire. He had joined the army at the age of 15 and had served against Tipu Sultan, as a military observer with the Austrian army, in Ireland, Holland, and Switzerland. But since 1799 he had been a Member of Parliament, and had only reached the rank of colonel by seniority in 1805. Sir Samuel Auchmuty had been born in New York, of a family ultimately of Scots origin but which had settled in County Longford in the Irish Midlands a century and a half before. He had joined the army in New York as a Loyalist volunteer in 1776 and had served since then in India and Egypt (with Baird, Beresford, and Popham). He had five years' seniority as colonel over Craufurd.

Rear-Admiral George Murray had been born in Chichester, where he still lived when on shore, but his family origin was in the younger branch of the Murrays of Elibank. He had been in the navy since he was 11, and had served in North America, at the Cape, the East Indies, the Baltic, and most recently as Captain of the Fleet for Admiral Nelson at Trafalgar. Rear-Admiral Charles Stirling was the son of a Scotsman who had joined the navy, and his service mirrored that of Murray – North America, the East Indies, Spanish waters – but he had also served in the West Indies. He had most recently commanded the Rochfort squadron in the blockade of France. Rather unusually, both admirals had served time as prisoners of war, Murray in France in 1779–1780, and Stirling in America in 1781 and again in France in 1798, and both had commanded in battle, both in single ship actions and in full battles.[32]

(It is of interest, and may be significant, that many of these prominent Scots were related in a distant way. Murray was of a younger branch of the Elibanks, who had intermarried with the Earls of Cromartie, one of whom had raised the 71st Foot; there are Stirlings in the family tree as well; and Baird was related to the Cromarty family also. Further, there are strong North American connections; Admiral Stirling's mother came from Philadelphia, and two of Lord MacLeod's daughters had gone to South Carolina when the family was attainted after the '45, where they married six men between them. Auchmuty was not the only Loyalist.)

These men were well experienced if not yet at the top of their professions. All had been involved in distant seaborne expeditions in the past. This fact almost persuades that Craufurd's expedition might have had some prospect of success. But the admirals were tougher, more direct types, than Popham, and the generals had more military ability than either Baird or Beresford. Auchmuty in particular had risen by ability, never having purchased a rise in rank in his career. These men were not about to hare off to the South Pacific without seriously considering their, and their men's, chances of survival.

Craufurd's and Murray's expedition was all arranged by the end of October, but then, as with Auchmuty's force, changes were made which delayed their setting out. The 9th Dragoon Guards were added, but were to accompany the expedition only for the first part of the voyage, for they were intended to go direct to Buenos Aires, and another frigate was added as an escort.[33] Then a naval scheme was developed which gave the convoy an escort of four line-of-battle ships only as far as the Cape Verde Islands but not supposedly beyond. Craufurd's convoy, with this special escort, finally sailed on 12 November, but without the intended escort under Rear-Admiral Murray, which was to take the transports on from the Cape Verde. Murray, in the 64-gun ship *Polyphemus*, with a shifting collection of other smaller ships, was delayed by adverse winds and finally got away only on the last day of the year.[34]

Then, just two days after Murray at last sailed, news arrived from Lisbon that Buenos Aires had been recaptured by the Spaniards. This was not actually confirmed until 25 January when letters from Popham arrived, but Windham at once sent out warnings to his expeditions, none of which reached their destinations, and the Admiralty sent the *Fly* sloop off in chase of Murray and Craufurd, with new instructions that they were to go straight to Buenos Aires if the news of its loss turned out to be correct.

In the meantime Lord Howick, the Foreign Secretary, drew up a paper in which, for the first time, a serious attempt was made to sort out what to do about Buenos Aires, rather than just sending expeditions all over the globe. There is among his papers an undated memorandum which may well be the one Howick read to the Cabinet on 12 February.[35] He remarked that, of all the Spanish dominions in South America, Buenos Aires was the best to possess if Britain was going to acquire any at all. Howick had been studying some geography – it was high time someone in the Cabinet did – and pointed out that Buenos Aires was separated from the rest of South America 'by an immense plain which as to population is little better than the desert, and then by a chain of mountains very difficult if not impracticable to an army'.

This was the land across which Craufurd, having taken Valparaiso, was to establish communications with Beresford in Buenos Aires; it seems that this was the first time the Cabinet – including Windham, who had written those orders – had heard of this 'desert', across which the 71st were at that very time trudging as unarmed prisoners.

Howick agreed that Buenos Aires was accessible to naval power, but Britain would have to control the estuary – though his geographical researches had not alerted him to the difficulties faced by big ships approaching the city. Britain would, by its naval power, be able to put in reinforcements if necessary and any Spanish counter-attack would have to be mounted over a distance of 'three thousand miles'. But he did not consider the possibility of local resistance.

Howick then suggested that the government had five possible future options. Two – abandonment of the conquest, or maintaining only a military and naval post in the estuary – were dismissed without delay. The third idea was to organize the conquest as a colony, in which case certain measures were required, including a 'considerable' British garrison, repatriation of all Spaniards – meaning, presumably, the *peninsulares* – recruitment of the local Indians into a military force, and the possible emancipation of the slaves. It all sounds very much like the treatment being meted out at that time to the Cape Colony. A fourth option was to declare the place independent, install a new government, and evacuate the British presence, except for a naval yard; in this he envisaged the continuation of a formal protectorate in which all the trade would be British, and therefore all the profits, though how this was to be achieved was not clear. The fifth option was to make it a colony and actively to encourage settlement – he mentioned Germans, Northern Europeans, and Irish as possible emigrants. When the Spaniards had 'melted into the emigrants', he envisaged a form of self-government.

All this was to be considered alongside the information that Lord Grenville, never more than a momentary enthusiast for the South American adventure in any case, had heard from one of his correspondents, John Barlinder, who worked at the West India Dock. His letter was dated 27 January, two days after the loss of Buenos Aires was confirmed. Barlinder condemned Popham's conquest as 'unfortunate' and 'rash and undigested', and included some home truths about the area; Buenos Aires could not be approached by big ships; Maldonado was unsafe and could provide no supplies; Montevideo was 'absolutely necessary' for any attempt to hold the area. He thought 10,000 troops would be needed at the minimum, plus artillery and a permanent squadron of twenty or so ships.[36]

At some time also, and perhaps January or February of 1807 is the most likely time, the Prime Minister acquired a paper giving a breakdown of the possible military strength of the whole Viceroyalty of Buenos Aires. Whoever compiled it included everything and everybody – regulars, militia, artillery, and volunteers – but omitted the gauchos, who were the true strength of the region. He counted almost 19,000 men by including every unit from Buenos Aires city to Potosi and Paraguay.[37]

When Howick read his paper to the Cabinet, however, it was probably already too late to prevent further commitments, quite apart from the fact that he was in a minority of one on the issue, and several expeditions had already gone out. Nearly a fortnight earlier at another Cabinet, poorly attended, the matter of Buenos Aires had also been raised, as a result of the news of its reconquest. Windham had already sent orders for Auchmuty and Craufurd to join forces, and they would presumably take in the troops Backhouse had landed at Maldonado as well as Beresford's force, if those men had been released from captivity. So Windham suggested that the command was now big enough for a more high-ranking officer, and he suggested Sir John Stuart, who had won the little, useless, battle of Maida the previous year and was now back in London. Lord Grenville countered with the name of Sir George Prevost, but dropped him in favour of Lieutenant-General John Whitelocke.[38]

The appointment of Whitelocke was agreed. The reasons are various, but the one which did not get any serious consideration was whether he was any good as a commander. That was presumably regarded as the army's business, and since the army had already promoted him to Lieutenant-General it had to be assumed that he could command troops and fight. But the Prime Minister's acceptance of Whitelocke's name perhaps had more to do with the job he already had than the one he was being appointed to. Whitelocke was Inspector-General of Recruiting, and on New Year's Day Grenville had mentioned, in a letter to Windham about something else, that he wanted to abolish the whole office of the Inspector-General. He thought two or three clerks could do the job instead of an expensive general. The appointment of Whitelocke to a distant command was, therefore, for Grenville, a splendid opportunity for some administrative pruning, and within a fortnight or so of Whitelocke's sailing to South America, the Inspector-General's office was accordingly abolished.[39] But this was not much of a reason for appointing a man to a difficult and distant military command.

Whitelocke was, in fact, a most strange choice for such a command. His early career had been in the West Indies, when he rose from lieutenant in

1782 to colonel in 1795 with the local rank of Brigadier-General. As such he took part in the fighting at Saint-Domingue in 1796, commanding a force in action for the only time before his appointment to the Plate in 1807. In 1799, after a spell in Guernsey, he became lieutenant-governor at Portsmouth, an important office carrying with it control of all the troops in the area. He was remembered by one officer as 'a most formidable personage', at least on parade, 'looking every inch a general', and by another officer as snarling at him that 'we ought to be shot for breaking through the quarantine laws'. He also had a reputation for using foul language, seemingly as a means of endearing himself to the ordinary soldier, but without realizing that this usually had the very opposite effect. From 1805 he was Inspector-General of Recruiting. That is, apart from the episode of fighting at Saint-Domingue, Whitelocke's career had been as an administrator.[40] Now he was to command a large army in an attack on a hostile city, the approach to which was by sea and by way of a very awkward landing. He had no training whatsoever for any of this.

Most of the troops Whitelocke was to command were already at or approaching the River Plate, but he was assigned a further 1,600 men to take with him, including his own regiment, the 89th Foot. But when he actually sailed he took his passage in a fast frigate, *Thisbe*, and left these troops to follow at the pace of the convoy.[41] As a result he never received them.

The final result of all this activity was that, when Whitelocke's convoy sailed, early in February, no less than six separate convoys were on their way to the River Plate, only one of which had so far reached its destination, while one of them never did arrive. There were now no less than eight general officers involved, and two admirals, not counting Popham. All of these troops and generals arrived in dribs and drabs at the River Plate over a period of nine months, giving the *portenos* a long period in which to make proper preparations to receive them.

Chapter Ten

Montevideo

The reinforcements sent in batches by General Baird from the Cape arrived in the Plate estuary on various dates in early October. Until then Popham had been attempting, without success, to extract the British prisoners from Spanish hands by his letters to Liniers, Sobremonte and Huidobro. Not only were the soldiers of the 71st, the St Helena Regiment, the artillerymen, and the dragoons captive, but Popham had lost virtually all the marines of the ships – over 200 men – and 120 of the sailors as well.[1] In the face of this inability to persuade either Liniers or Huidobro to return the men he could do nothing but wait for something to happen, for orders for his recall, for reinforcements to come, for his provisions to be exhausted, or for some agreement to be reached with the Spaniards by Beresford.

So the arrival of the reinforcements was welcome, if only by providing a possible new area of action. The colonel of the 47th Foot, Thomas Backhouse, the senior soldier, insisted that an attempt be made to take Montevideo, but when that failed, he settled for a landing at Maldonado, a small town at the northern corner of the estuary, which was taken with no difficulty. It was theoretically guarded by the fortified island of Goritti, but Popham ran out his guns at the island's castle next day, and it surrendered at once without resistance. This now provided a useful anchorage, the troops in the transports could recuperate on a base on land after their long incarceration on the ships, and nearby cattle could be rustled to supplement the rations, which were now becoming alarmingly short (see map 13).[2]

The occupation of Maldonado, however, scarcely advanced the British cause very much. They had enough troops – well over 2,000 in all – to hold the place, but not enough to advance any further; equally the Spaniards were unable to retake the place, while its occupation by the British was a standing threat of further attacks. On the Spanish side there were further effects, for the occupation of the town widened one of the fundamental cracks in their defences. Responsibility for recovering the village lay with the governor of Montevideo and the Banda Oriental, Ruiz Huidobro. He did not have the strength to tackle a British army of 2,000 men, supported by the guns of the fleet and those from Goritti, so the town was distantly blockaded by light horsemen, and Huidobro sent for help from Buenos Aires, no doubt recalling how Montevideo had gone to Buenos Aires' assistance when Beresford occupied it. The request was conveyed by a delegation from the Cabildo of Montevideo to that of Buenos Aires, but this had no effect. They met only hostility, for the two cities had been arguing ever since the reconquest of Buenos Aires over who should get the credit. The Montevidean appeal was unsuccessful.

It was clear that Montevideo was on its own, and that the city, or so all the signs suggested, would be the next British target. Preparations to meet the expected attack were made, partly prompted by Viceroy Sobremonte, who had also been rebuffed in Buenos Aires, and so had gone to the Banda Oriental. But he was disliked almost as much in Montevideo as he now was in Buenos Aires, and his assistance was resented. In return, and quite reasonably from his point of view, Sobremonte refused to put a Montevidean, Jose Gervasio Artigas, in command of the Spanish horsemen who were blockading Maldonado. Instead he gave the command to one of his own men, naval Lieutenant Abreu, who took with him some men from Montevideo and those whom Sobremonte had brought from the interior. They stood to fight the British at San Carlos, some kilometres inland form Maldonado on 7 November, but were beaten; Abreu died of his wounds. The light cavalry continued roaming about the grassland, driving off the cattle, and ambushing British patrols, but they were refused permission to mount a serious attack. The fact that Artigas would also have been beaten in such an attack on the town, which would thus weaken Montevideo's defences by reducing the available manpower even further, both in number and in morale, did not salve Artigas' hurt pride.[3]

The paralysis of the Spaniards meant that it was only the arrival of still more British reinforcements which would break the deadlock. Rear-Admiral Stirling arrived on 3 December, but, of course, he had not brought any troops with him, though he did bring a victualler ship, which helped relieve the shortage of food. He also brought orders to replace Popham, who made a tremendous fuss about leaving, and did not actually go until 26 December. Stirling had also brought General Sir George Grey, who was on his way to take over from Baird at the Cape, and this would undermine Popham's position even more. Popham's annoyance seems to have been partly an attempt to avoid having to go back to Britain before a new success in the Plate, and partly to avoid travelling by way of the Cape, for he had a guilty conscience about not keeping Baird informed of the loss of Buenos Aires.[4]

Auchmuty's forces arrived on 5 January, another 3,000 men, and this now provided the strength to allow the British to break out of the cul-de-sac which was Maldonado. Auchmuty quickly noted that the troops at Maldonado had no artillery, no stores, only four days' provisions left and no hope of getting more, and he decided that the place could only be held if it was supplied from the sea; it was, that is, a liability. Evacuated, however, Maldonado would cease to be so, and Auchmuty would have a force of 5,000 men to employ elsewhere. The decision was painless and rapid. The day after his arrival Auchmuty had persuaded Stirling to provide canvas for 3,000 sandbags – and he had decided to attack Montevideo.[5]

The embarkation of the Maldonado force was accomplished on 13 January in no more than two hours. Only Stirling comments on this, and then in severely factual terms in his Admiral's Journal (which is a most useful source for all these events).[6] The facts, however, are worth noting – embarking 2,200 men in a couple of hours without interference from a highly mobile enemy was an achievement which demonstrated qualities of planning and organization by both Auchmuty and Stirling which at once put the whole expedition onto a new and more professional plane, well apart from the improvisatory opportunism displayed by Beresford and Popham.

The Spaniards in Montevideo were meanwhile making preparations for the attack they could see was imminent. It seems that for a time Viceroy Sobremonte, who based himself in Montevideo in December and January, assumed or hoped that the British could be confined to Maldonado by the gaucho cavalry, despite the defeat of his forces at San Carlos. He did not have sufficient power in the Banda Oriental to expel them, and Buenos Aires would give him no help. He was informed of the main developments on the British side, and soon after Stirling's arrival he issued a proclamation calling on the people to arm themselves to defend the city. He followed this up three days later by proclaiming a state of siege, and feverish preparations began to make the city more defensible.[7] Auchmuty's arrival made the threat even more urgent (see map 16).

The British forces landed a few miles west of the city on 16 January, in a process very similar to that at Losperd's Bay at the Cape a year before. The troops were to land in three divisions. The first, commanded by Brigadier-General William Lumley, consisted of the riflemen of the 95th, the light battalion, composed of the light companies from several foot regiments, and the 38th Foot, commanded by the man Popham had asked for, Colonel Spencer Vassall. Admiral Stirling described the landing in his journal:

January 16. The transports were very slow in coming in, not withstanding a variety of signals, accompanied with guns and shot to enforce obedience and the consequence was that most of them did not fetch where they were directed and might have done. The enemy showed about 3,000 men with 6 pieces of artillery on Carretta Heights but the covering vessels effectually prevented their approaching the beach to give annoyance ... [M]ost of the transports having taken an anchorage I made the signal with the general's concurrence for the first division of troops to get into the boats. About 11 the signal was made for the troops to put off and row for the shore, and the general was with them before they could form. It rained excessively hard till towards two o'clock, and there was great fatigue and trouble in landing the troops, but by 4 the whole army with all the artillery were on shore without the least accident of any kind. The General advanced towards the enemy in the haze, but on the weather clearing up which it did towards 3 we could see his troops in motion up the hill and the Spaniards retreating before him and his skirmishing parties. The evening was beautiful, the water smooth and the wind northerly. Towards sunset the army having gained the heights, the firing ceased. One British soldier was killed, and two were wounded. A great many of the enemy suffered. The ships on shore landed the horses, but the boats were too much fatigued to move the cavalry from the line of battle ships.[8]

Auchmuty was much briefer:

I landed on the morning of the 16th to the westward of the Carrettas Rocks, in a small bay about 9 miles from the town. The enemy were in great force with guns on the heights when we disembarked but he did not advance to oppose us and suffered me to take a strong position about a mile from the shore. A trifling cannonade and some firing at the outposts commenced in the afternoon and continued occasionally during our stay on the ground.[9]

No one described the events on the shore, but the use of the light battalion and the riflemen means that these skirmishers immediately scattered across the beach in loose formation, shooting at the Spanish troops. The Spaniards had been unable to contest the landing because, like the Dutch at the Cape, they could not predict where it would take place – and anyway the British boats went somewhat astray. The shallower-draft warships went close inshore to provide an intimidating covering fire. Captain Wilkie some thirty years later gave an account of what probably happened:

> In fact, there is no situation more trying to the nerves of the soldier than when he is in progress to land on an enemy's shore, pent up in boats as close as they can stow, and perhaps exposed to a heavy fire; prevented from firing themselves, and having no other comfort but the 'give way' cheers of the men in the boat towing them; they have nothing left for it but the old woman's consolation when she lost her snuff box – patience. When the boats do strike the beach, the bustle, hurry, and feeling of insecurity, rather increase; the soldier, encumbered with an immense weight, is somewhat chary of accidents by water; and this feeling was rather sharpened by the recollection of an accident that happened in landing at the Cape: a flat boat, containing 60 men of the 93rd Regiment, after touching the beach, broached to, and was upset by the surf; all the men, encumbered with knapsacks and arms, were drowned. In general, I may say, it is the most critical time of a soldier's life – at least as regards the feelings of security between his getting over the boat's side and joining his company on shore. Here the great value of discipline becomes apparent – and even the minutiae of discipline. By the numbering of files, every man jumps at once into his proper place, his personal anxiety immediately diminishes – and when, by an equally rapid process of other companies, the whole battalion completes its formation – then 'Richard is himself again'.[10]

Wilkie is in fact describing the second part of the first phase of the landing. The light infantry had gone first, and now came the rest of the 38th, to provide a solid defensive force which would protect the landing place. Several hundred disciplined infantry, screened by a thousand skirmishers, and backed up by the guns of the supporting vessels, was quite enough to deter any Spanish counter-attack, apart from some distant shooting, inevitably inaccurate.

Auchmuty called back his light forces, leaving strong picquets to deter any surprise night attack. The troops settled to a damp night on shore, feeding on the supplies they were carrying with them. Next morning the landings continued. Admiral Stirling was diligent in his nuts-and-bolts account:

> 17 January. Landed the horses from the line of battle ships, and artillery seamen to make up the number 300 which were commanded by Captain

Palmer of the *Pheasant*. Order for the principal agent for transports to cause three days' provisions to be cooked and sent on shore tomorrow for the army. *Unicorn* was directed to send on shore 310 gallons of spirits for the troops ... The merchantmen were to anchor off the town to make a diversion. There was a good deal of fighting today on the heights. We lost another man and had two wounded. A great many of the enemy fell. They had 12 pieces of artillery today, which reached us although our shot fell short.[11]

The Spaniards kept up an intermittent cannon fire during the day, and several times Spanish forces grouped together on the British left, apparently with the aim of mounting attacks along the road which led close to the sea. These gatherings were regularly broken up by fire from *Encounter* and an armed transport, and the army suffered no serious inconvenience.

Both sides rested on the 18th, a Sunday. The British had to organize themselves, and Auchmuty and Stirling had to plan the advance, which now looked to be difficult, for it was clear that the Spaniards were intent on fighting hard before allowing themselves to be penned up in the city. There, planning was also proceeding, and with the intention of disputing the British advance, but also in recognition of the fact that the likely outcome of any fight in the open was a British victory, and so the city would have to stand a siege. The Spanish reaction was exactly the same as was Beresford's attack on Buenos Aires, perhaps because the same man, Sobremonte, commanded in each case.[12]

Auchmuty organized the advance on the city in two columns, one under Colonel Browne of the 40th Foot and Colonel Backhouse, along a track about a kilometre from the shore; the other was under Auchmuty himself and Brigadier-General Lumley along another track a further kilometre inland. The second column was the stronger, for it was clearly going to meet the main Spanish force. No doubt the Spaniards were conscious of the smaller column steadily marching to outflank them. Auchmuty described the advance in his later report to the Secretary of State:

On the 19th we moved towards Monte Video. The right column under the Honorable Brigadier-General Lumley was early opposed. About 4,000 of the enemy's horse occupied two heights to his front and right. As we advanced heavy fire and round and grape opened up on us but a spirited charge in front from the light battalion under Lieutenant-Colonel Brownrigg dispersed the troops opposed to him with the loss of a gun. The enemy in the flank did not wait a similar movement, but retreated. They continued retiring before us and permitted me, without any further opposition except a distant cannonade, to take up a position about 2 miles from the Citadel. Our advanced posts occupied the suburbs, and some small parties were posted close to the works, but in the evening the principal part of the suburbs was evacuated.[13]

Auchmuty's rather dry account may be supplemented by Sergeant Landsheit's more vivid and personal memories, not least concerning the general himself:

An hour before dawn ... we stood, according to custom, in our places; but, as the day broke, we received very satisfactory proof that the Spaniards had not been idle; for a formidable array of infantry, cavalry, and artillery was already in our front. They were drawn up on some heights about a couple of miles in the interior, and formed, with their wings thrown forward, three sides of a square; while their cannon, dragged by bullocks, were so disposed as to bring a cross fire on every point by which we might be expected to approach them. Sir Samuel examined their array carefully for a minute, and then ordered the advance, which our troops obeyed with the alacrity which English soldiers always exhibit when about to be led into action.

Our dragoons were not yet entirely mounted. The squadron of the 20th [of which Landsheit was a member], with the 21st and such of the 9th and 17th as landed, had horses; and a portion of them including our troops, were directed to move forward; but we were not well handled. The officer in command led us to the brow of an eminence, just within point-blank shot of the enemy's artillery, and there, finding that they had got the range, he halted. Several men and horses were killed and wounded in consequence, and more would have suffered had not Sir Samuel rode up. He rebuked our commandant in good round terms, desired him to move down into the hollow, and keep his wits about him, as he would be needed very shortly. The old man was yet speaking when a shot took his horse in the hip, and knocked the leg to shivers. Of course, Sir Samuel fell to the ground as if slain; and his staff (all of whom were with us prodigious favourites) crowded round him to ascertain whether he was hurt. 'There's nothing the matter,' said the gallant old soldier. 'I'm not hurt in the least. Just help me get up from under this horse; and John' – calling to his groom – 'fetch my charger'.

It was done in a moment, and I need scarcely add, that the perfect unconcern of our brave chief was not without its effect on the courage of his followers. For, no sooner was he on his legs than he gave us some work to perform. 'Charge that gun, and that, and that,' said he, 'they will annoy the infantry as they come up.' On we rushed at a gallop; and sabring the cannoneers, were in possession of three pieces e'er another shot had been fired. Meanwhile the rest of the troops were advancing to the attack with all the regularity and precision of a field day. The 95th, spreading through the sand hills, opened the ball; other regiments followed in column: and the enemy's wings were driven in upon his centre, a scene of dreadful confusion ensued. They fled in all directions, our people marching after them, as fast as was consistent with the preservation of their ranks.[14]

(The good sergeant's account is ghosted, and published thirty years after the event; this may account for the small mistakes in his account. The 9th Dragoon Guards were not present, not yet having arrived; the British casualties he rather exaggerates, at least by implication, since the monthly return for 1 February shows only two of the cavalrymen killed in January. But the general account may be accepted, and the story of Auchmuty's little incident rings true enough. It is just the sort of incident to be remembered, and it is revealing of why the soldiers liked him.)

The Spanish force had been commanded by Viceroy Sobremonte, who was thus once more let down by his troops, and who once more could be conveniently blamed for yet another defeat.[15] Yet he could only use the weapons he had available, and the only fighters he had were the undisciplined horsemen and barely trained townsmen of Montevideo. He had no infantry of sufficient steadiness or numbers to oppose a professional army 5,000 strong, supported by water-borne artillery. He did have roughly equal numbers, half Montevideans, and half men from those he had brought from the interior. At least he did not merely wait to be attacked, but repeatedly brought his forces out to dispute the British moves, at the landing place, and on the march. But the repeated defeats can hardly have helped morale in the city.

Nor did Sobremonte even now submit to a siege. Auchmuty described what happened next:

The next morning the enemy came out of the town, and attacked us with their whole force, about 6,000 men, and a number of guns. They advanced in two columns, the right consisting of cavalry, to turn our left flank, while the other, of infantry, attacked the left of our line. This column pushed in our advanced posts and pressed so hard on our out picquet of 400 men that Colonel Browne who commanded on the left ordered three companies of the 40th under Major Campbell to their support. These companies fell in with the head of the column and very bravely charged it. The charge was as gallantly received and great numbers fell on both sides. At length the column began to give way, when it was suddenly and impetuously attacked in flank by the Rifle Corps and light battalion, which I had ordered up and directed to the particular point. The column now gave way on all sides, and was pursued with great slaughter and the loss of a gun to the town. The right column, observing the fate of their companions, rapidly retired without coming into action.

The loss of the enemy was considerable, and has been estimated at 1,500 men. Their killed might count to between two and three hundred. We have taken the same number of prisoners, but the principal part of the wounded got back into the town. I am happy to add that ours was comparatively trifling.[16]

Again a less detached account can be found, this time in the diary of Captain Jennings of the 40th Foot, the regiment which was most closely engaged, since it formed the picquets which were the Spaniards' main target:

On the 20th, the enemy made a vigorous sortie with a force of about 3,000 men divided into three columns taking different directions. That which attacked the centre advanced with such rapidity as to drive in all our picquets of which they killed and wounded a vast number. A reinforcement however from the 40th Regiment having been sent out to the support of the centre of the line, the enemy was speedily repulsed with the loss of several hundred killed, wounded and prisoners and their whole force retreated with precipitation into the city. On our side the loss was considerable. Major Campbell of the 40th was slightly wounded and Lieutenant Fitzpatrick killed. Captain Rogers of the regiment was also slightly wounded and between eighty and a hundred men killed and wounded. The rest of our army suffered but little.[17]

Admiral Stirling added an important detail:

> If they [the Spaniards] had only gone a little further to have enabled our small body to have charged ... very few of them would have returned. The sight was fine. The covering vessels were directed to annoy the retreat, and boats were sent to bring off the wounded.[18]

Once more, the implication of large numbers of dead and wounded is not supported by the statistics. The 40th Foot suffered only seven dead in January. The wounded are not noted separately, but the regiment had 115 sick on 1 February; however, all regiments had a substantial sickness by this time, and not all the sick had been wounded. If Jennings in the regiment can exaggerate his own side's casualties, it follows that the figures for Spanish casualties he supplies are also likely to be exaggerated, though it seems clear that a good number really had been inflicted. Other British accounts claimed 'several hundred killed and wounded', or 'about 500', or even '2,000'; as usual the further in time from the action, the greater the figure; probably even Auchmuty's estimate is too high. The British loss was not negligible: Auchmuty's casualty return noted one officer, one drummer, and 18 rank-and-file killed between the landing and the sortie, and 123 wounded.[19]

Repeated defeats in the open did not convince the Montevideans that further resistance was useless. The city had been prepared for a siege, and that was now what the British had to undertake. Admiral Stirling described the scene in his journal:

> I went on shore to see the general and found him encamped about 1½ miles from the beach and 2 miles from the fortress. He had parties advanced within 600 yards of the Citadel, where he is preparing to erect batteries, and he had complete possession of a town which is near the fortress. The ground which the army occupies is not adapted for defence against an enterprising enemy, nor is there any commanding situation near from whence the approached could be covered. A letter was sent to the governor, Don Pascual Ruiz Huidobro, offering to let him have his wounded men, provided he would consider them as prisoners of war and permission was given to bury such of the dead as were yet laying on the ground, which he very readily accepted. In a letter which Don Huidobro wrote in reply, he acknowledges the barbarity in mutilating our men that were wounded: he said it was by Indians and mulattos not by the Spanish troops. I believe one is just as bad as the other.[20]

Stirling had realized as soon as he arrived that the only way the British could rule in the Plate area was by physical conquest and occupation. There was no basis for supposing any of the Spaniards would welcome British rule, though that was not to say that they would continue to oppose it after the conquest. No British officer, except perhaps Beresford, still a prisoner on the other side of the river, realized that the key to the situation was to offer independence, and even if they did come to realize it, none of them was of a sufficiently disobedient character as to promise independence when this was not part of their official instructions. Popham might have, in the end, for he was clearly sympathetic to the aspirations of Miranda, and had passed his obsession on to others, but he had become obsessed with getting the prisoners back. And anyway, he had been disgraced.

His offer of terms rejected, Auchmuty settled to a siege. He had been told the city's defences were weak – they were certainly old and old-fashioned – but one look convinced him otherwise. Stirling sent heavy guns on shore for his use, 24-pounders, with 300 rounds each and powder and wads to match, and a battery of 4 of these guns was established. This took until 25 January. It was hard work. One soldier, who was admittedly a new recruit to the 71st, one of the party sent to the Cape as replacements before it was known that the regiment was collectively captured, and sent on with Backhouse, clearly never realized the physical effort he would be required to exert. 'My limbs bending under me with fatigue, in a sultry climate, the musket and accoutrements that I was forced to carry were insupportably oppressive.'[21] But the batteries were dug in and the parapets built. Three days later another battery of six guns was set up, firing at the southeast tower of the Citadel, which was thought to be weaker than the rest.

The Spaniards resisted well, as Stirling noted:

28 January. At daylight the general opened his six 24-lb battery at 300 yards' distance which he expressed himself well satisfied with, but the enemy continue very obstinate, and bring up fresh guns in lieu of those dismounted, as well as open fresh embrasures. The firing was discontinued on both sides in the evening. Captain Beaumont of the 87th Regiment and one man were killed and eight wounded in the course of the day. A party of about 400 men were sent in the country for stock but they were not successful. Ten of the enemy were killed in a skirmish, and four of our dragoons [men of the 20th Light Dragoons] getting drunk were taken prisoners. A dysentery prevails among the

troops and seamen on shore, which although disagreeable, has only occasioned the death of two soldiers ...[22]

The Montevideans were able to keep open the means of supply and communication across the harbour, which was too shallow for the big British ships. The small ships could be threatened by the guns of the city, particularly those of Fort St Philip. *Staunch* and *Encounter* once made the mistake of anchoring too close to the city, and were damaged fairly badly before they could be got out. Stirling was scathing in his comments on this. Auchmuty placed a two-gun battery to command this water route, but never succeeded in cutting it. Viceroy Sobremonte had left the city before it was invested and he was the organizer of this supply route, and of the horsemen who prevented the cattle rustling. Undoubtedly successful in all this, his leaving the city was too reminiscent of his conduct at Buenos Aires to be appreciated by the beleaguered population. Sobremonte was in fact a considerable nuisance to the besiegers, according to Admiral Stirling:

30 January. There was not much firing on either side, as our great dependence was a breach battery intended to be erected in the night, about 500 yards from the south face. A party of 250 men went into the country, but were obliged to return without doing anything as they met with the army under the viceroy Marquis de Sobremonte, consisting of 8 or 900 horse, with 12 pieces of artillery which hover about 6 miles off.[23]

In addition Liniers at Buenos Aires had organized a column to go in relief of Montevideo. He and the Cabildo had finally appreciated that a British victory at Montevideo would pose a new threat to Buenos Aires (though so would a Spanish victory). The viceroy and the governor were his and the Cabildo's enemies, and if they could claim a victory over the British, and a much greater victory than that of the *portenos*, the viceroy's authority would be restored. Liniers in particular would suffer as a result. From what happened later, it seems probable that the relief column had contingent orders besides those concerning Montevideo.

The column came in two sections. An advance force of 500 was commanded by Brigadier Pedro de Arce, who had commanded at Quilmes the year before, and this was followed by about 2,000 under Liniers' command.[24] The *portenos* had to march by land, and *Cherwell* and *Protector* were stationed off Colonia for the express purpose of preventing reinforcements arriving there. The arrival of this force would put Auchmuty in an impossible position; his options would be to submit to a close land blockade while continuing the siege, or to lift the siege to confront the *portenos'* army and that of Sobremonte, with a probable sortie from the city taking him in the rear, or he would have to withdraw. On the night of 1 February, 500 men – Arce's force – slipped across the harbour to reinforce the city garrison. Auchmuty was in danger of being caught between two armies, each equal in number to his own.

On 1 February, Stirling went ashore again with an ultimatum for Auchmuty:

I mentioned that the powder was beginning to draw very short in the fleet, as well men of war as transports and merchantmen, and that we could not supply ammunition for longer than three days, although it was my intention to reduce the ships to 10 rounds each ...

A speedy termination has become absolutely necessary on every consideration. Want of powder must oblige the general soon to raise the siege and the consequences of retreat are incalculable. There can be no doubt a British army consisting of 5,000 soldiers and 800 seamen and marines with three field pieces would beat any force that could be brought against them in the field but we have already seen that 4,000 men well mounted can harass us and even the 800 horse under the viceroy prevents any supplies being brought in. Nor can the general detach after them with any prospect of success, as they are so well mounted whilst our horses are miserable animals. There is much confidence placed in the strength of Monte Video, that until we get it, the whole country will continue in arms against us, and consequently any retrograde movement will be dangerous. My stock of provisions is small for the number of men to be fed, we have great difficulty in getting it on shore even in this fine weather ... When our stock is exhausted I fancy there would be great hazard in embarking the troops if the general was to make Buenos Ayres his object. In Chico Bay they could not embark if the enemy had any enterprise or spirit whatever. If they retreat to Carreta Bay the transport would not bear up there, and a westerly wind would occasion too much surf for the boats to land ... [25]

In addition all the army's provisions were now coming from the ships, and Stirling and Auchmuty were buying supplies from the merchantmen they would be convoying. But their prices went up.

Most of Stirling's sailors were on shore, manhandling the guns or shifting supplies, so that at times the line-of-battle ships had no more than 30 men on board out of a normal crew of 300 or more. The personnel returns made that day (1 February) show that Auchmuty had 5,000 officers and men able to fight, but he also had a sick list of over 500. Casualties had been light since the landing, no more than 34 dead and 5 men taken prisoner (and two deserted), but sickness was claiming casualties now. As Stirling had noted, there was dysentery in the primitive camp, which partly lay in the area used by the citizens of Montevideo as their refuse dump. This sickness could be expected to get worse.[26]

Auchmuty therefore had now only two days in which to conclude the siege, either by victory or by withdrawal. By the third day he must be able to pull his troops out, possibly facing attack from two directions, and he must keep enough powder under his hand to give his troops a fighting chance. He was now concentrating his battering on the city wall, between the Citadel and the South Gate, by constructing another six-gun battery within 600 yards of the wall. There it was vulnerable to bombardment from the Citadel but by next day a breach had appeared which, under more leisurely conditions, would have been thought of as just the beginning, but now was judged to be worth attempting. Auchmuty could wait no longer.

The plan was to storm the breach which had been made in the wall near the South Gate, using the riflemen and the light troops, and the three largest regiments, the 38th, the 40th, and the 87th. The rest, the cavalry, the 47th, and the fragments of the other regiments, along with the marines and the seamen, were detailed to protect the rear under the command of Brigadier-General Lumley. Auchmuty was clearly apprehensive of interference from the landward side, either from Sobremonte's men, only six miles away, or from Liniers' force from Buenos Aires, which was about the same distance away, but separate from it.

The riflemen of the 95th, commanded by Major Gardner, grenadiers under Lieutenant-Colonel Brownrigg and Major Trotter, and the consolidated light companies under the command of Majors Campbell and Tucker, were the assault force. Out of them were formed the forlorn hope, to be the first in the breach, a company of the 38th under Lieutenant Everard of the 2nd Foot, who had been rescued from the *Volontaire* at the Cape. The main bodies of the 38th and the 40th were to follow in succession to exploit the breach once it had been penetrated; the 87th was to move to the north and wait to be let in at the North Gate. The assault was to begin at 3.00 am, with the aim of gaining surprise.

Surprise was actually not possible. The Montevideans were as alert to the situation as the British, they knew that the relief forces were nearby

(Arce's reinforcements had already arrived), and they knew the breach had been made, though it was not considered a practicable proposition by the professional soldiers among the Spaniards. Nevertheless precautions were taken since it was obvious that the British must attack soon. The breach was blocked by bales of hides, but this was not done until dark partly to protect the workers in the breach, and partly to keep the British in ignorance of the measure. The guns in the batteries on the walls and in the forts were kept alert all night. The streets inside the city leading to the breach were blocked by guns, the rooftops manned by soldiers. Infantry was stationed near the breach ready to intervene as necessary. The guns facing the breach were loaded with a mixture of round shot and grape. There was little or nothing more that Huidobro could have done. The odds were clearly against the assailants.

Captain Jennings gives the best description of the assault:

Having effected a breach of about six feet wide near the South Gate to the town it was resolved to attack the fortress by assault and agreeable to this determination every preparation was made to proceed to the storm on the morning of the 3rd of February. On the evening of the 2nd of flag of truce was sent in to summon the garrison to surrender but to this no answer was given other than 'that it was their intention to resist to the last extremity'. Orders were given to the besieging army to be under arms at 11 o'clock on the night of the 2nd, which accordingly were obeyed. The storming party was composed of the grenadiers of the line, the light battalion, and the Rifle Corps, immediately supported by the 38th and 40th Regiments. The 87th had orders to station themselves at the north gate there to remain until it should be opened from within by those who might have cut that way thereto through the town. The night was extremely dark and with much difficulty the troops could make their way to their different stations. The remaining part of the army was posted in the rear and on our right flank to secure us from any attempt on those points. The storming party commenced its march at about midnight and was received as they approached within range of musketry by a galling and most destructive fire from all the batteries. Owing to the extreme darkness of the night the breach was with much difficulty discerned, and it was rendered less perceptible from the chasms having been filled up from within by hides and other materials so as to bring it to its former level, but the advance party having once scaled it by the means of scaling ladders and throwing down the newly raised work rendered the passage free for those following. The greater part of the storming party made good their entrance by it long before day light although opposed by a commanding fire of great guns and musketry from the batteries and principal streets leading to it. The scene within was now dreadful, our troops dealt carnage wherever they moved carrying everything before them ... The 40th Regiment twice missed the road to the breach and were exposed to a most destructive fire of grape from the Citadel and shot yard batteries; however, when they got into the town they make good for the delay and in the course of an hour after the entrance the town and citadel were entirely in our possession. The slaughter on both sides was immense but not greater than might be expected from the gallant manner with which the town was defended and the no less valiant and determined manner it was attacked.[27]

Sergeant William Lawrence of the 40th Foot also remembered some details, having taken part in the assault as a member of the forlorn hope:

Captain Renney of ours commanded the forlorn hope. The ladders were placed against the hides of earth, and we scaled them under heavy fire from the Spaniards. We found the earth better stuff to encounter than stone, and though our poor captain fell in the breach whilst nobly leading on his men, we succeeded in forcing our way into the town, which was soon filled with the reinforcements that followed us. We drove the enemy from the batteries, and massacred with sword and bayonet all whom we found carrying arms; the general's orders being not to plunder or enter any house, or injure any woman, child, or man not carrying arms, or fire a shot until daylight. On our approach to the gunwharf of the town, we found some 20 or 30 Negroes chained to the guns, whom we spared and afterwards found very useful, chiefly in burying the dead.[28]

No chronicler or diarist appears to have been with the 87th; General Auchmuty explains:

The 87th Regiment was posted near the north gate which the troops who entered at the breach were to open for them, but their ardour was so great that they could not wait. They scaled the walls and entered the town as the troops within approached it. At day light everything within our possession except the citadel which made a show of resistance but soon surrendered and early in the morning the town was quiet and the women were peaceably walking the streets.[29]

Once inside the city, parties of British troops set off in all directions, hunting down any of the enemy they could find. The wall was captured along its whole length and by daylight the city itself was under British control. Governor Huidobro was captured and brought to Auchmuty by 5.00 am. He offered to surrender if granted the honours or war but Auchmuty refused. He had no wish to let these men go, and had been fully informed of the apparent breach of a similar agreement by Liniers. He insisted on collecting prisoners, perhaps with the intention of offering them in exchange for the 71st. So Huidobro withdrew his offer of surrender.

The Citadel held out. Sergeant Lawrence tells what happened, though he delicately refers to the cathedral roof as 'a tower':

> The governor said he had nothing to do with this, so Sir Samuel sent a flag of truce to know if the commander would give the place up. The answer being 'No', three or four riflemen were placed on a tower sufficiently high and near to the Citadel for the purpose of, if possible, picking out the general and shooting him. This was soon effected, for on his appearing for a walk on the ramparts in his full uniform, one of the men shot him dead: and when the Spaniards found that they had lost their commander, they soon became disheartened, and lowering the drawbridge, came out to the Citadel and gave themselves up. Part of our troops immediately took possession, pulling down the Spanish colours and hoisting the English flag from the town and Citadel in their stead.[30]

The British casualties are fairly heavy, 7 officers and 115 men killed; 19 officers and 274 men wounded, many of whom soon died of infected wounds, including Colonels Vassall and Brownrigg, a casualty rate of well over ten per cent of the whole army, and perhaps double that of the units employed in the assault. On the Spanish side the count was more perfunctory, Auchmuty giving only round figures of 800 killed and 500 wounded. He gave a preliminary total of 2,000 prisoners, and claimed that a further 1,500 had either escaped across the harbour or had 'secreted themselves in the town'. Later a more detailed count was made, showing 105 offices and 1,282 men as prisoners, with 876 'artisans' and 191 slaves.[31] He could thus justify his

2,000, but not his extra 1,500. If he overestimated the casualties in the same ratio, the dead would come down to 500, and the wounded to 300. But, as one soldier commented 'scarcely a family that had not the melancholy task of tendering their care to some wounded relative while performing the last offices to those who had met an untimely fate'.[32]

On the other hand, the British were proud of the fact that very little looting or disorder took place:

> One of the singular things, and, I may say, that adds a feather to the cap of the troops employed in the attack, is that it remains perhaps the solitary instance of a town taken by storm in the night, in which no instance of plunder or outrage took place ...[33]

And Captain Jennings noted the same in his diary:

> Great credit was due to the conquerors for the orderly and good conduct after the assault, the moment the town was in our possession all further hostilities ceased on both sides, and in the course of that same day everything appeared as quiet within the walls as in time of profound peace: few instances of pillage or of disorder occurred. And where any such was discovered the authors were punished on the spot ... God was mercifully pleased to protect me, as heretofore, and with the exception of lassitude and great fatigue, I suffered nothing else during the course of the siege.[34]

The Navy was at last able to get into the harbour. Admiral Stirling was quick to react, and pleased with the results:

> I ordered the *Pheasant*, *Staunch*, and *Lancaster*, armed with carronades, to push into the harbour as soon as Fort St Philip surrendered, but they could not prevent a frigate and two gun brigs from being burnt although they saved the other vessels and took possession of Rattones Island.
>
> The town and citadel of Monte Video are very strongly fortified. I understand there are 160 pieces of cannon mounted, besides mortars and howitzers, with an immense quantity of ammunition. There is a small naval arsenal walled in, very commodiously adapted for stores. In the harbour are two or three corvettes and smaller vessels, one or two of which seem well adapted for this river.[35]

In his report Auchmuty gave his considered opinion of the value of his conquest:

> It is strong and amply supplied with artillery, and a great quantity of fixed ammunition. We should want powder if a siege was greatly protracted. We also want artillery men. But how to provision the troops requires much deliberation. If the country is open, meat may be had in abundance, and cheap, but flour is very dear, and difficult to be obtained. Fuel is extremely scarce. Forage there is none. Should the country be shut up from us, we must live on salt provisions. At all events, if it is determined to hold this place as a post without further operations, large quantities of powder, flower [sic], spirits and salt meat should be immediately sent out.
>
> The capture of Buenos Aires might make an alteration in the behaviour of the natives, but at present they are inveterately hostile. My force, after leaving a garrison in this place, would be unequal to the attempt, for though I should not fear meeting them in the field, they would soon harass me with their desultory attacks, nor could I keep in subjection an open town of 70,000 hostile inhabitants. In my opinion, it will require a force of 15,000 men to conquer and keep this country.[36]

A rather more considered and independent estimate of the general situation is provided by Lieutenant-Colonel Richard Bourke, a young officer (he was still under 30), who had risen from ensign in nine years. An intellectual soldier who had some legal training, and had been appointed supervisor at the Royal Military College the year before; he acted as quartermaster-general at Montevideo, and, more to the point here, he had been asked by Windham to report privately to him. His letter is long and detailed, and he managed to see the wider picture, but also to fix his eye on the essential points:

> Having outsailed the convoy I arrived at Maldonado near a fortnight sooner than the rest of the fleet [he had sailed in *Staunch*, which had been sent on ahead from Río de Janeiro], and had there an opportunity of conversing with the few people of any expectation who remained in the place. Considering always how small a force England has as yet been able to send out or keep up for the purpose of foreign conquest I endeavoured in the course of these conversations to discover how far the inhabitants of this province were inclined to favour us, and whether they would prefer an English to a Spanish master. I was generally

assured that the prejudices of religion were not to be overcome, and that whatever commercial benefit might be derived from such a charge, still it would not render it acceptable. That it was true the great mass of the people were heartily tired of the Spanish yoke, but that their wishes were entirely turned towards independence, and the establishment of a republic or federal government similar to that of North America. That the submitting to an English master would be the greatest possible blow to this project, and that on this account as well as others they would strenuously resist us. But if we could be prevailed on to enter into the designs of the revolutionists who are (with the exception of the natives of Old Spain), the whole of the population of the province, and could be induced to afford them the protection and support of our troops during the first struggles, we might obtain in return the most valuable commercial advantage. That few then would be required for the purpose, but that the country could not be conquered without a large army, nor preserved without a greater. This with little deviation has been the language of the people of this town, and I have had opportunities of conversing with some of the principal magistrates on the subject. I have not been able to get hold of any of the priests as they keep as much as possible out of the way. I have never heard a word of an English party, of which so much was said in London about the time of our sailing, nor do I believe that such a party ever existed. It would in my opinion require 20,000 men to occupy the principal points in the province, and those garrisons being placed in the midst of an adverse population must at all times be on the alert and adopt vigorous measures for their own security, which would at the same time elevate the animosity of the people.

This is as far as I have been able to collect the state of politics of this country. I have confined myself to this topic as being perhaps of the first importance, and because I feared any erroneous representation both as to the dispositions and power of the colony have found their way to England.

As to myself I have had some fatigue and a little illness in consequence, from which I am now set for recovery, and propose taking a party to reconnoitre the interior of the country, of which we have as yet a very confined knowledge.

I shall never like this country for a residence, and do not propose bringing out my family, but to return to England as soon as an opportunity occurs. If you could assist me in this view, you could add one more obligation to the many already conferred on me.

PS. It required some nerve to pass the breach.[37]

Colonel Bourke's overview quite rightly ended with this brief tribute to the troops. He might also have pointed to the commanders. It also required 'some nerve' to launch the attack on the breach in the first place. But Auchmuty's reports are strictly factual, and so are Stirling's, and if no one else does, it is well to point out that they had accomplished a notable feat of arms. Auchmuty's conduct of the approach march, and the siege, attacking a strong fortress with inferior numbers and poor resources, while being threatened by two other armies, can scarcely be faulted. But he could not have accomplished this without the steady and willing co-operation of Stirling. Most unusually for a naval commander, Stirling was generous to a fault with his own fleet's resources, in manpower and in materials. In fact one of the few naval commanders whose co-operation with the army was as intelligent and wholehearted as Stirling's was Popham. But both Auchmuty and Stirling had realized very quickly, as Popham never did, that the British were even more unwelcome as rulers than the Spaniards. Neither, however, was audacious enough to disregard instructions so far as to adopt a possible alternative policy: Independence. And Bourke, who did appreciate the situation, could not do so.

Chapter Eleven

Advances and Escapes

The capture of Montevideo induced Liniers' *porteno* contingent, which had approached independently of the viceroy, to retreat. The two forces, together with whoever had escaped from the city, probably outnumbered Auchmuty's force, but only if they were united. But they would not join. Auchmuty took the opportunity to extend the area of his authority:

> After getting possession of Monte Video, Sir Samuel Auchmuty detached parties into the country, to watch any attempts on the part of the enemy, and to protect the inhabitants who could be encouraged to bring supplies to the markets. Canalon, about 20 miles above the garrison, was occupied by a detachment of 200 men; and another was posted at St Lucia, about 20 miles further.[1]

One player was now removed from the table: the viceroy himself, who was arrested by the *portenos*. Auchmuty had tried to treat with him, after the capture of Montevideo, and this was perhaps the trigger for his arrest. Auchmuty reported the event in his next report to Windham, together with his impressions of the opinions of the people of his conquest:

> When I last had the honour of addressing you, I had so lately gained possession of this fortress and was so little acquainted with the country that I could not presume to give more than a general opinion of the disposition of the inhabitants. I had every reason to believe that they were without exception inimical to us. Previous to the surrender of Monte Video, I could place no confidence on any information I received, nor did any person superior to the lowest class come over to me. After its capture a sullen silence pervaded every rank, and for some time by the best informed account the principal citizens appeared ignorant of the most trifling of occurrences.

The seizure of the viceroy by the inhabitants of Buenos Ayres, an event certainly very important in itself, first gave me an insight into the views of many of the leading men and convinced me that however inimical they were to us, they were still more so to the present government.

… I wrote to the viceroy demanding that our prisoners taken at a Buenos Ayres should be delivered up agreeably to the capitulation and declaring that all the prisoners we had taken should without exception be sent to England if the demand was not complied with. In reply he acquainted me that he wanted the orders of his sovereign before he could take any steps respecting his prisoners. This answer I conveyed to the governor [Huidobro] and the Cabildo, assuring them that much as I regretted the necessity I was reduced to, I should certainly send away the prisoners. I was now requested to write to the Cabildo of Buenos Ayres and was informed that they alone could comply with my demand as the viceroy had no authority whatever and the province was under their orders.

I now determined to send to Buenos Ayres to demand the prisoners and at the same time to offer terms to the inhabitants if they would surrender, but I waited until a force I had directed to advance into the country had begun its march. The intention of the march of the corps was to oblige the viceroy to fall further back, to open the country, and to try how far it would be convenient to advance by land to Colonia. The viceroy retreated on the first information of this approach and fell in with the corps sent from Buenos Ayres to apprehend his person. He was conveyed a prisoner to that city.[2]

But almost at once two other players re-entered the scene. General Beresford and Colonel Pack escaped from their captors. Beresford later explained the circumstances:

… [O]n the fall of Monte Video it was determined by those exercising the chief authority at Buenos Ayres to remove me, and those officers stationed with me at Lujan, to a town in the interior called Catamarca, about 800 miles from Buenos Ayres, they having certainly resolved not to permit me to leave the country during the war … In pursuance of this intention an oidor Basso, one of the royal Audiencia, and a Señor Garcia, an attorney, but now a lieutenant-colonel and deputed by the Cabildo, came on the 5th of February to Lujan and commenced by seizing all my papers, and those of all the officers with me, placing me under a close sentry, as were also the other officers. Not having everything prepared for our removal, they did not think fit to communicate to me their intentions on that subject till the 8th, nor would they send us off till the afternoon of the 10th, when without having any opportunity of providing ourselves with the comforts or even necessaries for such a journey, we left Lujan. On the 16th, at a place near to Arecife, 40 leagues from Buenos Ayres, two Spanish officers, one Senor Liniers's secretary, came to me under pretence of a mission from him, but with proposals of a singular nature from a principal person and which I shall have the honour of personally explaining to his Majesty's ministers but circumstanced as I was I refused to comply with, or give any opinion upon. Finding me determined on this subject, the two gentlemen, after assuring me of their entire devotion to me, and of the abhorrence of the whole town for the conduct held towards me and my troops, then proposed to me to take me to the British army at Monte Video, which they represented there would be no difficulty in accomplishing, and that they considered in asserting my escape they were acting for the good of their country (they are both South Americans), and according to the wishes of the principal inhabitants of Buenos Ayres.

After much consideration, and having failed in every effort to get an officer to our army to give a true account as well of what related to ourselves as of the state of the country in general, and fully aware that, ignorant of the nature of the people as were and must be our commanders (as I myself had been), they would not only find it impossible to procure just or true information on the real state of things, but would run the chance that befell me of being deceived and betrayed. I determined to hazard every personal risk for what I considered of the utmost consequence to my country. What the consequences of detection would have been to me, His Majesty's ministers may judge from the virulence of passion excited by my escape, and expressed in the letters of the present supreme authorities at Buenos Aires which are transmitted by Sir Samuel Auchmuty.

It was agreed that another British officer would accompany me, and Lieutenant-Colonel Pack, wishing to be the person, we set out on the 17th February, of necessity in want, to Buenos Ayres, where we were obliged to wait three days, and at a time when we thought our situation desperate, and an escape seemed impossible, we were fortunate enough to effect it on the evening of the 21st, and the next morning got on board His Majesty ship *Charwell*, a little below Ensenada.[3]

Charwell, in fact, had been positioned as it was in part to collect escapers. Already it had picked up an American, William White, shortly after the fall of Montevideo. White, who had been busy as an intermediary between Beresford and Liniers earlier, and so had quite reasonably incurred *portenos* suspicions, and who will reappear in these events, had 'some interesting intelligence to communicate':

> On the 22nd of February we were fortunate enough to discover another boat to the SW; got underway, made sail towards her, and found two British officers on board of her, and to our no small satisfaction, proved to be General Beresford and Colonel Pack, who had made their escape; took them down to the Monte Video.[4]

Auchmuty, in accordance with his instructions, now offered to serve under Beresford, who was locally superior to him, but Beresford decided he ought to go back to Britain, presumably to shore up whatever political and military support he could find. Colonel Pack, however, whose regiment was still in captivity, decided to stay, and demanded a court-martial to clear him of the charge of having broken his parole to the Spaniards. He was, predictably, cleared, and was then employed by Auchmuty to extend the area in the British occupation by the capture of Colonia on the north shore directly opposite Buenos Aires. Auchmuty reported it in his arid way:

> May I beg you will acquaint the Rt Honble Mr. Windham that I have taken possession of Colonia del Sacramento, with the corps under Lieutenant-Colonel Pack, without any opposition. It is also my intention to take possession of the fort of Sta Theresa, situated on the frontier towards the Brazils and commanding the only pass from Brazil into the province.[5]

Once again Sergeant Lawrence's recollections expand on the general's report, and the sergeant also gives some indication of the difficulties all this gave to the inhabitants:

> After staying in the town for the time stated, a thousand of us were dispatched up the River Rio de la Plata to a small place called Colonia, where an army of Spaniards about four or five thousand strong were lying. We landed with ease, and the enemy retreated out of the place after firing a few shots, leaving it in our hands, so that we again found

ourselves for a time in comfortable quarters. We placed pickets of two or 300 men round the place, and fixed a *chevaux de frise* in the gate, formed of very sharp and pointed swords stuck very thickly into a beam which was made to turn on its axis; rather an awkward instrument to face if one is not used to it. Duty in this place was rather hard, owing to there being so few of us, and such a number on picket or at work building some batteries for our better protection.

At the picket house, which was some distance from the town, there lived a soap-boiler and tallow-chandler, who was very kind to us while we were there on duty, killing a bullock almost every night for our use, as he only required the skin and tallow, and anyone may suppose that 200 hungry men knew what to do with the rest of it. An incident took place during our stay at his house which will show how well disposed he was towards us. We had passed a very quiet week there, when one night the Spaniards passed our picket secretly in the darkness, fired a volley into the town, and then immediately retreated. Our picket only just managed to get through safely into the town, leaving one of our men asleep in the house, and he must certainly have met his death if he had been caught there singly; but the tallow-chandler, though himself a Spaniard, concealed him under a quantity of dry hides while the enemy was scouring the place in search of stragglers, and so saved his life. In consequence of this surprise, still heavier duty was afterwards put upon us, the picket having to be augmented to prevent further annoyance.

Two or three days after this had occurred the tallow-chandler was sent for to join the Spanish army, no doubt because their general suspected him of favouring the English, but he would not go until he had obtained our colonel's advice, which is that he should go by all means, and if he could conveniently come back with full particulars of the enemy strength, he should be rewarded. As far as I can remember, he had been away for about ten days when he again made his appearance with the requisite information.[6]

Lawrence's *naïveté* is touching, for it is all but certain that the chandler had provided the Spaniards with the same information about the British. It is significant that, when it came, the Spanish counter-attack was mounted by just about double the force Pack had under his command. There seems no record of the tallow chandler's name, but he was clearly an ingenious and brave fellow.

Auchmuty's conquest had its effect beyond the area under his control (map 13). When Popham's expedition arrived in the river, an Englishman, John Mawe, a mineralogist, was in Montevideo. He was arrested and sent into the interior, to live at a place called Barriga Nigra, 200km from the city. He was released when the city was captured; the place thus implicitly recognized British authority, even if no soldiers came near the place.[7]

Stirling sent a ship to have a look at Santa Teresa, which was deemed to be too strongly fortified to be worth attacking.[8] In fact, Auchmuty had now run up against the basic problem which sooner or later affected every British commander in this campaign; shortage of manpower. In Buenos Aires Beresford had never had enough men to hold the city after the initial surprise; at Maldonado, 2,000 soldiers could do no more than hold the place; at Montevideo, a bigger force of 5,000 troops – plus the 9th Dragoon Guards, who arrived late in February – were able to hold the city, capture Colonia, and establish control over the neighbouring countryside, but no more. There was always another place further off, which was under the control of the Spaniards, and from which their horsemen could raid into the British-controlled territory. Above all, there was Buenos Aires, seething with resentment at its past humiliation, on the verge of revolution – if the arrest of the viceroy had not pushed it over the edge – and profoundly fearful of the next attack.

The victory of Auchmuty's men at Montevideo was clearly the reason for the decision to move Beresford and Pack further away, and which persuaded them to make their escape. The rapid development of a commercial prosperity in the conquered city – it, unlike Buenos Aires, was now free of the British blockade – and the relatively good treatment of the citizens were also no doubt seen as threats by the uncertain government in Buenos Aires. This pressure was all the greater since Rear-Admiral Stirling distributed his ships so as to establish control over the whole estuary, and tried to prevent ships reaching Spanish-controlled ports. They were not always successful:

I understand from Buenos Aires that five English ships have got in since the recapture and I am of opinion that the underwriters ought to enquire into the circumstances of their going there before they make payment. Lieutenant Street of *Staunch* informs me he chased one vessel with English colours flying close to the Rio Chuelo, and that the master of another expressed regret he had not been allowed to proceed. In thick weather vessels may certainly get in without being seen by our cruisers, but I am told the Spanish flag is always flying on the fort, and I believe no man can go in there by mistake from any other than a fraudulent motive.

An American ship called the *Bengal* which I suppose insured at Lloyd's from the great secrecy observed, ran onshore at the Island of Goritti, and from Captain Downman's [of *Diomede*] report should not recover without due enquiry. She was afterwards towed up here by two of her countrymen and has since gone to pieces, but from the appearance of the cargo strewn about the beach it does not look as if the master expected the owners would suffer by any loss.[9]

Other ships came straight to Montevideo. James P. Robertson, still a teenager, had learned Spanish on the voyage from Greenock, and polished it after he reached Montevideo with his father. He noted that within a week the signs of the battle had disappeared, and that in a month the place was becoming more confident in British rule – a development he attributed, probably rightly, to Auchmuty. He also emphasized the commerce which came from the new regime; there were 'foreign troops, merchants, and adventurers of every description' all through the city.[10] James Paroissien arrived at the end of February, by which time he estimated there were 150 ships in the harbour; and by May British merchants had brought in goods worth £1.2 million. Since 'Monte Video was by itself incapable of such commerce, the city had become the centre of a far-flung contraband trade with Buenos Ayres and other parts of the viceroyalty'.[11]

The escape of Beresford prompted the government in Buenos Aires to move those of the prisoners who were still fairly near the city further away. Captain Gillespie's memories were of a relaxed time in San Antonio at first:

At daylight of the 16th we renewed our labours that after crossing an arm of the river passing close to it we reached the village of St. Antonio de Araco. After great trouble another officer and myself procured a small hut at the rent of three dollars a month behind the house of an inhabitant. Our abode had been recently devoted to a flour granary, and our contract was that it should continue so, but for form's sake that it should be entitled our house. We however were contented with our lot … The village became our resting place for three months, and yielded pastimes of fishing, cricket, hunting, and riding.[12]

His comment that this lasted for three months is significant, for it is clear that the escape of General Beresford and Colonel Pack in early February seriously worsened the officers' conditions of detention, but also in some cases woke them from their contentment. Lieutenant Fernyhough felt the escapers were justified, even though he and his comrades were then sent further inland:

> February the 7th. We now heard of the surrender of Monte Video to the British forces under General Sir Samuel Auchmuty. Towards the latter end of the month we were informed that General Beresford and Colonel Pack had effected their escape to Monte Video, and that the remainder of the officers who were of their party at Lujan were sent into the interior under a strong guard. We were not at all surprised to hear of this; that the Spaniards had broken their faith with us and had intended for some time to remove us into the interior of the country; we felt perfectly justified in attempting to escape whenever the opportunity presented itself.
>
> February the 26th [four days after Beresford's escape succeeded]. An order was sent to Don Felipe, from the Cabildo to deprive us of our horses, and keep us closely confined to the house. After existing sometime under this unpleasant restraint, about the middle of March a guard of soldiers arrived to convey us up the country.
>
> The officer commanding the party informed us that we were immediately to proceed to Salto, a small fort situated on the frontiers, where the whole of the officers were to rendezvous, and to set out from thence together.
>
> The night we left our kind host, Don Felipe, we had some idea of attempting our escape, by the way of the River Parana, but the officer of the guard, who suspected something of the kind, had planted his sentries around the house.
>
> The next morning we took our leave of Don Felipe, with the most grateful recollections of his kindness, and he seemed much hurt at the conduct of his government in sending us further into the country. He rode with us some distance, and at parting recommended us to the officer of the guard, requesting that he would do everything in his power to make us comfortable during the march.
>
> We passed through St. Antonio de Araco, where we were joined by Colonel Campbell and his party ...[13]

Captain Gillespie's group was ordered to move up country, but they felt themselves hard done by, and the solution they adopted could not have pleased the new *porteno* government, already very nervous:

The Spanish commandant was very soon apprised that the prisoners at his guardia would not advance an inch until their arrears were adjusted to the utmost farthing and that if force was used, it would be met with force. Things remained in this state without a settlement during eight days … He adopted the expedient … of assessing the villagers in an amount equal to our necessities under an official promise to refund in better times.

The whole detachment set out from Salto de Areca upon the 30th of March.[14]

Ensign Gavin was also moved on, joining the party of officers of which Fernyhough was one, as part of Colonel Campbell's group. He remembered matters a little differently:

February 1807. We were informed of the escape of General Beresford and Colonel Pack across the River Plate to Monte Video then in possession of the British – and got orders to proceed further into the interior. I was sent with Colonel Campbell, Major McKenzie, etc., to St. Ignacia, a quinto or country house belonging to an extensive landowner, 40 leagues north of Cordova. We passed for the first week through the same kind of country as from Buenos Ayres, but destitute of wood and water. We each had a horse and a new saddle and bridle, with bullock wagons to carry our little remaining baggage and women. We got vessels provided for us to carry water for five or six days, and our only fuels were bullock dung and withered weeds. Afterwards we got into a country scarcely passable for a kind of prickly thorn and the prickly pear.

We were well supplied by our landlord Don Pedro Gomez with good bread, beef and mustard, paying him well for the same … We had a captain's guard of Spanish dragoons. We also received three months' pay from the Spanish government – a dollar a day. Through the whole of the country we traversed we scarcely met an inhabitant, except at distances, where large towns were traced with streets and squares, with a wretched mud fort or perhaps a dismounted gun, and an unfortunate corporal with two men sent to keep the natives in awe.[15]

Beresford's and Pack's escape was not seen by all the British prisoners as necessarily a praiseworthy action. Captain Pococke, with characteristic perverseness, described it in his increasingly scrappy diary as 'highly blameable', before being moved further into the country.[16] Others were inspired to emulation, not always with success. Gavin briefly recalled two attempts:

> From this place [the mud hut mentioned above] Major Tolley and Captain Adamson made their escape to the River Paraguay, which falls into the Plate, and after innumerable hardships obtained a boat, hiding during the day and rowing all night, levying contributions of provisions on any house where no male person was to defend it, and arrived in safety at Monte Video. Captain Jones, encouraged by this success, formed a plan to follow their footsteps but while waiting for an issue of pay, unguardedly made his attentions so public that the Spanish captain knew to the hour when he was to set out, with his servants disguised as Creoles, and the route he was to proceed, and allowed him to proceed about six leagues, and in a wood secured them both and carried them prisoners to Cordova – there kept them closely confined during our captivity.[17]

The main difficulty in escaping seems to have been the sheer distances involved. It was thus sensible for potential escapers to make their attempt before being moved even further inland, and at the same time it was equally sensible of the *portenos* to move their prisoners away from the British dominated coast, for it was obvious that it was distance which was the main deterrent – unless, like Captain Jones, your intentions were all too obvious. (Jones later became the commanding officer of the regiment, so the escapade did not harm him among his peers.)

In Montevideo, meanwhile, Auchmuty was busy administering his conquest, extending the area under his control, and investigating what was going on in Buenos Aires. As a man who had lived through the preliminaries and the first years of the revolution in North America, he may well have been unsurprised at events, and perhaps he had a quicker understanding of what was going on, and of the significance of what he heard. But he needed a closer view than he could get from Montevideo. Communications were by no means closed, and Admiral Stirling refers at times to information from Buenos Aires in a casual way, showing that it was a normal matter. But Auchmuty also had his means. For example, he sent Major Campbell with a flag of truce to the city, ostensibly with despatches, actually to keep his eyes open. Campbell reported afterwards:

I have the honour to state to you that agreeably to your orders, I proceeded with the flag of truce to Buenos Aires in the *Cherwell* and anchored about 6 miles from the town. At 10 o'clock I went with the flag in one of the sloop's boats towards shore when a gun boat with a flag of truce, mounting an 18-pounder with a match lighted and a good supply of small arms, met me some distance from the shore, and at my own particular request took me on board, as I said I wished to deliver my dispatches in person, and we agreed that my boat should return back to the ship and that he should on a white flag being hoisted on shore, come for me. I had a handkerchief tied round my eyes agreeably to the custom of war and after landing proceeded in the midst of a mob, to the Citadel or general's house. When I entered the house I found a great crowd of officers and people of all descriptions round me, and pressing in so much that the door was obliged to be shut to prevent more from entering.

On my inquiring for the general or the person who had the chief command, I was introduced by the officer of the navy who conducted me on shore to General Liniers. I then delivered my dispatches and on the general's receiving them the crowd was so great that gathered round him, that he could hardly open them, some reading over his shoulder, others holding the paper by the corners that they might be the better able to see the contents of them.

After a great deal of conversation regarding my mission the general told me they had the greatest confidence in their numbers, and that the sword must decide, at the same time adding that it did not depend on him, as a council must be held.

I was asked to dinner. The table was large and crowded, and every attention was paid me by the General and his staff, but a short time after dinner a person ran into the room saying my boat was coming towards shore with a white flag, on which some of the people at table got up and said we must be prisoners. Their expression was: 'Liniers, they must be prisoners, they have broken the truce.' Others said that we should not be prisoners and the dispute ran so high and in such a manner that General Liniers found it necessary to take me into his own room, and send one of his aides-de-camp for a guard, to turn away the mob, that I might get on board, requesting that I would not come on shore any more but that he would send me the answer on board.

From what I could see that seemed to be a great deal of party work among them and I thought that General Liniers was in a disagreeable situation and had little authority. I was the more strongly confirmed in that opinion from his not being able to silence the dispute about determining the lieutenant of the navy, the boat's crew and me prisoners, which ran so high that a junior officer offered to draw on a senior, without paying the least attention to the General's order, as well as from the white flag having been hoisted on shore without the general's knowledge, which must have been done by some party with the intention of breeding a disturbance or as a pretense to detain us prisoners; in short there seemed to be no subordination among them.[18]

The complacent remarks of James Paroissien and John Robertson about the situation in Montevideo are not wholly accurate. The military men were more conscious of, and closer to, the possibilities of insurrection. Sergeant Lawrence remembered how:

[A] sergeant and a corporal of the Spanish army came in disguise and tried to enlist any of our men who would join their service; and unfortunately a sergeant named Goodfellow, one of my own regiment, accepted their proposals, tempted by the heavy bounty they offered. But while passing out of the town in disguise with the Spaniards he was met and recognized by the general himself and his staff: a most unlucky encounter for the three runaways, for they were brought back again and put on a charge immediately and a court-martial ordered on them next day. Our colonel, however, implored so hard for our sergeant's life on account of the regiment's late good conduct in the field, that the General granted it, and changed the sentence to transportation for life: but the Spaniards were not quite so leniently dealt with, for they were tried and hanged, to make sure that they could not repeat their mischievous practices.[19]

It was widely remembered that the possibilities of marriage to eligible Spanish daughters was held out as a bribe to British soldiers. Lawrence recalled:

Another case of desertion was that of an officer's servant, who went away with the greater part of his master's clothes, taking with him likewise a Spanish lady; he was lucky enough to get off safe and nothing was heard of him afterwards. This was not at all a rare temptation, though, that was put in our soldiers' way; for I was myself offered a fortune by a Spanish gentleman, together with his daughter, if I would desert and remain in the country. Whenever he met me about he would treat me to anything I liked to name, which I sometimes found very acceptable, and he would often give me money as well, in hopes of gaining me over in time.[20]

But Captain Wilkie also remembered an incident with its lighter aside, but with a serious basis:

Reports have been circulated [for] some days that it was the intention of the Spaniards to rise upon the garrison; and for that purpose quantities of arms had been introduced into the town, and were concealed in the houses. As these reports gained some consistency, the officer in command thought it prudent to be on the sure side, and a search for arms was determined on. The town was divided into districts, and allotted to each regiment. We marched to our stations at daylight; and the search was pursued immediately. It was rather ungallant to turn out so many senoras and senoritas from their warm beds at that unseasonable hour; and it ended without anything to warrant the reports that had got abroad, but in this hunt after arms we lighted on a quantity of property belonging to the Spanish Philippine Company, which had been landed and concealed in Monte Video. It consisted, for the most part, of Chinese work-boxes and fancy articles, fans, card-boxes, etc., which had been intended as presents for the different branches of Napoleon's family; and the ciphers of their names are figured on the different things.[21]

It is clear that occupation armies behave in much the same way, no matter what their origins. There is no reason to suppose that the relative quietness of the Montevideans was a sign of contentment with their city's situation. Even if they were, the relative calm in the city from February onwards was to be much disturbed by the arrival of more troops and a new commander in May and June.

Chapter Twelve

Buenos Aires: The Second Attack

The expeditions and reinforcements sent from Britain converged on the River Plate, arriving over a period of five months, from Auchmuty's troops in January to the 9th Dragoon Guards late in February, to Craufurd's expeditionary force in June. Whitelocke arrived in May, but the troops he started out with, held up by foul winds in the doldrums, missed all the action and only arrived in September. Their absence probably made no difference to the outcome.

The crucial group, because it was the largest, was Craufurd's. Convoyed by the squadron of four line-of-battle ships commanded by Captain Robert Stopford, the expedition reached Porto Praya in the Cape Verde Islands in mid-December, and waited there for a month. Stopford was supposed to hand over to Rear Admiral Murray, but Murray did not get away from Portsmouth until the end of the year. On 11 January, therefore, Craufurd persuaded Stopford to split his force, send two of his ships back to Britain with the news, and sail on to the Cape with the others and the convoy.

Murray arrived at Porto Praya six days later, and sailed on at once. In addition to these two fleets, the *Fly* sloop had been sent with Windham's and Tom Grenville's new instructions for both Craufurd and Murray, as a result of the news of the recapture of Buenos Aires by the *portenos* the previous August. All three – Stopford, Murray, and *Fly* – sailed much the same course southwards through the Atlantic without seeing each other – the *Fly* missed Murray at Porto Praya by only a day. They, and other vessels, arrived at the Cape successively in early March. Admiral Murray reported the bombardment of news and orders he received to the Admiralty on 23 March:

> You will be pleased to inform their lordships that the *Haughty* gun brig arrived here on the 15th inst. She was sent on by Captain Stopford with an account of his approach and with directions to return to him at the Cape if Table Bay should be thought unsafe for the transports to enter.

On the 18th the *Campion* army victualler arrived from the convoy, Captain Stopford having taken some provisions out of her on this side of the line and left her to proceed here, as she had detained the convoy by her bad sailing.

On the 19th His Majesty's ship *Nereide* arrived from off Monte Video with dispatches from Rear-Admiral Stirling to Sir Thomas Troubridge or the senior officer at the Cape, giving an account of Monte Video being taken by assault on the 3rd February last.

On the 20th inst. His Majesty's ship *Theseus* arrived having left the transports two days before standing in for Table Bay, and being desired by Captain Stopford to come here. The same day the *Fly* sloop arrived from England last from Porto Praya with dispatches from Sir Thomas Troubridge or the senior officer for Brigadier-General Craufurd and for myself dated the 1st and 2nd of January. I likewise received a letter for Captain Stopford informing me of his arrival in Simons Bay with the transports and *Paulina*.

… As General Grey wished to send a transport with some provisions and powder for the army at Monte Video, I shall send her under convoy of the *Fly* sloop who will take dispatches to Rear-Admiral Stirling and will I hope sail 25th inst. I shall by the *Fly* sloop inform Rear Admiral Stirling of my intentions as to my future proceedings in consequence of their lordships' orders dated the 2nd December.[1]

Craufurd only very reluctantly accepted that the logic of the new situation at the Plate meant that he would have to abandon his own expedition. He argued it out at great and rather tedious length in a letter to Windham, but in the end, inevitably, he decided to head for the River Plate, but he could not avoid hoping it was all a mirage:

I have, … in concurrence with the admiral, determined that unless any intelligence that may be received whilst we are here should induce us to alter our plans, we shall proceed from hence to the Plate as soon as the squadron and transports can be watered and victualled and otherwise prepared for sea, which I have reason to hope will be the case in about 10 days from this time.

If in the course of 4 or 5 weeks after our arrival in the Plata affairs should be in such a state as to induce Sir Samuel Auchmuty to think it right that this detachment should proceed on its original voyage, the admiral seems to think that we should be about three months from the

Plata to New Holland, and allowing two months from thence across the Pacific Ocean we should arrive upon the coast about the month of December.[2]

Craufurd's was the last of the British forces to arrive in the Plate. By then Whitelocke had been there for a month, and had gained a good notion of what the situation was. He had been commendably eager to take up his post, and had made a serious effort when in Montevideo to apply his skills to this new British conquest. It is well to remember that the British assumed that their possession of the city would be permanent, and that they would, perhaps with some difficulty, retake Buenos Aires. After all, it had been captured originally by only 1,600 men; Whitelocke had many times that number; its conquest was confidently expected.

He had to wait until his forces were sufficiently augmented by more reinforcements before making any serious attempt. He knew his own group was on the way, and he may have known that Craufurd's force would also join him. So he could wait. Meanwhile he could do what he did best, administer the area already under British occupation. The presence of the considerable colony of British troops and merchants amid a Spanish-speaking population stimulated the production of a bilingual newspaper, the *Southern Star/La Estrella del Sur*, which first appeared on 23 May. It was, of course, in part a British propaganda sheet, but paid its way in large part by advertisements, which gave a notion of the activities above all of the British merchants. The leading articles reflect British policy, such as it was. He could also organize and regulate the Customs House and the market.[3]

Whitelocke's work as governor was competent, and had the post of governor and commanding officer been separated, with Whitelocke in the former role and Auchmuty in the latter, things may well have turned out differently. But Whitelocke combined the two positions, and he had been sent to take Buenos Aires so that was what he had to attempt. It was a task which would take the full strength of all his forces and had best be attempted as soon as possible. In Buenos Aires Liniers was building up his military strength. When Murray and Craufurd reached the Plate, Whitelocke kept the men on the transports, and swiftly organized the embarkation of all the troops on shore, except for a small garrison left at Montevideo under Colonel Browne of the 40th Foot. The outposts inland had been coming under attack, first at Colonia, then at Canalon, which, along with the news from Buenos Aires, clearly indicated a rise in Spanish confidence and strength. Colonel Pack, who had been reinforced by the 40th Foot and eventually had over 1,000 men at Colonia, reported to Whitelocke what had happened:

> Having obtained information on Saturday evening that the enemy had taken post at St. Pedro, 12 miles from here, I resolved upon moving to attack him and commenced my march at 3 o'clock the next morning … leaving the garrison under the command of Major Pigot of the 9th Light Dragoons. We arrived at St. Pedro at seven o'clock and found the enemy strongly posted on an eminence with his front and flanks secured by a deep and marshy plain, over which there was only one pass scarcely practicable, and that defended by four 6-pounders and two howitzers. The bravery of the troops however soon overcame all difficulties. They crossed the ford reduced to a front of less than sections, many up to their middle and under a heavy fire from the artillery. After having effected a passage I formed the troops and advanced to the attack without firing a shot. The enemy's cavalry soon gave way, but the infantry to my surprise stood until we approached within a few paces, when they fled in disorder, throwing away their arms and ammunition and leaving us in possession of their guns and camp, with one standard and 105 prisoners, including the second-in-command and five other officers; had it been possible to bring our guns and cavalry across the ford I am confident that we should have taken or destroyed the whole force of the enemy, which consisted of upwards of 2,000 men.
>
> The chief loss fell on the 40th Regiment, which corps supported most gallantly its well-established character, and indeed the bravery evinced by the whole of the troops in this affair merits my warmest recommendation.
>
> NB. The enemy in the above affair left 120 men killed on the field, and a number of wounded.[4]

But the Spaniards were only driven from the field, not destroyed, and their cohesion was clearly much greater than it had been in earlier conflicts, witness Pack's 'surprise' at the length of time they stood awaiting attack. They had a new commander, Colonel Javier de Elio, recently arrived from Spain, and he probably had had a major effect.[5] The post at Canalon had to be rescued a few days later, probably from the same force:

Colonel Mahon of the 9th Light Dragoons [i.e. the 9th Dragoon Guards], was detached, on the morning of the 12th of June, with 500 men to support Lieutenant-Colonel Backhouse, who was stationed at Canalon with 200. This officer had been summoned to surrender on the former day by a particular hour, or that he should be attacked by 1,400 men, who were ready to follow up the summons; he thought it prudent to retire, and was met near Monte Video by Colonel Mahon, who took back with him the two field pieces belonging to the retreating party. The Spaniards, apprised of the approach of Colonel Mahon, retired, and this officer not being able to come up with them, returned on the 14th.[6]

Since these attacks had been organized from Buenos Aires, Whitelocke's decision to attack the source was sensible, but he was compelled also to abandon the outposts, in order to concentrate all possible forces into one for the assault. He was under no illusions as to the difficulties he and the troops faced, as General Craufurd recalled:

On my arrival at Monte Video Lieutenant-General Whitelocke proposed a walk round the works, and on our return through the town desired me to notice the peculiar construction of the houses, their flat roofs encompassed by parallel walls, and other circumstances, which, as he observed, rendered them particularly favourable for defence; and he certainly would not expose his troops to a contest so unequal as that in which they must be engaged if led into so large a town as Buenos Ayres; all the inhabitants of which were prepared for its defence, and the houses of which were constructed similar to those of Monte Video.[7]

The invasion fleet gathered off Colonia, then crossed to land at Ensenada, 30 miles from Buenos Aires (see map 14). Colonel Bourke, who was now Quarter-Master-General of the invasion force, stated the strength, which was no more than half that which Auchmuty had said was needed for the task and much less than he himself had suggested was needed:

The forces landed at the Ensenada de Barragon on the 26th of June consisted of 8,522 rank and file, including 150 unmounted dragoons. It was provided with 18 pieces of artillery, and 206 horses and mules for conveyance; there was also a large quantity of ordnance embarked, and a reserve of artillery of some heavy pieces, mortars, and howitzers; there were entrenching tools for 1,000 men; six pontoons and camp equipage for 1,000 men; but no horses had been embarked for its conveyance.[8]

The landing, at Ensenada, was a good deal farther from the city than Beresford's landing at Quilmes. Again this made sense. Because of the greatly increased military strength of the city, he could not risk being caught with only part of his forces on shore. The landing at Quilmes had been slow and difficult; shallow water had prevented ships approaching, and even boats could not reach the shore; and then there had been that uncomfortable swamp. Beresford would probably not have chosen to land there had he known about all this. Whitelocke did know, and the existence of an easier approach from Ensenada, which was an outpost of the city, and was sufficiently far from the *portenos* forces to allow the landing to go ahead without interference made it a much better choice. He had sent Colonel Bourke in the *Fly* to examine possible landing places, but it must have been known all along that Ensenada was the only place with access easy enough for a landing, and close enough to the city to allow the troops to get there reasonably quickly.

The force divided for the march towards the city. The light troops under Craufurd went first, then the First Brigade and Brigadier-General Lumley – these two were eventually joined under General Gower – and last the Second Brigade under Auchmuty, who had Whitelocke with him. The march was wet and uncomfortable:

> The country is almost all level and covered with long clover that reached to our waists, and large herds of bullocks and horses, which seemed to run wild. The weather was very wet. For days I had not a dry article on my body. We crossed many morasses in our march, in one of which I lost my shoes, and was under the necessity of marching the rest of the way barefooted.[9]

Supplies were difficult, partly because the approach march was taking a good deal longer than expected. Lieutenant-Colonel Lancelot Holland was with Craufurd's brigade, and kept a detailed diary, and noted that at Reduction, a village near the Quilmes landing place,

> we found an abundance of wheat, enough for all the men. General Gower sent us from his quarters two sheep a company, and some biscuit found in them. This was a most acceptable supply to the men, most

of whom had not eaten since yesterday morning, and were very much worn and fatigued. We arrived on our ground about four o'clock having marched about 12 miles.[10]

Any stragglers were in great danger from the bands of local light horsemen who hovered near the column:

An incident took place here, which was attended by the death of two men, a corporal and a private, and likewise the very narrow escape of a second private. They were engaged in plundering one of the Indian huts, when the inhabitants fell on them armed, and, catching the corporal round the neck with a lasso, soon dragged him away, at the same time knocking the private down and stabbing him; the other private only escaped back to the regiment after receiving a sabre-wound which carried the skin and hair off the back of his head. This was a great glory to the natives; they stuck the corporal's head on a pole and carried it in front of their little band when on the march. They also made use of the rifle and ammunition they had taken from him to fire at times into our camp, but fortunately it was a very harmless sort of practice.[11]

Otherwise no serious opposition was encountered until the suburbs, but this was because no attempt was made to cross the Rio Chuelo where Beresford had crossed, at the bridge. Liniers had brought out his forces to contest their passage at that point, and these were now much more numerous, better trained, and much more formidable than a year earlier. So most of the British turned and crossed the river upstream where it was narrow. A detachment under Colonel Mahon remained at the site of the bridge. Liniers marched his forces in parallel on the city side of the Chuelo, and so reached the suburbs first, at a place called the Coral de Miserere, where cattle were butchered for the city market. General Gower reported what happened when the two forces met:

I have the honour to report to you for the information of General Whitelocke that the advanced corps under my command, consisting of three companies of the 95th, light battalion, 36th and 88th Regiments, with two 3- and two 6-pounders, advanced from the position I had taken up in front of the village of the Reduction and after marching a considerable distance from the badness of the roads I crossed the Chuelo at the Chico Pass, from whence I continued my route through very strongly enclosed and difficult ground, till the head of the column arrived at the junction of two roads about 500 yards from the Coral de Miserere. At the same moment that we discovered the enemy, they commenced a heavy though after the first round not well directed fire of shot and shells, my artillery having been left in the rear, under the protection of three companies of Brigadier-General Lumley's brigade, owing to the inability of the horses to bring it up at the same time at which the infantry marched. I directed an immediate attack to be made on their left flank, with the bayonet, which was executed by Brigadier-General Craufurd in the most perfect manner with his brigade, and he was well seconded by the gallantry of the Lieutenant-Colonel Pack and Major Travers, the officers and men of the 95th and light battalion, that in five minutes the enemy's force though strongly posted behind hedges and embankments gave way, leaving about 60 killed and 70 prisoners with all their artillery, consisting of nine guns, one howitzer, three tumbrils with limbers complete.

I beg to state that the conduct of every officer and soldier engaged was admirable and that I am also under great obligations to Brigadier-General Lumley for his exertions to take a share in the action, but which alone the very exhausted state of his regiments from the severity of the march prevented. Immediately after I formed I found that he had taken a position on the right of the light Battalion to support it in case of a re-attack. I am happy to add our loss has been but trifling, not exceeding 14 rank-and-file killed, five officers and 23 rank and file wounded, the exact returns I have not been able to obtain.[12]

After the short commons of the approach march, food was located at last:

We finished a day's work [on July 3] by taking possession of the houses in front for the night; where we supped on pigeons, ducks, and fowls, garnished with plenty of aquadente and country wine. Such a scene I never before witnessed. A few women were left in the houses, and were, with a few exceptions, treated with respect; but everything eatable and drinkable went to destruction; such a slaughter of poultry! such rummaging in holes and corners! such preparations for dinner! such hallooing, laughing and noise! Our poor fellows seem to forget all the hardships past, their meagre diet and their spiritless march.[13]

The fight had in fact seen the defeat of the main *portenos* force, commanded by Liniers in person, who then went missing for a time – he only just avoided being captured. Colonel Elio had to report this to the Cabildo, where Martin de Alzaga stimulated defensive measures, using similar ideas to those adopted fruitlessly at Montevideo – blocking streets with ditches and guns, summoning back into the city the detached groups still at the Rio Chuelo (allowing Colonel Mahon's group to cross at the bridge). Alzaga defined a relatively small area which was to be defended, centred on the Fort, the Cabildo, and the Plaza Mayor, and the immediate neighbourhood.

Whitelocke arrived a day later with the Second Brigade. He made his headquarters in the house of the American, William White, who had fled from Buenos Aires in February, and had been picked up by *Cherwell* in the estuary. His house was at the rear of the city, rather separated from the rest of the built-up area.

It is clear that neither Auchmuty nor Craufurd had much respect for Whitelocke, and Craufurd at one point almost disobeyed a direct order because of this. Furthermore, Whitelocke had devised no plan of his own for attacking the city, though he clearly understood its difficulty, as his conversation at Montevideo with Craufurd shows. He seems to have been rather disconcerted by the fact that the British had reached the outskirts at a different place than he expected. It was General Gower, another soldier who had seen little or no action for years – he had been assigned to a garrison battalion for years and owed his present position to his membership of the family of the Marquis of Stafford – who provided the plan which was used (see map 17). Neither Craufurd nor Auchmuty were consulted, though Colonel Bourke, and Colonel Torrens (Whitelocke's military secretary), made some comments. When the plan was explained to the commanders at headquarters on 4 July, none of them had anything to say, other than that they wished to reconnoitre their lines of approach first. So Whitelocke set the next day, 5 July, for the assault. The scene of the briefing, and its limitations, was recalled by Craufurd – not perhaps a wholly impartial witness:

The disposition was afterwards read and explained on the plan ... [It] was for an attack to be made at 12 o'clock that day... I did not understand from anything that passed that either myself or the other brigadiers were called there to give their opinion upon the propriety of the dispositions, but for the purpose of being made acquainted with the detail of it. Sir Samuel Auchmuty and Colonel Pack suggested that a little before daybreak on the following morning would be a better time than noon on that day for advancing into the town; and after some consultation the commander-in-chief determined to defer the attack to the morning of the 5th. While we were in this room a Mr White, who had resided a considerable time in Buenos Ayres, gave us some information, which we afterwards found to be perfectly correct, respecting the dispositions and arrangements which the enemy had made in the town since the evening of the 2nd.

Mr. White told me and several other officers in General Whitelocke's room that he was informed by people who had lately left the town that the enemy had strongly entrenched themselves and placed heavy cannon in all the streets leading into the great square where he had concentrated the principal part of his force.[14]

The plan Whitelocke adopted was based on the geography of the city, which was laid out in a rigidly gridiron system, the streets leading off at right angles to the river bank. Each regiment was assigned two parallel streets along which to advance, as far as the river. The effect was that each half-regiment was separated by the intervening blocks of buildings. Further, the orders were that the soldiers were to attack with guns unloaded, using the bayonet, while two corporals were to march at the head of each column with crowbars to break into the houses. This idea Whitelocke – or Gower – had got from Auchmuty's practice at Montevideo, ignoring the very different circumstances. (But at his court-martial, this was the one charge of which he was acquitted; the unloaded muskets clearly made sense to the judges.) The actual result was that the columns rushed along as fast as they could, ignoring the houses they passed, so that the Spaniards either retreated before them along the streets, or they took cover in the houses – and then emerged once again once the attackers had passed, to take them in the rear. This is clearly not what Whitelocke had intended, but he certainly did not make clear what else they were to do, other than to reach the river bank. Nor did he give any idea of what they were to do then. The assumption seems to have been that by reaching the river all opposition would have been removed.

Within the city, the initial panic as the news of Liniers' defeat at the Coral subsided under the pressure of working to dig the defences. The detached groups came back in, Liniers returned, and a new determination took hold. This was helped by the delay in the British advance asked for by the commanders.

The rival plans of attack and defence were both liable to lead to defeat. Alzaga had concentrated his defences into a very small area, where, if the British had realized this, he could have been besieged. Liniers, however, accepted the situation – his forces had already been beaten in the open, so holding a built-up area was probably easier – and distributed his forces around the area defined by Alzaga's works.

The British plan is regularly condemned by all who discuss these events. 'Curious and unpractical' is the summary judgment of one historian, and this has been the general conclusion.[15] None, however, have made any suggestion as to what should have been done in its place. It is convenient to blame the plan, of course, since it did result in defeat. But the only way to capture the city was to attack it, and given its geography the only way to do so was along the streets. It may have been better to move more slowly, taking time to clear out rooftop ambushes, but there were not many of these. The plan produced by Gower and accepted by Whitelocke and all the rest of the general officers was the only possible one. The fact that it ended in defeat was due to the resistance of the *portenos*, who comprehensively defeated the British attackers at all points. Blaming the plan disguises that awkward but indisputable fact.

The army the British were attacking was much larger, stronger, and better armed and equipped than that which had defeated Beresford in August the previous year. Various administrative measures had allowed Liniers to recruit volunteers to reinforce the existing forces so that he now commanded not 2,000 or 3,000 men, but a properly organized army three times that size. One part was composed of *peninsulares*, with units named for the various provinces of Spain – Catalonia, Andalusia, and so on – and comprising six regiments of from 200 to 600 men, giving a total of about 2,200 men, at least on paper. These were infantry.

The call for volunteers produced eight units of cavalry, with varying titles, but all but one formed in Buenos Aires; they were each about 200 strong, giving about 1,500 men in total. A variety of infantry units also emerged, the most important being the three battalions of *Patricios* with a total strength of about 1,300 men; several smaller units, including a battalion of Marines, added another 900 or so to the infantry. Artillery units, amounting to about 1,000 men, were also formed, and they were equipped with guns from the Fort. The total of Liniers' army was thus perhaps 7,000 or 8,000 men, more or less what Whitelocke commanded, but they were assisted by the population of the city, and were fighting in defence of their homes and their families.[16]

During the delay insisted on by the British commanders, a summons to surrender went into the city. This was the second such summons. Major Gideon Roach had been sent in first, had met Colonel Elio and had been rebuffed. Now, after the British plan had been unveiled, another envoy, Captain Samuel Whittingham, went in. He was at first refused access to Liniers, but met Colonel Hilarion de la Quintana, the former commander of the Fort, who eventually did take him to see Liniers. The reply was that, reasonably enough, if Whitelocke wished to avoid bloodshed and killing people, he could simply not attack.[17]

The military proprieties having been observed, the attack began next morning, signalled by a cannon shot. On either flank of the advance, the British columns were successful, for they met virtually no resistance, which was concentrated in the central area, round the fort. In the north, Auchmuty reached the Plaza de Toros, and captured the nearby barracks with few casualties; in the south, half of the 45th Foot seized control of the Residentia, a well-built friary. But in between there were a variety of British disasters. The 5th Foot's experiences were recorded by Major Henry King in his diary, which is the most detailed account which survives, giving a clear insight into the difficulties and confusions of the attack:

Having received verbal instructions from Sir Samuel Auchmuty relative to the attack, and being shown the different roads by which the columns of the brigade were to penetrate on the preceding evening, at six o'clock the next morning, Sunday 5th, the columns were ready at the different entrances; and on the commencement of the cannonade in the centre, advanced in quick time. I led the left wing of the 5th Regiment, and on entering the town I dismounted, and the column pushed forward, the front rank of the leading section with charged bayonets. On our charging down the street four pieces of cannon were abandoned to us by the enemy, they having first shot all the horses. We proceeded without halting to the River Plate, which we reached without opposition. On getting to the river I halted my column and looked about for the most eligible houses to occupy a position in; at that moment Major Miller and Captain Rose of the 87th came to my street, both badly wounded, calling for a surgeon and stating that the 87th were dreadfully slaughtered in their advance, and that Captain Considine and Lieutenant Barry of the grenadiers were killed. Soon after the colours (one stand) of the 87th came from the left, with many of their men, the colours having been very much cut up and broken by the enemy's cannon. I extended the 5th about 50 yards, and having previously broken open a house we took some prisoners and found a soldier of the 71st (John Smith), who joined us, though I was suspicious of him as I concluded him to be a deserter. I occupied the top of the house, and planted the regimental colour of the 5th on it. At this moment a galling and heavy fire of musketry opened on me from the right; I detached Captains Clark and Drury with their companies to occupy a church at a short distance, and to break into other houses; one man was killed and two wounded on the top of the house with me in a short time; and the lower part of the house was occupied by assistant-surgeon Bone, where he dressed the wounded. I occasionally detached parties to attack stragglers of the enemy whenever seen, which sometimes occurred when they were endeavouring to run away from the left. About nine o'clock the king's colour of the 5th was planted on the tower of the Church near, and we mutually cheered each other; the firing on the left from the Plaza de Toros, which much galled my position, completely commanding it, was silenced soon after, and it surrendered to the 38th and 87th Regiments. Many prisoners were brought in to me, who I placed on top of the house; and the firing to my left having completely ceased I determined to move to the right and attack a house where a French colour was flying. Having left a sergeant and 12 men to guard the wounded and prisoners, I formed my men in the street before the house I had occupied and advanced up the street to the right, our colour in front. On advancing some distance I received a heavy fire from the tops of houses etc., and in consequence broke open a house on the opposite side of the street to the one we intended to attack, about 150 paces from it, and where it was my intention to retreat should we fail in our attempt. On breaking the door we entered the courtyard, and the men being formed, sallied up the street, but received so heavy of fire, and sustained such loss, that I returned to the above house, and had the wounded brought in. I sent Captain Phillips to take the wounded to the first house, where Mr. Bone was, and to go to the church to Lieutenant-Colonel Davie to request him to send a reinforcement. I then formed my men again in the yard, having had in the above attempt three or four killed, and many wounded; however, my men wishing it, I again determined to attempt to get into the house where the French colour was displayed, and reached a large green door, which resisted our efforts to break it; at the same time the fire of the musketry disabled many of the men, so that another retreat became necessary. I here was struck on the head with a spent ball, which dropped at my feet, without doing me any injury, and received a wound in the left arm, which turned out, contrary to my expectations at the moment, to be slight; we retreated with loss to the courtyard of the former House. I sent Sergeant Maiden with the wounded to Mr. Bone; and observing that the enemy had brought two field-pieces and were firing grape, and also being informed they were endeavouring to surround us, I determined to retire, if possible, to my first position. Having kept the enemy from working their cannon by firing from the door up the street, we retired under a very heavy fire and turned to the right, where I found part of the 36th. Not being able to retreat to my first position as I had purposed, from the grape from the enemy's cannon raking the whole street, I left some killed behind me, and Drummer Downie mortally wounded in the courtyard of the last house. I, however, exercised that discretionary power which in my opinion every officer in danger has a right to do, and knowing I could no further advance the service where I was, I preferred proceeding to where I could more advantageously annoy the enemy, without risking the certain and total destruction of the few gallant fellows with me. Captain Ridge received a contusion on his leg from a musket ball in this last business. I was here joined by some men, and Captain Ridge soon after informed me that a party of the enemy were advancing up the street, and wished to charge them; on which the 5th were formed and advanced up the street, each section extending across it, the front rank of the leading one at the charge. On nearing the enemy we observed them waving their hands, making signals not to fire and an officer with a white handkerchief came forward, as we supposed to surrender them prisoners. I halted, ordered my men to remain formed across the street, with charged bayonets, and to wait, for orders. On the Spanish officer advancing I went up to him, and made him understand he was a prisoner, which he assented to, and shook hands with me. His men followed him close, some mounted with swords in one hand and pistols in the other. I concluded they were all about to surrender, as did Captain Ridge: and I made signs to them to lay down their arms, which not being obeyed, I seized two or three, and threw them to the ground. At this moment, one man presented to me, and I parried the muzzle of his piece with my sword, and one of my men rushed forward and made a thrust with his bayonet at the Spanish officer, he, however, jumped aside, and the bayonet only tore open his clothes. He called out to his men 'No! No!' and I also with difficulty restrained my men, though I suspected some treachery; yet Captain Ridge still thought they were to surrender, and kept back his men. The Spaniards had now accumulated in great numbers, being drawn up in ranks ready at the charge across the street; and the Spanish officer, squeezing my sword wrist, as I understood, asked for my sabre; on which I put the point to his breast and demanded his, which he instantly unbuckled and gave me. I buckled it around my waist, and ordered Mr. Dundas to take him prisoner to Brigadier-General Lumley. At this moment Mr. Harvey, who carried the colour, called out they were trying to seize it; and some men said they were taking their arms; on which I hesitated no longer, but gave the order to charge, when the scoundrels immediately turned and ran, and galloped off as fast as possible, turning down the first streets they came to. The above-mentioned officer and about 12 of his men paid the forfeit of their lives for this treachery. This plan, I found afterwards, of endeavouring under a flag of truce to mask their real design of surrounding our party, had frequently been practiced during this day. I did not pursue the enemy, but determined to break open another house, and establish myself in it; and having borrowed a pickaxe from Lieutenant Lalor of the 36th, was in the act of doing so, when I received an order to form a junction with the right wing of the 5th to move on and join the right wing and retreat to the Plaza de Toros. I accordingly ordered the 5th to move on and join the right wing, and retire to the above position, the enemy saluting us with round and grape on our retreat, which accelerated it without destroying any of our men. We reach the Plaza de Toros about three o'clock; where we found Brigadier-General Sir S. Auchmuty, the 38th and 87th, and were immediately joined by Brigadier-General Lumley with the 36th.[18]

Both sections of the regiment thus retreated northwards along with the 36th Foot and all of them joined up with Auchmuty's troops at the Plaza de Toros, leaving the northern half of the city along the riverbank in Spanish hands.

Across the city Craufurd commanded the light troops – the grenadiers from the various regiments and the men of the Rifle Regiment – in advancing along two streets north of those used by the 45th. Colonel Holland was with Craufurd, and notes what happened in his diary:

In passing through the town with General Craufurd we were not much annoyed, there was little firing at us. We advanced till we came to the waterfront, we then turned to the left [i.e., towards the fort] and fell in with Colonel Pack. He had been very roughly handled, and was retreating to a post called the Residentia some distance on the right. Pack himself had five balls in his clothes, two of which had wounded him slightly. He had lost a great number of officers and men killed and wounded; some were left in the street and a few were with him. They had been shot from the houses.

The 45th Regiment had advanced on our right without opposition and taken possession of the Residentia, a strong building on the skirts of the town. After Colonel Pack had placed his men, he himself with his grenadier company joined us. There was a large cathedral at the bottom of the street by which Colonel Pack had advanced. General Craufurd determined that we should possess ourselves of this and maintain it until we knew the fate of the columns of the left.

We burst open the doors with cannon shots and posted our riflemen all over the top of it that they might drive the Spaniards from the tops of the neighbouring houses, from which they kept up a very hot fire on us. In this, however, they could not succeed. We were still quite sanguine. In the cathedral (which is called Santo Domingo) we found the colours of the 71st which Pack was delighted to have recovered.

On entering the cathedral we had expected to find it full of soldiers, there were however very few. Two monks were badly wounded, one lost his arm, the other was shot in the breast. We collected together all the frightened monks and friars, of whom there were many, and protected them and their altar plate with sentries. It was difficult to prevent plunder, the cathedral was rich and magnificent.

Meanwhile the enemy fired through every hole and window at us, wounding many of our people. We heard nothing of the other troops and the enemy were bringing guns to bear on us. We entered the cathedral about eight, at twelve Liniers sent an aide-de-camp to summons us to surrender, saying the army was defeated and the 88th made prisoners ...

Colonel Pack had left Colonel Cadogan with three companies of the light infantry at a little distance from us, in a post which he did not consider good; we heard no firing in the quarter of it and apprehended he was taken. The Residentia, where the 45th were posted was very distant from us (six squares) and could not hope to gain it under the fire we should be exposed to. We had a hundred wounded men and officers in the cathedral. The enemy were firing grape shot at us, and they were bringing more guns down. We expected soon to have the place about our ears. The troops were alarmed and jaded. At four o'clock General Craufurd consulted Colonels Guard and Pack and Major McLeod [of the 95th] concerning the measures to be pursued, and it was agreed to hold communication with the enemy; a flag of truce was hoisted. This produced a Spanish officer who said our troops were either taken, killed or retreated, that General Liniers was willing to receive us as prisoners of war, but that he would make no other conditions with us. After some conference we sent him back with some proposals, he returned and said General Elio was at the door wishing to speak with General Craufurd, who went out, there appeared a dirty ill-dressed man to meet him who called himself General Elio. He was surrounded by a riotous armed rabble hooting and screeching and whom we expected every moment to fire on us.

Colonels Guard and Pack having agreed with General Craufurd that we were reduced to the necessity of surrendering, General Craufurd settled with this Elio that we should give ourselves up prisoners of war.[19]

Craufurd himself later explained his reasons for surrendering:

Immediately after we regained possession of the building [i.e. Santo Domingo], which was very close to the enemy's main position, a considerable fire was directed from the surrounding houses against all those parts of it from which we could annoy the enemy, and the roof not being flat, it consequently was much less disadvantageous than the buildings of the town generally were. Till 12 o'clock I had no reason to suppose that any considerable disaster had befallen any part of the army, and when about that time a Spanish officer with a flag of truce approached the convent, I flattered myself that the other columns had established themselves as near the enemy's positions as I had; that General Liniers had judged it expedient to capitulate ...

Between 12 and one o'clock a considerable column came into the street on the west side of the convent, apparently with the design to seize a three-pounder which the narrowness of the entrance prevented us bringing in. I immediately ordered all the Rifle Corps from the different stations in the building, and also ordered to be taken down the colours of the 71st, which we had found on our first entrance into the convent, and had displayed on the top of it. While I was thus preparing to evacuate the post, the enemy were on the point of seizing the gun, but were attacked with such vigour and bravery by the grenadier company of the 45th, headed by Colonel Guard, and a small party of light infantry under Major Trotter, and they were compelled to give way. But the fire from the houses close to the convent was so fierce that about 40 men of the 45th were killed and wounded in the course of two or three minutes; Major Trotter was also killed: and finding the impossibility of effecting any thing, I ordered the remainder to retire back into the convent, which we continued to defend till about half past three o'clock ...

I assembled the field officers, Colonel Pack, Colonel Guard and Major McLeod, who commanded the detachment of the artillery corps. I told them that in my opinion to retreat was utterly impossible, that it was completely in the power of the enemy to annihilate the remainder of the brigade, as being then in a very heart of the town with only 600 men. It appeared clear to me, that all the rest of the army had been obliged to retreat, and in the circumstances, after waiting about eight hours on the post I had been ordered to occupy, in expectation of orders I had been taught to believe I should receive, I did not think that the sacrifice of the remainder of the men would either conduce to the honour of his Majesty's arms, or prove in any way advantageous ... I had the entire concurrence and sanction of all the field officers I had named, they being the only persons in the convent acting as such ...

A flag of truce was in consequence held up by us to the enemy, who on their part, in the close of the day, several times approached with flags of truce, but merely for the purpose of enticing us out, and then firing upon us. Our people after this naturally fired on their flags of truce, so that it was a considerable time after we displayed ours that they took any notice of us. At length an officer approached, with whom I had a conversation in the presence of Colonel Pack and I believe of Colonel Guard: and finding that no other terms could be obtained, I thought it better to surrender the remainder of my brigade as prisoners of war. The number which surrendered I believe to have been about six hundred rank and file.[20]

The net result of these attacks was that half of the 45th held the Residentia in the south, and Auchmuty with a much bigger force of the survivors of four regiments in the Plaza de Toros on the northern edge of the city, but neither of these turned inwards to assist in the assaults on the central fortified part of the city. In between, the light troops, half the 45th, and both parts of the 88th Foot, had been forced to surrender. Of the fifteen columns which had attacked, five had surrendered. In addition almost 1,200 officers and men were recorded as being killed, wounded, or missing shortly afterwards.[21]

Some of these were clearly in the captured units, but it is clear that there had been substantial British casualties. Colonel Bourke stated later that he made a return of the 'effective strength' available to Whitelocke after the day's fighting: 5,441 rank-and-file – a loss of about 3,000 men.[22] The Spanish casualties as reported later in a published account in the *Gazeta de Madrid*, were about the same in killed and wounded, but they had lost few prisoners.[23] Since the rival forces were originally about equal in number, the balance was thus heavily in favour of the defenders, who also had more men to begin with.

Whitelocke had stayed at his headquarters during the attack, but he had not made any attempt to find out what was happening, nor had anyone made any attempt to tell him. He appears to have intimidated even Auchmuty into believing he was properly in command, and apparently also believed that the plan would work automatically, without supervision. It was only next day when he received a summons to surrender from Liniers that he had any inkling of things going wrong. Eventually he rode to the Plaza de Toros where the full horror of what had happened was revealed to him.

His options were to renew the assault with the men he had, or to land artillery from the ships to blast his way into the city, as recommended by the senior artilleryman present, Captain Augustus Frazer, though this would result in the destruction of the greater part of the centre of the city; or give up. To add to his problems, the not-unsubtle threat was made that a renewal of the assault would cost the lives of the British prisoners. He knew enough of conditions in the city to find this a credible threat.

Whitelocke gave in. Gower was sent in to see Liniers, and a bargain was struck: the *portenos* would give back their prisoners, both those taken in this attack and the 71st and their fellow marines and sailors taken the year before; and the British would evacuate the estuary, including Montevideo.[24] No one on the British side protested – until later.

Chapter Thirteen

Release

The men who had been captured in the second attack on the city were taken to be held in the Fort, which had been also the scene of Beresford's surrender. The officers were concentrated in one area, the men in another. Colonel Holland describes the officers' situation from his usual lofty vantage point, incidentally providing a good picture of the strains the Spaniards were operating under:

We were ordered to march out without arms. It was a bitter task, everyone felt it, the men were all in tears. We were marched through the town to the fort.

Nothing could be more mortifying than our passage through the streets amid the rabble who had conquered us. They were a dark-skinned people, short and ill made, covered with rags, armed with long muskets and some a sword. There was neither order nor uniformity amongst them.

We were led into the house of Liniers at the fort where we were ushered into a room filled with British officers. We found all those of the 88th who had escaped being killed or wounded. Colonel Cadogan with the officers under him. A General Balbiani, a little waspish fellow but civil, received us and made us sign a parole not to serve against Spain or its allies till exchanged. There were in all between 60 and 70 officers in two large rooms, well guarded. They brought them some biscuit and a lump of flesh smoked and quite beastly; there was nothing but bricks to lie on.

General Balbiani gave General Craufurd and me some supper at his own table; he also gave him a mattress to lie on. I lay on some boards beside him.

July 6. In the morning Balbiani gave General Craufurd and me some chocolate for breakfast. Nothing could be more civil than his treatment, as well as that of the other officers. They appear to live in a dirty uncomfortable manner. Balbiani is second-in-command and quarter-

master-general, he however makes his own bed, wipes the table, etc.
He and his staff sleep all in one room on mattresses, not taking off
their clothes. They seem to consider washing as a very unnecessary
operation and do not frequently shave. They are great smokers of
segars. In general they seem civil, illiterate, ill-educated people. There
are, however, some exceptions, a few of them have read and seen the
world. They have mostly a smattering of French or Latin. Their dress
is deficient, and appears more regulated by fancy than uniformity.

Amongst these people the half were merchants of the place who
had taken arms and received their rank from Liniers. After breakfast
we returned to our fellow prisoners, whom we found enveloped in
smoke. They are become greater admirers of segars than the Spaniards
themselves. They had some very good biscuit brought in for breakfast
for which there was a general scramble.

At three o'clock General Liniers invited all field officers to dinner.
We were met by about an equal number of Spanish. The dinner was
pretty good without any state or display; it was carried off very well.
Liniers is a good-natured talking man and does not seem to possess
talent. At the end of dinner General Gower came in to treat with
Liniers, in consequence of a letter he (Liniers) had sent with a flag of
truce in the morning. They were long closetted together.[1]

If Colonel Holland felt uncomfortable at being made a prisoner by an army he
describes as a 'rabble' with neither 'order nor uniformity', the problem faced
by Colonel Pack was dangerous rather then awkward. His original attack and
capture of the city, his escape from captivity, and his new participation in the
second attack (and at San Pedro), had made him a desperately unpopular
man among the *portenos*. He had to be rapidly sequestered in the Fort,
guarded by three priests. He was eventually smuggled out in disguise and
sent to Whitelocke.

The behaviour and treatment of the ordinary soldiers in the attack was
very different from that of their commanders, and they were accordingly
dealt with in a very different way. A soldier whose memories were recorded
later recalled what happened:

During the time we were charging to the streets, many of our men made
sallies into the houses in search of plunder; and many were encumbered
with it at the time of our surrender. One sergeant of the 38th had made
a longish hole in his wooden canteen, like that over the money drawer in

the counter of a retail shop; into it he slipped all the money he could lay his hands on. As he came out of a house he had been ransacking, he was shot in the head. His full canteen burst, and a great many doubloons ran in all directions on the street. Then commenced a scramble for the money, and about 15 men were shot, grasping at the gold they were never to enjoy. They even snatched it from their dying companions, although they themselves were to be in the same situation the next moment.

[After capture, w]e were all searched, and every article that was Spanish taken from us; but we were allowed to keep the rest. During the search, one soldier, who had a good many doubloons, put them into his camp-kettle, with flesh and water above them; placed all upon the fire and kept them safe. There were about one hundred of us, who had been taken in that church, marched out of prison to be shot, unless were produced a gold crucifix of great value, that was missing. We stood in a large circle of Spaniards and Indians. Their levelled pieces and savage looks gave us little to hope, unless the crucifix was produced. It was found on the ground on the spot where we stood; but it was not known who had taken it. The troops retired, and we were allowed to go back to prison without further molestation.[2]

The prisoners remained in ignorance of the events outside, as did the sailors in the ships in the estuary:

About noon on the 6th the gun boats opened against the castle, whence some heavy pieces were directed at them. This cannonading continued but half an hour, without doing much damage on either side, three or four shots only having struck the castle, one of which dropped in the Spanish general's room.[3]

Colonel Holland was continually astonished at the behaviour of his captors:

July 7. In the morning a pushing Irishmen, a Captain Carrol of the 88th, who speaks Spanish, and contrived through this to get intimate with the Spaniards, seeing me in a dirty uncomfortable state offered to procure me a clean shirt and a razor. This was not a proposal to be neglected. I followed him not knowing where he was leading – to my astonishment he brought me to the room where Liniers, just got out of bed, was dressing; he very coolly told him what he had brought me there for, and Liniers, immediately himself fetched me a razor, shirt, etc., after which he was half an hour looking for a new toothbrush for me. He talked all the time, fast and to little purpose. Whilst I was with him not less than ten ill-looking Spaniards, some military, some civil, passed into his room without ceremony, with loud complaints against the English. Their manner is that of a people on a footing perfectly equal ...

The field officers dined again with Liniers. In the midst of dinner some of the townspeople came to demand Pack, and Liniers had the greatest difficulty in getting them out of the room, there was a vast bustle and confusion, Liniers in a prodigious passion. At night General Balbiani with Liniers' orders disguised Pack like a Spaniard, procured him a horse, and sent him into our lines, accompanied with one of Liniers' aides-de-camp. The people are excessively irritated at him and if not prevented would certainly destroy him. They appear to desire the destruction of us all, and our situation would certainly be most critical if the English were to assault the town.[4]

As soon as the treaty was arranged, perhaps remembering the problems caused by the delay in releasing the men of the 71st, Liniers arranged for the new prisoners to be liberated, once again, of course, without their arms. A man of the 95th remembered being received by Whitelocke himself with a chilling comment:

The evacuation of the country having been agreed to, our release followed accordingly. Then we marched out of prison ... We passed heaps of our own dead, all stripped and unburied. When they arrived at the Retiro, the first person we met was General Whitelocke. 'Gentlemen,' said he, 'I am glad to see so many green jackets together again. I can assure you I have had much uneasiness on your account, for I expected that fellow Liniers to put you all to death.'[5]

The process is detailed by one of the officers held in the Fort:

On Wednesday the 8th the English officers were escorted from the castle to El Retiro. In their way, along the beach, they beheld the melancholy spectacle of a heap of our brave fellows who had fallen in the streets of St. Pedro: they were stripped perfectly naked, and thrown together on this spot. The Spanish officers returned with all the countrymen in our possession; and in the afternoon many of our privates were brought in, and the whole exchange was effected the next day, excepting only such of our wounded as could not be removed with safety. The re-embarkation commenced immediately.[6]

There were considerable inducements to the prisoners to remain in Buenos Aires. Major King had found one of the 71st, whom he called 'John Smith', during the fighting. This would seem to be a soldier of that name who had joined at the Cape – his name may well have been actually 'Johann Schmidt', but the regimental clerk made only a perfunctory stab at correctitude in spelling foreign names. He had joined on 22 March, and is recorded as having deserted on 13 August, the day after Beresford's surrender, when most of the Germans recruited at the Cape joined the Spaniards, but he was also noted as being present early in 1808, back in Ireland, so Major King seems simply to have handed him over to his regiment, who then took him back, assuming he was one of the released prisoners, and carried him home with them without any investigation.

Another near thing was the agonized decision of Donald MacDonald, again of the 71st. This story is told in the *Journal of a soldier of the 71st or Glasgow Regiment*, originally published in 1819 and repeatedly reissued since. This is certainly a vivid tale, though it is certainly not a 'journal'; in fact it is ascribed in some areas – in the Bodleian and British Library catalogues, for example – to Captain Samuel Pococke, no less, as a ghost writer. Now Pococke did keep a journal, and this may be the basis for the account. Yet the soldier is depicted as joining the army in 1806, when Pococke and the 71st were already in South Africa, and it has proved to be quite impossible to identify the soldier from the regimental records, despite the clues the author has scattered in the account – or perhaps they are deliberate misdirections. (A recent identification as Joseph Sinclair may be correct: Sinclair joined as a volunteer from the second battalion, and embarked for the Cape on 14 August; he is said to be from Dunfermline in Fife, and was aged 22, a swarthy man with grey eyes and light brown hair.)

But the real problem is not his precise identity but the truthfulness of the account. It is very likely – the matter will recur – that his story includes elements from a whole series of experiences, not to mention pure invention. Nevertheless it may well be that Pococke – if he was the author – used the memories of a particular soldier. And the story of Donald MacDonald's dilemma and decision, much romanticized, may be true enough:

Donald MacDonald was quite at home all the time we had been in South America. He was a good Catholic, and much caressed by the Spaniards. He attended mass regularly, bowed to all processions, and was in their eyes everything a good Catholic ought to be. He often thought of remaining in Buenos Aires under protection of the worthy priest; he had actually agreed to do so when the order for our release arrived. We were to join General Whitelocke on the next day, after fourteen days confinement. Donald was still wavering, yet most inclined to stay. I sung to him 'Lochaber no more!' the tears started into his eyes – he dashed them off – 'Na, na! I canna stay, I'd maybe return to Lochaber nae mair.' The good priest was hurt at his retracting his promise, yet he was not offended.[7]

There are problems with all this, beginning McDonald's 'fourteen days' confinement', which is impossible – but if Pococke was the author he was not present in Buenos Aires at the time. However, there really was a soldier of that name in the regiment, and these details fit his dilemma. He came from 'Monteith' in Perthshire, which is presumably the Port of Menteith, and he joined the regiment at Callander, close by. He was 25 years old in 1807, dark complexioned, with grey eyes and black hair, and only 5'4" tall. Early in 1808 he is noted as 'a five-year-man', which means he had joined before 1803. The *Journal* depicts him as a Catholic, and as a MacDonald from the Highlands, he could well be. He had been a shoemaker before joining the army.

However, there are other problems with the account, which cast doubt on the very possibility of these events. He is credited with additional pay as from November 1806, which appears to have been granted to some of the prisoners released in August and September 1807. Yet the soldier of the *Journal* did not join the army until after MacDonald had left Britain, and did not reach the River Plate until after the regiment had been captured, so he cannot have met Donald until after the latter was released from his captivity. So the story of singing to him, and persuading him to return to his regiment cannot be true. It may be true as an experience of Donald MacDonald at the hands of another soldier, or even of Captain Pococke, who was eccentric enough as an officer to go out of his way to persuade a man like MacDonald not to desert, and then to have written up his story later, adjusting reality in the process. It may also be that this was a story handed round the regiment after the men's release, and versions of it feature in more than one of their published reminiscences.

The evacuation agreement stipulated that the British would be out of the estuary and out of Montevideo within two months. In that time the prisoners who had been sent to the interior had to be returned. That meant still more walking for them. The journeys they had been on had begun after Beresford's and Pack's escapes and some had been on the move more or less ever since.

Lieutenant Fernyhough's party had joined up with that of Colonel Campbell, which included Sergeant Gavin. Fernyhough's memoirs are a transcript of his diary:

March 30th. Salto. All the officers being now collected, in order to proceed up the country, we commenced our march, coming about fifty waggons drawn by oxen for the use of ourselves and servants to sleep in, as well as for the conveyance of the baggage.

April 2nd. We arrived at Roxa [probably Rojas], another of those frontier jobs. Here we halted, in order to provide ourselves with a little bread; being informed that it was the last place at which we should be able to procure anything, as we were going to enter the Pampas, where should not be seen any habitation for some time. This is generally called 'putting to sea'. After providing ourselves, we proceeded, and soon entered upon the Indian country …

We got information about April 8th of the Indians having declared war against the Spaniards, and that large bodies of the former were near us. This rendered it necessary to alter our route to the northward, and proceeded by the great post road, which runs from Buenos Aires to Cordova. This change afforded us great pleasure; for we had already remonstrated with the Spanish officer, respecting the danger and inconvenience to which we were liable in travelling through the Indian country.

We understood that some of our men had preceded us on this road, and that the Indians proposed putting them to death. We were informed, before leaving Salto, that several had been murdered; indeed, we saw the remains of some by the road side …

April 28th. We arrived at the village of Salta, situated on the banks of the Tercero, about 600 miles from Buenos Aires, and 60 from Cordova, in which district we now were. We had a very different prospect before us to the one we had been accustomed to on the commencement of our journey; instead of an extensive plain, we were in a mountainous country, extremely well wooded.

May 1st. An order arrived from the governor of Cordova, for us to proceed to the valley of Calimuchita, which lies at the foot of the mountains we then had in view. We set out the next morning much disappointed at not being permitted to proceed to Cordova.

May 5th. We arrived at the place called St Ignacio, in the valley of the Calimuchita, after a fatiguing journey of 60 days, living in carts all the time, and during the night sleeping under the canopy of heaven, exposed to all weathers. Such is the consequence of captivity, as such is the fortune of war.

There was only one building in this place, which appears to have been a college, belonging to the Jesuits, dedicated to St Ignacio. Thirty officers were put into this building, and the remainder distributed in different places about the valley. We understood this place was to be our residence till further orders.[8]

Captain Gillespie also reached San Ignacio on 5 May. He had been on the move since 31 March, but he had also had to fend off the attentions of Captain Martinez, who had been sent by Liniers to see if Gillespie still had the list of *portenos* who had shown a willingness to take up Beresford's offer of British citizenship. Gillespie eventually wrote to Liniers on June 6 claiming that the documents were on the line-of-battle ship *Diadem*, but he had in fact hidden them in Buenos Aires before he was dispatched on his travels.[9] So Captain Martinez and Liniers had to do without.

Gillespie's situation was affected once more by an escape. That of Beresford and Pack had sent him to San Ignacio; a little later that of Major Tolley, Lieutenant Adamson, and the sailor Snow sent him off again:

We did not arrive at St. Ignatius until 1 p.m. of the 5th of May ... It was soon found that this spot was too small to contain more than a third of our number ... Accordingly Lieutenant-Colonel Campbell and others were lodged at St. Rosa four miles off; the naval officers were removed to Cordova, and the remainder were permitted to establish where they could in the country.

Soon after these officers disappeared preparations were made to transport the others from the different quarters in separate divisions towards the mountains and one detachment was put in motion towards Rioja early in June ... The Spaniards often tauntingly jeered us, as we had invaded their country in search of gold, we might depend upon having enough of it before we left them; and there is little doubt but that our final destinies would have been placed among the mountains of Potosi.[10]

This possibility was one which many of the prisoners feared, above all that they would be compelled to become slave labourers in the mines. But above all the officers particularly felt the humiliation of their situation. Officers and men recorded their experiences in different ways. They were, of course, as are all prisoners, vulnerable. In some cases their treatment was kindly, as was recalled much later by Private Kennach:

> About this time the governor of the place granted permission to any of the inhabitants, who had a mind, to select one or two of the prisoners if they were agreeable to reside with them. A gentleman, an Old Spaniard, and his lady, a Creole, selected me – for what cause I knew not – but the effect proved good; they carried me along with them to their hospitable home, for so it proved to be. They had no family and were both very delicate, and, so far as I could learn, had few relations; the whole establishment consisted of three slaves – one man and two women – who were very kindly treated. I had now changed from a prison to a comfortable home ...[11]

This treatment was in part the result of Kennach's own humility, but it was also his luck to fetch up with a kindly jailer. At the same time it must be remembered that he (or his ghost writer), was writing forty years after the event, when his memory had clearly acquired a rosy glow, when he had had time to assimilate others' accounts and perhaps internalize them, and he was aiming his account at a certain Victorian sentimentality. Others, however, suffered:

> We had not been here long before two of our people were murdered in a barbarous manner. A man and a woman, belonging to the 71st Regiment, were attacked by assassins; their cries were heard by three of my brother officers and myself, and we ran to the spot, but arrived too late. We found them weltering in their blood ... We learned afterwards, that they were attacked by five or six fellows, with knives; the man defended himself and wife as long as he could, but at last fell through loss of blood.[12]

The difference is, perhaps, the presence of the soldiers and his wife with the group of officers. The officers' assumptions of superiority, which comes through in every account, might be met with the equal Hispanic arrogance of Don Felipe at San Antonio, or by Kennach's 'Old Spaniard', but it would grate on their guards and non-lordly Spaniards. And the man and his wife were the only targets that the locals could reach.

Fernyhough describes his experiences in the west:

> We remained in this vile place, shut in along the mountains, until the middle of July, when an order arrived for our removal 300 miles farther up the country. Now every reasonable person would have thought that we were quite far enough from the scene of action, for it was utterly impossible for us to hear of anything that was going on in the River Plate, as we were already about 700 miles from Buenos Ayres.
>
> According to this last order, we were to be separated, and travel in small parties, and instead of being allowed carts, we were to travel with mules. This arrangement was made on account our route lying to the mountainous district, scarcely passable by carts.
>
> We now began to provide ourselves with a covering of some kind, to shelter us from the clemency of the weather, particularly during the nights; for such were the hostile feelings of the Audiencia towards us, that nothing of the kind was to be allowed from the Spanish government, who seemed determined to treat us with the most unrelenting severity.
>
> [W]e had now and then a battle with our guard. The captain was worthless and unprincipled. Some of his soldiers had a pique against my servant: one night, after we had gone to rest, two or three of them seized him by the hair of his head, and dragged him to the stocks, which were about 40 yards from the house. We heard his cries, and the whole of us immediately turned out in our shirts, armed with good sticks, attacked the guards, about thirty in number, who were armed with swords and muskets, drove them from their post, and released the man. This was a bold enterprise for unarmed prisoners, nevertheless it was the cause of them treating us with more civility in future.
>
> July 15th. The first party of officers set out this day, nine in number, on their march; and a second party (in which I was to go) was to follow in ten days or a fortnight. We now began to despair, and to give up all thoughts of seeing England again: we hoped our country would not forget us, and fondly lingered after our homes. We expected our destination was to the coast of Chili, where we would be lost to the world; and to be sent to the mines was certain death.[13]

Events in the estuary seem to have triggered the successive decisions about the prisoners. Beresford's escape was in part the result of the capture of Montevideo, and these two events together provoked a decision to send the officers further inland, no doubt reaffirmed by the escape of Tolley and Adamson. In July a new decision, to move the prisoners still farther off, was probably in part the result of the threat to Buenos Aires by the arrival of Whitelocke and the new force under Craufurd. However, before they could go very far, the news of the treaty, and the decision to release them arrived:

> The first party had not been gone many days, when a man was dispatched to bring them back. A messenger had arrived from Buenos Ayres with a dispatch, containing an order for the release of all the English prisoners in South America. This order was communicated to us during the night after its arrival. We were almost frantic with delight, congratulating each other on the prospect of revisiting our native land. We only awaited the arrival of the carts, to convey us down to Buenos Ayres, where we were ordered to appear as soon as possible.[14]

The message travelled quickly, to Fernyhough's group about 21 July, but it took another ten days to reach Gillespie. The officers who were with Gillespie reacted, he recalled, in a particular way, which marks them as men of their time:

> While we were assembled at our Saturday's club on the evening of the 31st of July, our landlord at the cottage, Don Ortiz, peeped his head into the door, and then entered into the room with one of his sons, and the captain of the guard, scarcely able to announce to us the glad tidings of our immediate return to Buenos Ayres, our release from captivity, and our embarkation for England ... The whole of us instantly with one accord and with melody in our hearts sang 'God save the King'.[15]

Ensign Gavin does not seem to have been so excited, or grateful, or impressed:

> We lived here very comfortably until the month of August, when we were informed that we should soon be on our way to England; that the British government had sent out a force of 10,000 men under a General Whitelocke, who was obliged to surrender with his whole army to the Spaniards, and that one of the articles of capitulation was our release.

We laughed at the idea, as we took Buenos Aires with about 1,000 men and could have marched all over Spanish America with 10,000 …

On arrival at Buenos Ayres we were marched along the river side and embarked in boats for Monte Video. We could observe that the fortifications of the town were much improved from the time we took it. On our arrival at Monte Video we were inspected by General Whitelocke, and a motley crew we were, without arms, and mostly dressed in nankeen jackets and trousers.[16]

Private Kennach's experience was more personal, and perhaps more painful but also perhaps more the product of his imagination. It paralleled that of Donald MacDonald, which lends a certain verisimilitude to the story of the Perthshire shoemaker; on the other hand Kennach may be repeating in a new version the story of MacDonald, which was surely going through the regiment after 1807. Nevertheless here is Kennach's version:

[B]efore being committed to sit at table it became necessary to instruct me in the principles of Christianity. Accordingly a padre, their confessor, attended the house daily for some time; he commenced with telling me that the British were fine looking people, good soldiers and seamen, but withal they were a nation of heretics, and enemies of Christianity. He then pointed out the beauties of the Roman Catholic religion, and after enumerating a host of saints concluded by telling me that none would be eternally saved but Roman Catholics. I was then instructed to say the Lord's Prayer, creed, ave Maria, and also to make the sign of the cross. I thought there was no harm in learning the Lord's Prayer and creed in the Spanish language. After I had learned these different articles which I soon did I was declared fit to be baptized and enrolled among Spanish Christians.

I had by this time by study and practice learned a considerable part of their language. I was now to be baptized, take the oath of allegiance, become a Catholic and a subject of Spain. I told them I had taken the oath of allegiance to the king of Great Britain, that I was bound to maintain his laws and nothing would induce me to betray my country. They told me to destroy the principles of Protestants was to build up the true church and serve God; I told them that the people of Britain had liberty to think and choose any principle of religion they may deem best and that there were many principles of religion in Britain and that all expected to be happy.

I had now lived six months with this excellent family and had everything the heart could wish, and had acquired some knowledge of the customs and manners of the people; and I have every reason to believe that the people with whom I lived were interested in my future happiness and prosperity. They had a niece, a pretty brown lady, who frequently visited the house and seemed to be much interested in my welfare; she told me that her uncle had no family, how he had a large landed property and in the event of his dying would fall into the hands of those who had already too much, and that from her own knowledge she was certain that by me taking the oath of allegiance I would undoubtedly receive part of her uncle's property. This was no doubt a snare laid for me but I was prepared to avoid it.

By this time the governor of the place had received intelligence of the defeat of the British in an attempt to retake Buenos Ayres, and, at the same time agreeably to the articles of capitulation, to send home the British prisoners as soon as possible; this brought matters to the point. The domestic circle was formed, the old padre sat president, I was told the attempt to take Buenos Ayres by the British had failed, how their general and his army were made prisoners, and how foolish it was for me to attempt to run the chance of a long and dangerous passage to Britain when I had it in my power to live in peace and comfort. I told them I had only one choice left. My kind benefactor and his amiable lady then told me that all I had to do to make me happy was to take the oath of allegiance to his Catholic Majesty, be baptized and become a subject of Spain and they would share their property with me and everything else I could wish.

I thanked him kindly and told them I had sworn allegiance to one sovereign and that it was out of my power to betray my country. The temptations to remain in South America were very strong, it took great effort to resist them and I must confess I was more than once like King Agrippa with Paul, I was almost persuaded to become a Spaniard.

The prisoners were very healthy, only one died and the inhabitants actually became much attached to them, so much so that they supplied them gratis with every kind of fruit the place afforded, they insinuated themselves so far into the favour of the prisoners as to cause a great number of them to desert and betray their country.

I now parted with my kind benefactors, Don Pedro Bertaran and his amiable lady, Maria Gracia, whom I sincerely loved; and now after a lapse of 42 years I still remember them with a grateful heart. We were all assembled and commenced a long and dreary march across Lapampa, nothing extra occurring and after a march of 28 days safely arrived at Buenos Ayres, dropped down La Plata in lighters and went on board British transports in Monte Video, set sail for Old England, the land of liberty ...[17]

It took a long time for these distant prisoners to return to the estuary, and some, of course, never did return. The problem of deserters was always present in the expedition. After the return of Whitelocke's expedition from Buenos Aires to Montevideo, investigations and recriminations began, and the collapse of morale produced an outbreak of sickness:

Some few days after our return to Monte Video ... a general court-martial was ordered to assemble, for the trial of the infamous characters who had so basely deserted to the Spanish standard, at the moment the bodies of their slaughtered comrades strewed the streets. Above fifty of these wretches had been given up by Liniers, to the great satisfaction of the whole army, the British prisoners having met with more insolence and abuse from their countrymen serving with the Spaniards when we entered the town than from the country rabble. The railings and scurrility of these vagabonds, particularly towards the officers, gave offence to the very Spaniards.

The hardships which had been endured now broke out in disorders among the troops. Dysenteries and fevers were increasing to that degree as to crowd all the hospital ships, the hospital on shore being appropriated to the wounded, who in general were doing very well.[18]

These expellees, however, were clearly the men the Spaniards did not want. Generally they were quite happy to give deserters refuge. Desertion had continued all through the British presence in the Plate area. Ignoring for a moment the prisoners of Beresford's expedition, and looking only at the period since Auchmuty arrived, the cavalry lost nine men by desertion under Auchmuty's command, until the May muster, and the infantry twenty. Meanwhile the navy lost, with fewer men than the army, no less than eighty men – and it was probably more difficult to get away from the ships than from the army. In the months of action which followed, recorded in the musters of June and July, the cavalry lost another nine men, and the infantry only five. The navy lost another fifty. (Whitelocke claimed that 170 had deserted before the end of June, though this may be an exaggeration.)

The navy's losses in these six months were spread over the whole fleet, but it is noticeable that the bought-in ships at the Cape (*Rolla*) and at Montevideo (*Dolores, Paz*) leaked a greater proportion of their men. All these were small ships, but between them they lost thirty-seven men, more than a quarter of all those who 'ran'. The reason, of course, is that these men had been transferred from other ships and the captains had taken the opportunity to rid themselves of their worst characters.

In the period covered by the August and September musters, which included the attack in Buenos Aires and the return to Montevideo, desertion was somewhat greater from the navy – sixty-six men ran – and very much greater from the army. The men by now had greater opportunities to desert, and, with the knowledge that the whole force was going to be shipped away by early in September, this was their last chance. They must also have been aware that any deserters, especially those with some skills, would be welcomed by the Spaniards. The cavalry lost twenty-two men, almost all from the 17th Light Dragoons (nine men) and the 9th Dragoon Guards (twelve men). The infantry lost over one hundred men in that time, most of whom fled from four regiments, the 5th, 36th, 38th, and 45th. In fact, desertion was clearly very much a unit matter, as it had been all along.

During Auchmuty's time in command (January to May) only three of the regiments had lost men – mainly the 87th – and only two of the cavalry regiments. The 40th, 54th, and 71st, and the 21st Light Dragoons lost no men at all. This remained the pattern in June and July, though two men now deserted from the 47th. The reason is partly that the regiments which lost few or no men tended to be already low in numbers – only a hundred or so in the 71st, for instance, since the greater part of the regiment were prisoners – but it was also a function of command. The constant desertion of men from the 87th was surely a failure of the officers of that regiment. Some of the smaller units in the navy also tended to hold on to their men better than the larger ships, no doubt because of the greater intimacy of life on board, but also because the smaller ships were much busier in the shallow waters of the estuary – that is, unless they were the discards who were sent to man the bought-in ships. But in the last two months (July – September) almost every unit lost men. The exceptions were the technical units (engineers, artillery), the 6th Dragoon Guards, the 89th Foot – and once again the 71st. Altogether over 300 men deserted from army and navy between February and the departure of the expedition in September.[19]

The return of the prisoners from the interior took a long time. They arrived at Montevideo in the midst of preparations for departure, and saw only confusion. Ensign Gavin recalls:

One of the articles of capitulation was that Monte Video should be evacuated by every British subject on a certain day, and the confusion on that day was beyond description – hundreds of merchants who came with all sorts of merchandise from England lying on the beach with their goods and could not obtain a passage. The troops were, of course, provided for in the men-o'-war and transports.

The writer of this was sent, on the day of evacuation, by Colonel Tolley, on shore to purchase articles for the regiment, and brought a man with $2,000 on his back for the purpose; but the Spaniards, conceiving that it was plunder, detained us, and would probably have murdered us but for the interference of one of general Whitelocke's staff, who explained to them our mission.[20]

Captain Gillespie rather gleefully watched the final panic:

We arrived at Monte Video upon the 6th of September where all was in a state of confusion, owing to a recent order that had been issued for the re-embarkation of the English merchants and their goods, which was most unfortunately premature, for even until the last, venturers were hurrying down from the Upper Country to have made their purchases, as the whole of the interior was in the utmost want of European manufactures from the long suspension of all commercial intercourse with it. As we were all in a destitute situation with regard to money and clothes, General Whitelocke humanely gave directions for an immediate payment of bat and forage money to us.[21]

John Mawe, the civilian geologist, had accompanied the expedition against Buenos Aires in July, also watched with a certain detachment:

In the beginning of September 1807 we had just embarked for the voyage (to Río de Janeiro) when an order for the immediate evacuation of Monte Video by our troops was unexpectedly issued. As it had been generally believed that a prolongation of the time for giving up the place had been agreed on, the greatest hurry and confusion prevailed in embarking the troops as well as the baggage of individuals. About midday the whole was on board; a signal gun was then fired for the Spanish troops to enter and about three in the afternoon we had the mortification to behold their flag hoisted on the ramparts of this important military and commercial depot, which the British forces had a short period before so bravely and dearly won.[22]

General Whitelocke had done well to organize the evacuation – but then administration was his forte. We have no indication of his feelings, though his habitual anger is often mentioned. In his report he took refuge in the formal words which disguised all emotion:

Having arranged with the Spanish officer sent to assume the government of the place, that the troops should not embark until the wind permitted the ships to leave the harbour, evacuation was carried into effect with order and regularity, and the whole of the fleet, anchored in the roads yesterday evening, from whence it will sail to England whenever the ships are completely with water, for which purpose they are about to move up the river.

Having in my letter of the 23rd July expressed my belief that no exertion would be wanting on the part of the Spanish general towards a due fulfillment of the treaty by expediting the march of the prisoners from the interior, I now beg leave to report to your lordship that at different periods subsequent to the date of that letter, the whole of the officers taken with General Beresford arrived at Monte Video, with 449 men of the 71st Regiment, and 126 of the St Helena Corps, together with marines, seamen and merchants (in all 1089), as well as the whole of the wounded left in the hospital at Buenos Ayres.

The remainder of the original number captured at the time of General Beresford's surrender were stationed so far up the country as to not admit of their arrival previous to the expiration of the period of the treaty, and after making allowances for the numerous desertions which have occurred, arising from the strong temptations which the country offers, and the connections formed by individuals, I cannot estimate this number above 200 men, I did not think myself justified in detaining the army in this country for so comparatively thriving an object, when its services might be calculated upon in Europe, in consequence of my having already been enabled to report that nothing was likely to occur to protract the period of the evacuation, as specified in the treaty.

A large transport has been left to convey to England this last division of the prisoners with proper officers to take charge of them; and I have left instructions with the hostages (Captains Hamilton of the 5th and Carrol of the 88th Regiments) to expedite as much as possible the embarkation and sailing of these people from Buenos Ayres immediately on their arrival from the interior.[23]

Later, in his court-martial – he was, of course, found guilty on most charges – he explained his failure in these terms, which may also stand for his justification for concluding the treaty of evacuation:

I expected on my arrival to find a large proportion of the inhabitants prepared to aid our views; accurate information for the arrangement of future operations arising from friendly intercourse with them, and a body of cavalry formed, or at least the means of forming it. I found a country completely hostile, in which we could not by conciliation or interest procure a friend, either to assist or advise us, or afford the slightest information; horses, but no adequate means of feeding them; and which therefore, though well adapted for the armed inhabitants who turn them out when tired, and take others, could not, until time and possession had matured a new system, form an effective body of cavalry ...

The inhabitants becoming every day more and more exasperated, any attempts to maintain a footing in the country would be attended with the complete destruction of the whole force remaining in the country. To attempt keeping Monte Video we must have turned out 14,000 inhabitants: a measure utterly impossible in its execution, and a deviation from the spirit of my instructions. The court will perceive that the instructions I received were, in the strongest manner, to avoid any oppression of the inhabitants, which would expose us to the consequences of their hatred. I felt, therefore, satisfied that there were considerations of sufficient weight, in a military as well as a political point of view, to induce me to abandon a position which was only to be retained by the disposing of the inhabitants in a manner revolting to humanity and the law of nations. On the other hand I was anxious for the preservation of the lives of our brave troops in the town, and having no other means or hope of procuring their surrender but by agreeing to leave the Plata.[24]

Chapter Fourteen

The Consequences of the Invasions
in the River Plate

When the British fleet dropped down the Plate estuary from Montevideo in September 1807 it took with it the great majority of the soldiers and sailors and marines who had been captured in August the previous year as well as those released from Buenos Aires after the second attack. But not all of them by any means. A considerable number of the wounded men were too ill to be moved and they remained at Buenos Aires for the present. And, as the figures noted in the previous chapter show, there were others who had voluntarily remained behind (or 'deserted') as well.

There were still more men who had not yet been collected. These were the men, captured in 1806, who had not been able to get from their places of detention in the interior to Montevideo or Buenos Aires in time to join the evacuation. For them, and for the recovering wounded, a ship remained in the estuary until the end of the year, and men were collected as they arrived and could be moved. As a result the precise British losses could not be calculated until long after the evacuation was completed – and in fact no attempt to carry out such a calculation seems ever to have been made. Perhaps this was part of a collective British decision to forget the whole matter.

General Whitelocke had begun to send off the soldiers as soon as he could. He determined to retain a substantial force so as to be able to threaten the Spanish authorities if they seemed likely to break the agreement. But everyone on the Spanish side was only too pleased to see the British forces leave; they complied wholly with the agreement, though this tacitly permitted deserters to remain if they wished to do so – and were worth keeping. And they cared for the wounded devotedly.

Spanish nerves cannot have been soothed, however, by the arrival of yet another convoy with British troops. This was the force, mainly consisting of the 89th Foot, which had originally set out with Whitelocke in February.

It had had a desperately slow passage, having had great difficulty in getting out of the doldrums, and finally arrived, in great want of food and water, on 24 July.[1]

Whitelocke and Murray rapidly organized the onward passage of the 89th, which, along with the 47th, was to go to India. The 21st Light Dragoons and 87th Foot were similarly quickly sent off to the Cape, convoyed by Admiral Stirling, who was to take up his post of commander-in-chief of the Cape Station at last.[2] This removed over 2,500 troops from the estuary, and made provisioning the rest a little less difficult.

Provisions and watering were in fact Whitelocke's main problem, and he had to demand supplies from the Spanish authorities. The ships voyaging north back to Britain were poorly supplied even so, and in some cases were in a very bad condition. One ship, the *Princesa*, carrying members of the 71st Foot, sank on the voyage, and another, also with men of the 71st, was wrecked on the Cornish coast in the winter storms. And all the time men continued to die of sickness and of the effects of their wounds. Seven sailors out of the warships died on the voyage home; but 138 soldiers also died, nearly half of them from the 88th Foot, though all the infantry regiments lost men. And twenty-three sailors managed to desert as well.[3]

For months the record keepers of the 71st Regiment could not decide what had happened to many of the men who had been in captivity. Some men had died in the fighting at Buenos Aires back in August 1806, others had died in captivity, or on the voyage back to Britain. Other men had suffered so badly by their experiences that they were rendered unfit for further service, and were discharged when the regiment landed at Cork in December and January; twelve men were thus cast off to fend for themselves. And when the clerks wrote out their pay records they found eleven men in the regiment who didn't appear in their earlier records. These are listed coyly with a note in pencil that 'these men are not found previously in either battalion'. They were men who had either been filched from other regiments, or who had become mixed in with the 71st and had chosen to stay with it, or who had perhaps – though no record exists – been officially transferred. It is, however, suggestive that the names of all these men strongly imply Scottish ancestry. Their Christian names included Alexander (2), James (4), Dougal, and Robert (and three Johns); their surnames include Anderson, Steel, Craig, Johnson, Lindsay, Macaulay, and McCraw (and two Browns and a Bradley). A tentative suggestion might thus be made that a quiet poaching process had gone on, whereby Scots in other regiments had been persuaded to transfer themselves to a Scottish regiment.[4]

It is quite certain that the 71st had need of more men. The regiment's losses in killed and men discharged – and a few had also been left at the Cape and at St Helena for various reasons – amounted to almost ten per cent of its original strength, but its main loss was in men who had been left in South America. In January 1808 no less than 300 men were noted as being left there – out of an original strength of something over 700. In the next month 136 of these men arrived in Ireland and rejoined the regiment, having been on ships which were slower than the main convoy, but that still left 174 men who remained in South America, and they are so noted in the records. By March most of them were clearly regarded as having deserted, though even then not all of them were so branded. But there is no sign that any of these men ever turned up to rejoin.

So, in addition to the 306 soldiers of other regiments and the sailors of the Royal Navy ships who had deserted, the 71st contributed 174 men to the increase in the population of the Viceroyalty of Buenos Aires. The accepted assumption in the regiment, judging by the published histories, is that these men were mainly the Germans who had been recruited as 'volunteers' at the Cape: 'not more than thirty-six individuals were found to swerve from their duty and allegiance to the king and country', as one history published in India in 1908 put it, echoing an account in 1876, which simply said that 'few' failed to return. By 1952 this had become 'only thirty failed to rejoin and these nearly all Irish Roman Catholics or Dutch-Germans captured at the Cape'.[5]

None of these figures and guesses is even remotely correct, except in the recognition of the desertion *en masse* of the Germans of the Waldeck Regiment who had been recruited at the Cape – 'volunteers' is hardly an accurate description of the process. Seventy-three of those who remained in South America were men who had joined the regiment between January and April – and so at the Cape. That does not, of course, include Jacob Eckarts, the man shot for desertion in Buenos Aires three days before the whole regiment was captured. Eckarts may be taken as a typical example of the experience of these men. He had been virtually forced to enlist by being imprisoned in a damp and crowded battery at Cape Town for a month; he did not actually enlist until 19 February, after being captured at the latest on 21 January; he then spent forty-six days in the regimental hospital before he was carried, surely unwillingly, to South America along with the rest of the regiment. He had thus deserted as soon as he could. Shooting such a man was hardly calculated to encourage loyalty among his fellow enlistees. Those whose date of desertion is noted seem to have done so on 13 August, the day after their capture, though a few, like Eckarts, had gone earlier. Most of the Cape recruits had thus remained 'loyal' until the end of the fighting, but had then changed sides as soon as the *portenos* had recovered their city and made them prisoner. It is unlikely that the regiment missed them, though they did provide a useful excuse to account for the much larger number who deserted, especially since no serious count of those who left was made.

For that still leaves a hundred men who deserted and who were not enlisted at the Cape. They were, therefore, men who had been members of the regiment when it had left Britain, and this is confirmed by their names, for only one of them is a foreigner (Neptune Vero, no doubt an Italian who had wandered abroad). The rest all have British or Irish names. Applying the same criteria of origin as in Chapter 2, I calculate that thirty-one of these deserters were Scots, twenty-four were Irish, and the rest (forty-three men) are impossible to classify in such a way, though it is probable that most were Scottish or Irish; it is about the same proportion of unclassifiables as in the whole regiment, but the proportion of those who can be definitely identified as Scots and Irish among the deserters is rather different. In the regiment as a whole there were twice as many Scots as Irish, whereas among the deserters, the numbers are almost equal. The attraction for Irish Catholics of living in a country where they could worship freely, and perhaps even be treated as equal citizens – and be free of their greedy Protestant landlords – can be adduced as one likely explanation.

This must also have worked with some of the Scots as well. As it happens, however, the origins of a few of the Scotsmen is known. Two of them came from Edinburgh, three from Glasgow, and two from Lanarkshire, and one each from Stirling and Aberdeen, all, that is, from towns which were very largely Protestant in population; the few Irishmen whose origins are known (two from Tyrone, one each from Roscommon and Armagh), could be either Protestant or Catholic, but the odds are surely on the latter. Given the origin of the regiment it must be assumed that most of the forty-three whose origins cannot be assumed from their names were also Irish or Scots; a few were no doubt English, but the low proportion of identifiable Englishmen in the regiment as a whole (five per cent) implies that there were unlikely to be more than five of them among the deserters.

So the population of viceroyalty of Buenos Aires was augmented by another hundred men from Britain and seventy also from Germany; this was added to the merchants and ex-transportees who had been discovered living in the city by the regiment when it first captured the place. In addition there were 300 other deserters from ships and other regiments, and still more among the sailors and marines who were captured with Beresford and the 71st, who cannot be clearly identified. In a population of something under half a million for the whole viceroyalty from Patagonia to the borders of Peru, this number of additions – about 500 altogether – may not seem significant. But over half of these inhabitants were Indians, and only a quarter of those of European descent were men – perhaps 50,000. The deserters were concentrated very largely within Buenos Aires, with perhaps a few in other towns. Further, they were all men, and generally young. They amounted thus to about one per cent of the male *portenos*, and a substantial addition to the population of young, productive males.

What effect these men had on their new host society is difficult to estimate. Anglo-Argentine historians tend to magnify the influence, Hispano-Argentines to minimize it. But they clearly had some effect. They were all trained soldiers and sailors, for a start, and there was to be plenty of employment for such men in the next decades. Skilled sailors could find employment in the waters of the River Plate and its contributory rivers. Many of the soldiers had civilian skills; of the thirteen who remained behind and whose civilian occupations are known, four were weavers and five had been labourers, and others were a stocking-maker, a nailor, a painter, and a 'carver's gilder'; a British visitor in 1809, Thomas Kidder, remarked that 'boots and shoes are tolerably made here by English deserters from Whitelocke's army'.[6]

Forty years later Irishmen were working as labourers in the Argentine at a wage which would quickly provide them with the resources to set up in independence.[7] The demand was for 'hands' as much as skills, but skills were highly valued, and as former soldiers and sailors they were adaptable and will have picked up other skills than those they admitted to on enlistment. They were also, of course, trained to arms, and this was to be a valuable skill in the next fifty years in this region. This small group of men could have an effect on their new host country out of all proportion to their numbers.

They would also arrive with their own 'mind-set', which in many cases would emphasize personal independence and individuality. They were men who had, in most cases, volunteered to join the British army. Many of the Scots had done so at the bidding of their clan chief (as with the Sutherlanders of the 93rd), others at the insistence of the magistrates, still more at the bidding of economic deprivation, but they had in most cases deliberately chosen the life of a soldier. The sailors, of course, were likely to have been pressed, and this must be one of the main explanations for their greater willingness to desert. And now they had all volunteered in a different way, by making the individual decision to cut themselves off from that army or navy. Many of them, probably most, were not in general typical of Wellington's denigratory comment of the 'scum of the earth'. The Scottish Highland regiments, for example, eschewed the lash as a punishment, which indeed appears to have been much less used than in many other units.[8]

The influence of these men would be overwhelmingly, in political terms, for independence from Spain. At least two of them, William Brown, an Irish sailor, and Peter Campbell, one of Beresford's men (though not traceable in the later records of the 71st), played prominent roles in the independence wars. Brown is reckoned to be the founder of the Argentine navy, and for a time was Military Governor of Buenos Aires (as Beresford had been);[9] Campbell, also said to be Irish, commanded a river fleet on the Rio Parana for a time, and was later employed – by James P. Robertson or his brother – to control a large estate, which he did largely by displaying greater ferocity and skill with a knife and sabre than his underlings, and victims.[10]

Some of the merchants who came out so eagerly from Britain at the broadcast news of Popham's original conquest in 1806 remained in South America, and some of them survived and prospered. James P. Robertson – Campbell's employer – was joined by his brother, and became established in a profitable estate, and as a major trader with Paraguay.[11] James Paroissien developed an ability to manufacture gunpowder – a skill of surpassing importance in the wars which followed – and accompanied General San Martín in his crossing of the Andes and his victories over the Spanish imperial troops in Chile and Peru.[12]

Above all, however, the British attacks in the River Plate established the area in the minds of merchants in Britain as a likely place in which to invest or to trade, building on the old notion of South America as the place of wealth. There was a substantial emigration of Britons to Buenos Aires in the next decades. The later development of the Argentine as part of Britain's 'informal empire' in the second half of the nineteenth century is in part due to the exploits of Popham's and Beresford's expedition, and paradoxically, to the success of the *portenos* in defeating the British attacks.[13]

The direct effect of individuals, whether merchants or deserters, on the Argentine is thus difficult to discern, and recourse has been had to such historians' inventions as the 'mind-set' of the population and the 'informal empire' of Britain to estimate the overall result. But there is one aspect which can be stated clearly; the independence of the communities of the River Plate was very largely a direct result of the British invasions. When in 1806 the Viceroy Rafael de Sobremonte left Buenos Aires city for the interior of his viceroyalty, he did the right thing from a military point of view, for he was responsible for the whole of his huge viceroyalty, not just the city, and his remaining military forces were largely in the interior. But that was not how the *portenos* saw it. Nor were the Montevideans overjoyed, when they were besieged, to see the viceroy leave the city before the siege began, and who was even then unable to protect or relieve them. That is, his military moves were sensible, but not politically intelligent.

But the effects of the British attacks went much further. Sobremonte had used the royal forces to face Beresford at Quilmes and was beaten; he went to Córdoba to collect more royal forces; at Montevideo he again commanded royal forces. But the recovery of Buenos Aires, the defence of Montevideo, and the defeat of Whitelocke's attack on Buenos Aires were all conducted by local militia forces. It was not just the viceroys who were discredited but the whole royal regime. After that the news of the collapse of that self-same regime in the Spanish homeland was only confirmation of its powerlessness. The arrest of Sobremonte by the government of Liniers and Alzaga in Buenos Aires, and later the expulsion of other viceroys, was a clear sign of the complete loss of political authority by the royal government, and this became obvious above all when no protests resulted.

The removal of Sobremonte in February 1807 had left Buenos Aires having to defend itself with the threat of a new British attack ever present. It did get help from other parts of the viceroyalty, but the main effort was made by the citizens. Many years later the city government made a collection of evidence of the help it received; it is of limited historical value, being largely anecdotal, but it shows men from Peru and Chile coming to assist in the defence of the city, as well as some other towns within the viceroyalty.[14] The intendant of Paraguay brought 3,000 men to assist, leading the British to believe that the Indians had been mobilized against them.[15]

Liniers became interim viceroy in place of Sobremonte, and joined with Alzaga and Elio and the men from the interior in fighting Whitelocke's invasion. But the defeat of that invasion and the almost immediate removal of the British from the whole region also removed the pressure from outside which had compelled these various leaders and groups to work together. Liniers and Alzaga were effectively the leaders respectively of the *criollos* and the *peninsulares*, and these two groups each had the loyalty of part of the army. Liniers could count on the volunteers and militia whom he had recruited; Alzaga looked to the old royal army regiments who had not only lost their battles, but were much the fewer in numbers. In the next year or so political intrigues centred on Alzaga's attempts to secure the disbandment of the volunteers, but these failed, and then news came of the French invasion, with the deposition of King Carlos IV and Prince Fernan.

The former governor of Montevideo, Ruiz Huidobro, had been captured with the city and sent to Britain, but he was released and returned to Spain when an alliance of the Spanish insurgents and Britain was made. In the Plate the French invasions of Spain provoked further divisions. Viceroy Liniers had the loyalty of the provincial intendants, more or less, who proclaimed Fernan (Carlos having formally abdicated), but Fernan was out of communication. Liniers advocated waiting to see what would happen, which was only a way of allowing intrigues to go ahead. In Montevideo the new governor was Javier de Elio, who was a fervent royalist; in Buenos Aires one group suggested that Ferdinand's sister Carlota, wife of the King of Portugal and now living in Brazil, be imported as a constitutional monarch, but this idea collapsed in face of Carlota's absolutist ideas and unpleasant personality. Alzaga's group now became advocates of independence, but with themselves in control; the *criollos*, now including the Carlotists, also shifted towards independence, but were not at all willing to see the *peninsulares* ruling.

On 1 January 1809 the Alzaga group, in electing a new Cabildo for the coming year, attempted to impose a new junta as the provisional provincial government. They were guarded and supported by three of the Spanish regiments of the old royal army, who occupied much of the Plaza Mayor, together with a selected civilian crowd of supporters. But the intervention of the *Patricios* regiments, commanded by Cornelis de Saavedra, rescued Viceroy Liniers as he was about to give in to the Cabildo's demands.

Meanwhile Ruiz Huidobro had been sent out by the Galician *Junta* as the next viceroy, but he was not accepted, either at Buenos Aires or at Montevideo, because the *Junta* itself did not have any acceptable legitimacy. Then the *Junta* of Seville sent out the Marquis de Cisneros, who *was* accepted as viceroy and replaced Liniers. He held the office for a little over a year, but he also attempted to reduce the military power of the *criollos*, and was then deposed and expelled by another *coup d'état* in Buenos Aires.

This was the Revolution of 25 May 1810. The Cabildo was pushed into converting itself into a wider assembly, a *cabildo abierto*, in which the future was debated, with the majority eventually voting to expel Viceroy Cisneros and establish a governing *Junta* in his place – though the decision was taken by only a few hundred men, who were no more representative than Alzaga's Cabildo's attempted *coup*. But the *Junta* when it was formed included the viceroy, so that night the *Patricios* regiments visited and carefully threatened every Cabildo member they could find, so the new *Junta* came to include only *criollos*, with Saavedra as president.

The independence of Buenos Aires therefore was a slow process, taking from 1806 to 1810 in its narrowest terms. It had been resisted by those loyal to Spain – the viceroys, the bishop, many of the *peninsulares* – but they had little armed strength to support them. From then on the *peninsulares'* royal army was always outnumbered by the *criollo* militia and the volunteers. And, as in all revolutions, it was the armed strength of the victorious party which allowed it to prevail.

It had all begun, in an overt sense, with the first British invasions, but that only brought out into the open a long simmering desire for change, which the royal government could not or would not meet. The 'New Army' of volunteers and militia was recruited to defend the city when the royal army failed, but was then seized by the conflicting parties, divided and politicized. Thomas Kidder in the diary of his visit, which began in 1808, noted that:

> I have been greatly sorry to see numbers of Englishmen wearing the Spanish uniform. I have not had opportunity to ascertain satisfactorily the actual number, and therefore hope that 2,000, the number I have been told are in garrison here, and in quarters in Buenos Aires, greatly exceeds the truth. They have been tempted by the large wages given, which amount to $16 a month, to a private a very large allowance in a country where the necessities of life are cheaper than in almost any other. They are mostly very fine men, and have the grace to show some embarrassment at facing the English officers.[16]

It would seem that, even if the figure of 2,000 is wrong, some at least of the British deserters had joined in the local politics.

The 25 May revolution was, however only one stage in the process; it then became necessary to defend the revolution. Not long afterwards, Liniers, who was already suspect both because of his French origin and because of his loyalty to Spain, was detected as being involved in a scheme to return to a royalist government, and was shot.[17]

The removal of Cisneros from the viceroyalty was also not accepted elsewhere. He had been acceptable in other sub-provinces, where the intendants had operated in the name of Fernan VII. Several of those provinces of the viceroyalty reacted to Cisneros' arrest by refusing to accept *portenos* orders. Montevideo reactivated its anti-*portenos* feelings, and embarked on a long and violent period in its history, in which Jose Gervasio Artigas,

Sobremonte's old *gaucho* antagonist, dominated large areas of the Banda Oriental by his command of the horsemen of the plains. It also suffered an episode of Brazilian rule, until the city and its hinterland gained recognition of its independence as the Republic of Uruguay.[18]

An earlier outbreak of revolutionary fervour in Upper Peru, the later Bolivia, where the silver came from, had been suppressed by forces from Buenos Aires with much bloodshed. This was partly because in many areas the revolution there took a socially radical turn, so that the conservatives of all sorts, *criollos* and *peninsulares*, united to destroy it. But the May Revolution in Buenos Aires in turn destroyed that conservative consensus. A new revolution in Upper Peru broke out, was again attacked from the south, but this time the local royalist forces defeated the military force from Buenos Aires. Paraguay also refused to accept *portenos* authority after the May Revolution and fell under the rule of the first of its long sequence of dictators.[19]

Thus, almost as soon as its independence was achieved, the old viceroyalty broke into pieces. And meanwhile, Britain was assisting the Spanish insurgents in the homeland, and so theoretically hostile to the new revolutionary government. But markets were valuable in the time of Napoleon's Continental system, and the revolutionary government rejected overtures by Napoleon, who at one point sent the Marquis of Sassenay as envoy with a view to establishing the area as, at the least, a French protectorate, and its local enemies were equally insistent on rejecting him.[20] Spain did manage to make an attempt to recover its power in the estuary, but no Spaniard could bring himself to make any concessions to local feelings or aspirations, so all such attempts failed. The anti-*portenos* provinces thus gained independence mainly by default, though Buenos Aires itself took that independence by its own efforts.

The resort to violence, however, first in the city, then in the outlying regions of Upper Peru and Paraguay and Uruguay, and in the suppression of actual or suspected counter-revolutionary plots, steadily reduced the ability of the city to count on the loyalty of other sub-provinces of the old viceroyalty. It became a routine *portenos* matter to send out armed expeditions against dissidents, with the result that it was another half century before settled government emerged, and then it had to be a fairly loose federal system. As usual the revolution took unexpected turns. For a quarter of a century after the British invasions the men who had resisted them were the political leaders – Saavedra, Pueyrredon and others – but in the end the city fell under a military dictator, Manuel Rosas, which, given the military turn of events, as provoked by the British invasions, is not surprising.

The effect of the British attacks was therefore first, to militarize the population of Buenos Aires and Montevideo, then to undermine the authority of the viceroy. By defending themselves the *portenos* and the Montevideans developed a new self-reliance and an impatience with the ineffective imperial Spanish government. Ironically one of the main springs of their discontent was economic, in which the mercantilist Spanish empire was blamed for restricting the commercial opportunities open to the merchants – ironic because it was the British maritime blockade of Europe which was mainly responsible for the general collapse of trade. But the governments always get the blame, quite rightly.

Chapter Fifteen

Consequences in Britain and its Empire

I t was not only in South Africa and South America that results stemming from these South Atlantic expeditions can be traced, but also in Britain and its empire, sometimes clearly, sometimes less so. This is hardly surprising, for it is obvious that the empire had as great an effect on the homeland as the other way around. Taking its effect on the Empire first, it was inevitably South Africa which was the most important.

The capture of Cape Colony, intended to be permanent, was an important addition to the British Empire, but less for its own sake than for the control its occupation gave over the main sea route between Britain and India. The naval station which developed at Simon's Town (later Simonstown) became one of the principal bases used by the Royal Navy to dominate the South Atlantic and the Indian Ocean. And, of course, eventually South Africa became itself a great source of imperial wealth – but that was a development no one had looked to originally.

The fact that Baird took the 59th Foot with him on the expedition, used it in the Cape conquest, and then sent it on to India, is a good example of the use the Cape was intended for. But he also diverted two other regiments, and this may well have had serious consequences. The Indian career of the East India Company had brought it to the point of being an imperial power, though this, in 1806, was only a very recent development and (like the process of the revolution in the River Plate), the situation in India was by no means stable.

The Company had recruited its own army, most of whose men were Indians, and most of the officers British, though it was reinforced by royal forces from Britain, whom it in effect hired. The British officers tended to be less than sensitive to their Indian soldiers' concerns, and in 1805 and 1806 a scheme was hatched in the Madras army to make the men look more alike – the same uniformity whose absence Colonel Holland had deplored amongst the *portenos*. This involved replacing their turbans with round hats, removing facial marks and beards, and dispensing with earrings and other 'joys'. But all these had personal or social or religious significance for the men. Turbans were racial and caste symbols, caste marks were on the faces, beards for Muslims were religious requirements, and 'joys' were other caste or tribal markings. Clearly the importance of these items was not appreciated by the officers who originated the order, or if it was, they ignored it. When the order of implementation was made the men refused to obey.

This refusal was universal in the Madras army, and was accompanied by protests from those officers who understood their men's concerns. But it also came along at the same time as a series of rumours spread amongst the soldiers which suggested that the British intended to forcibly convert them to Christianity. This all happened at a time of peace, for since the conquest of Tipu Sultan and the capture of Seringapatam in 1795 and the defeat of the Mahrattas at Assaye in 1803, there was no enemy which seemed capable of meeting the Company army in battle. Relaxation inevitably followed, and the officers turned away from fighting to such vital matters as their pay, their perquisites – and attempting to impose uniformity on their soldiers – and the men now had the leisure (and now the incentive) to plan insurrection.

The result was, in July 1806 (about the same time as Beresford's force was attacking Buenos Aires), a violent mutiny centered on the fortress and palace of Vellore, about 150km inland from Madras. There were other outbreaks, but the one at Vellore was the most violent and the one which frightened the British most. Three regiments of Madras infantry carried out a careful and well-thought-out seizure of the fort, killing most of the British troops garrisoned with them, and brought out the children of Tipu Sultan, who had been sequestered in the palace there, as their figurehead leaders. The clear intention was to provoke, or inspire, a much wider rebellion in the name of the Tipu family, restore them to the throne of Mysore, and presumably drive the British out.

They failed, partly through their own inaccurate assumptions, and partly because of a swift British reaction. The word got to the 19th Dragoons at Arcot not far away, and they came out at great speed. Commanded by Colonel Rollo Gillespie they broke into the fort and carried out a reprisal massacre of the mutineers. Those who survived this were captured and many were later executed. The whole affair cost about 140 British and 400 Indian lives. But the mutineers had made no plans beyond the seizure of the fort, apparently assuming that their example would be instantly followed by other Indian soldiers, or that they had time to consider their next moves at leisure. In actual fact Gillespie's dragoons were accompanied by a force of Indian cavalry, who were just as keen to kill the mutineers as their British companions.[1]

Before the suppression was complete, however, word of the mutiny had spread rapidly. The British in southern India were very scared, quite rightly, since they abruptly came to the realization of their isolation as a small ruling group placed over the multitudes of Indian subjects who did not particularly like them. One of the first acts of the governor of Madras, Lord William Bentinck, on hearing of the mutiny was to send letters to all possible destinations whence help might come. One of these was the Cape. When the letter addressed to Baird arrived, he was suddenly confronted with the results of his casual way with his regiments. He sent off what men he could, and next year sent on at once more men as they arrived from the defeat of Buenos Aires.

Of course he was far too late for these men to have any effect upon the mutiny. That was over long before Baird was able to react. The real lesson was perhaps that it was dangerous to spread your forces quite so widely and thinly. It was quite possible to lose India while attempting to gain South America. Baird was replaced in Cape Colony in 1807 by Sir George Grey, and his carelessness with his regiments may well have been one factor in his removal – though changes in the party in power in Britain had as much effect. Lord William Bentinck was also recalled, for, although he had nothing to do with the issue of turbans and beards and caste-marks on soldiers' faces – and in fact was quite ignorant of the orders given – he was the governor of Madras and so was ultimately responsible. The soldiers who were responsible for the orders were also removed. The suppression of the mutiny brought an uneasy peace.

In Britain Captain Sir Home Popham had returned early in 1807, and was then tried at court-martial for a variety of offences, though he had clearly avoided any too obvious ones, and much of what he had done had been at least partly covered by his instructions, and as a commander-in-chief he had considerable discretion. He was, however, condemned, but then was quickly re-employed as Captain of the Fleet in the British attack on Copenhagen later in 1807. Baird – who was not subjected to a court-martial, despite joint responsibility with Popham for diverting the soldiers – also was soon employed again. (And Bentinck eventually served for seven years as Governor-General in India.)

In Britain the scattering of expeditions by the Grenville Ministry (misnamed, 'All the Talents') provoked scorn from its opponents in Parliament. (Other expeditions had gone to the West Indies and Constantinople.) The ministry was replaced in April 1807 by a new group of Pitt's followers, with the Duke of Portland (Bentinck's father), as Prime Minister, and with the intention of concentrating much more on the European war. This was all the more necessary in that Napoleon had now defeated Russia, and had, at Tilsit, compelled Tsar Alexander I to become his ally. Virtually all of Europe was now united against Britain. One result, already partly intended by the Grenville government, was the expedition to Denmark. But for the present any serious attack on the European continent was likely to be suicidal. The Portland government was driven to consider distant imperial expeditions, just as had been its Grenvillean predecessor.

As the battered regiments returned to Britain from the River Plate in July 1808, therefore, they had to be quickly reinforced, rested, and re-equipped (all their guns and muskets were left in South America). In Europe the Spanish King Carlos IV was less than co-operative with Napoleon, was compelled to abdicate, and this was followed by the imposition of Napoleon's brother Joseph as King of Spain, which in turn was followed by a widespread rebellion. One group of insurgents, the Galician *Junta*, asked for assistance from Britain, and this was agreed.

The request arrived just in time to divert a new British expeditionary force, to be commanded by Sir Arthur Wellesley, and which was intended to invade Mexico. The apparent vulnerability of the Spanish empire had been suggested by Popham's expedition, and there was, after the peace of Tilsit, no space to use the British army in Europe, despite the constant danger of invasion. So the Portland government had taken up the Grenvillean idea of an overseas expedition, despite their condemnation of these by the previous government. (But commanded by Wellesley it was more likely to be successful than one by Whitelocke.) Then the situation in Spain changed all minds.

Wellesley went to Spain and Portugal instead of Mexico and over the next six years was gradually metamorphosed into the Duke of Wellington, ascending by battles from knight to duke. The regiments he took on his first foray, in August 1808, included many of those which had been involved in South America. At Vimiero, for instance, he commanded the 2nd, 5th, 36th, 38th, 40th, 45th, 71st, and part of the 95th, all Foot Regiments, and the 20th Light Dragoons, among others.[2] One of the officers of the 95th was Lieutenant Harry Smith, who had been at the storm of Montevideo, and at Whitelocke's attempt on Buenos Aires. He had learned some Spanish on that campaign (where he was one of those who claimed to have been invited to desert, being offered the daughter of a Montevidean as inducement). His language skills enabled him to propose marriage, this time successfully, to his Juana after the storm of Badajoz in 1812. And thirty years later she was with him when he was Governor-General of the Cape Colony, and gave her married name to Ladysmith, the scene of one of the sieges of the Boer War.[3] Many others of the soldiers in Wellesley's force will have had at least a smattering of Spanish.

Harry Smith – by then a general, of course – was not the only survivor of the Plate campaign to reach high office. Colonel Bourke was Lieutenant-Governor of the Eastern Cape in the 1820s, and a highly successful governor of New South Wales from 1831 to 1837. Brigadier-General Lumley was governor of Bermuda, 1819–1825, having survived Wellington's contempt in Spain, and several others rose to high command in the army, in the Peninsula, in Britain, and in India. Captain Augustus Frazer (as a colonel), was commander of the Horse Artillery in the Peninsula; Captain Whittingham rose to Lieutenant-General in the same campaign; Baird was badly wounded at Corunna; Popham, as Rear-Admiral, conducted a notable campaign along the northern Spanish coast in 1812; both he and Stirling commanded for a time in the West Indian station – and Stirling was successfully prosecuted for corruption and was dismissed. Both Smith and Bourke clearly learned a good deal from their South American experiences, which they put into effect during their governorships. So the South Atlantic expeditions had their distant effects on several regions of the Empire. But they also had less direct effects on Britain itself.

One of these effects, of course, was on the army. One reason for the professional soldier Wellesley to command in Portugal in 1808 rather than allotting the post to the most senior general was his clear military competence. Apart from his Indian experience, he had commanded successfully in Denmark in 1807. Another reason was that he was a supporter of the government, indeed a member of it, as Chief Secretary for Ireland for the past couple of years, and his administrative competence had been shown in that post. One lesson from the River Plate expeditions was that it was clearly necessary to choose a commander for such an expedition who was a competent soldier, rather than one who was merely senior or whose job it was desired to eliminate. Whitelocke's court-martial, being held during 1808, showed up his lack of military command ability. (It also showed up the less than sensible measures of Windham and Grenville, for that matter.) So Wellesley got the Spanish command, and took with him many of the regiments which had survived the South American adventure. (Of course, he swiftly fell foul of the seniority rules when, having defeated the French at Vimiero, he found senior generals coming along to take over the evacuation negotiations from him; but they bungled the task so disastrously that Wellesley's conduct only stood out the more competently.)

Meanwhile, throughout the Napoleonic wars, the 93rd Foot remained in South Africa. It was called back to Britain in 1814. The people of Plymouth were reported to be astonished that the men, with pay in their pockets, chose to frequent churches instead, and to buy bibles rather than drink themselves stupid.[4] It was still almost entirely a Scottish unit, only 41 men out of 1,018 not being Scots. The regiment, if any of its pious members retained a sense of irony, may have been amused to be inspected on ceremonial parade by Prince Frederick of Orange, after having taken from his country one of its overseas possessions.

The next stage in the regiment's life, however, was not at all amusing. It was sent, with others, as part of the expedition to New Orleans, in pursuance of the war with the United States, which had begun in 1812. There it more than made up for its years of peaceful inactivity by losing three-quarters of its men, killed, wounded, and missing, in the botched battle for that city, notoriously fought after the peace have been concluded in Europe. More men from the 93rd died in that battle than of the 93rd, the 72nd, and the 71st in all the expeditions in the South Atlantic.[5] Perhaps their Calvinism, with its ingrained fatalism, was a consolation.

The battle, virtually the only victory for US arms in the war, allowed the United States to imagine it had won the war – so here again the 93rd lent itself to a shift in the historical developments. Without that victory the United States might have appreciated its overall defeat, and Andrew Jackson might not have reached the presidency. This would have meant a more intelligent economic policy by the federal government, and a good deal less cruelty and injustice to several Indian tribes.

Yet this was only the final element in the destruction of not just that regiment (though it was of course later revived and reconstituted with new recruits), but also of the society from which it emerged in the north of Scotland. For while it had been fighting the British Empire's battles in Africa and America, and having the profound effect it did have in the Cape, the relatives of the soldiers in their homeland had been subjected to a different campaign, and one which wrought far more destruction than any of the regiment's battles or military campaigns.

Those with a conspiratorial view of the past, or those with a fixed idea that the past was a class-war battlefield, may feel justified in regarding the absence of the regiment overseas as a deliberate attempt to head off trouble in Scotland. Most of the regiment had been recruited in 1800, and a new draft was added in August 1807. Those men were sent first to South America and then dispatched on by Whitelocke to South Africa, but they were also Scots. Since 1800, while they were in South Africa, the homeland of all these men from Scotland had been ravaged far more seriously than anything which had happened in the fighting in the South Atlantic. The Countess of Sutherland, who had required the men to join the regiment, had also required her factors to conduct a series of 'clearances'.[6]

The first of these clearances had taken place in the year the regiment was first recruited, 1800, but these were on a fairly small scale. They may have helped persuade some of the men to join, as an alternative to the life at home, which was becoming steadily more precarious. The main clearance began in 1807, in Farr and Lairg; one might note, if one had a conspiratorial view, that the regiment, whose recruitment had removed more than 1,000 of the young men from Sutherland, was by that time far away in South Africa, and would clearly be there for some time. More clearances in the Sutherland Estates took place in 1809, covering a large area north of the Dornoch Firth, in 1812 in Assynt, and in 1813 in Kildonan. The people were removed to new homes, or at least a new location, and so were separated from their lands and their means of livelihood, their places being taken in the main by sheep, all in the name of improvement and economic development (see map 18).

The men of the 93rd Regiment of Foot were therefore being used to support the clearance of part of South Africa, the Zuurveld and the land beyond the Great Fish River, just at the same time that their own homeland was being subject to the same treatment, and for much the same economic reasons. And the regiment must have known this. It was a very literate body of men – some acted as teachers, they purchased bibles – and letters were exchanged, just as part of the men's pay was sent home. There is, however, no trace of a protest by any of the men, and no sign that anyone in authority felt that the regiment might enter a collective protest, even though a polite sort of mutiny over social conditions was something of a tradition among Scottish Highland regiments.[7]

Yet for class-war devotees it is noticeable that the regiment was rapidly sent overseas once more as soon as it arrived from South Africa, and before its men had the chance to go home. The Countess of Sutherland's husband, the Marquess of Stafford, was a prominent supporter of Lord Liverpool's government. There is, however, no evidence for any connection between that fact and the dispatch of the regiment to the disaster at New Orleans.

Yet, even if the simplistic theories of conspiracy and class-war are rejected – as, of course, they must be, for lack of evidence, but mainly because they are nonsense – there arises a peculiarly acrid stench from these events. The areas which were subjected to clearance by the Sutherland factors recur repeatedly as the homes of the casualties at New Orleans. Families were moved from Farr and Lairg in 1807, and twenty-four men of Farr and Lairg were killed in 1815; the group of parishes of Dornoch, Rogart, Loth, Clyne, and Golspie, north and west of the Dornoch Firth, were the scene of removals in 1809, and thirty-nine men from these lands died at New Orleans; Assynt was cleared in 1812 and part of Kildonan in 1813; in 1815 eight men of Kildonan were killed and three from Assynt. In all seventy-five men from Sutherland died at New Orleans, a very substantial proportion not only of the regiment, but of the male population of the county.

By 1816, however, some of the men of the regiment were refusing to re-enlist, according to the *Annual Register* (and some had already taken their discharge in South Africa).[8] Given the economic depression settling over Britain at the time, which meant that continued employment in the army was attractive, the reason may well be connected with the Sutherland clearances, all the more so since the men were quite willing to enlist into other regiments. At least some of the men would do neither, and many emigrated.

In this they were joining a movement which had been taking people from Scotland for a long time. This, however, is not unusual, since every country in Europe has been a source of emigrants since the early Middle Ages. But Scottish emigration, particularly from the Highlands, had been increasing during the second half of the eighteenth century, though tending to be interrupted by such untoward events as the independence of the United States and the Napoleonic Wars. Emigration had, of course, being directed especially at eastern North America where part of New Jersey was largely Scottish; North Carolina, Nova Scotia and Prince Edward Island were other chosen destinations. In the post-war period also the dispatch of several parties of Scots to South Africa has already been noted in Chapter 5. The emigrants were largely driven on their away by hunger and unemployment – much the same at the time, of course – so that the emigration of those subject to the clearances is largely a continuation and intensification of the same movement.[9]

Another aspect of this movement was the participation of an increasing number of Scots in the expansion of and administration of the British Empire. The existence of an English overseas empire before the Parliamentary Union of England and Scotland in 1707 may have been one of the inducements to the Scots to sign up for that union, though it was probably only a relatively small one; Scots had actually infiltrated into the English empire before 1707 in an unofficial, clandestine way, and there was no perceptible increase in that participation for some time after the union.

There were three kinds of participation; emigration, military, and administrative. Emigrants had been leaving Scotland for centuries, but in the seventeenth century the main destination had been Ireland. Scots went in some numbers to the English West Indian islands, along with the small settlements of Scots in New Jersey and North Carolina on the northern mainland. There was no real increase in this general outward flow before about 1760, but the direction changed from Ireland to America, and after 1760 the predominantly Lowland origin of the emigrants was supplemented by a heavy outflow of Highlanders.[10]

This is where the emigration impulse intersects with military history. The recruitment of Highland soldiers in the Seven Years' War (1755–1763) had introduced a new and disturbing element into Highland society, for the soldiers who returned brought back information about the wider world which was new to most Highlanders, and which stimulated many of them to begin thinking of bettering that condition. Highland poverty was dire, with the rising population making matters worse. There might be other stimuli also. In one notorious case a group of Catholic MacDonalds emigrated to escape persecution by their Protestant MacDonald lord. A few were probably driven out by their 'improving' landlords, but there were not many of these yet. Some emigrants were sponsored on their way by their clan lord, or by the lord's tacksman. But most, in all probability, went because of the lure of free or cheap land, better and more food, and perhaps freedom.[11]

The recruitment of soldiers resumed for the American war, as with the 71st in 1777, though the possibilities of emigration were much reduced during and for some time after that war. This drained young men away from the Highlands, and most of them did not return. The development work of many improving landlords in the Highlands – not all of whom drove their people out – together with the independence of the Thirteen Colonies after 1783, which temporarily reduced the attraction of that land for emigrants, all combined to reduce the pressure for emigration and the attraction of the process. But Canada was available, and became more popular after 1783. And the continued recruitment of Scots into the army was a method of reducing the population pressure, particularly since so few of them returned.

All this very much contributed to the change in attitudes of the Highlanders towards the United Kingdom – for one cannot fight for a state without developing a certain loyalty towards it – and of the rest of Scotland and England to the Highlanders. Whereas they had been both feared and despised by the Lowlanders and the English in the rest of the country until after the rebellion of 1745, from the time of the Seven Years' War that image gradually changed into one of admiration. Their military valour was much admired, but particularly so because it was now directed so successfully overseas in the service of the United Kingdom.[12]

The new empire in India which came into existence just as that in America was collapsing, opened a series of new opportunities for a different class of emigrant. There had been Scots in the government service in the American colonies even before 1707, but they had not been numerous, for it was largely an English, indeed a London, enterprise. In India, however, by the second half of the eighteenth century their numbers made them conspicuous. Warren Hastings appears to have favoured Scotsman as his agents and in his time almost half of the cadets entering the Bengal army – nominated by him, in fact – were Scots. With Henry Dundas at the India Office in London from 1784 the proportion certainly did not fall in the last decade in the eighteenth century. So while the Scots regiments were conquering south India – the Mysore Wars 'sometimes looked like a conflict between Mysore and Celtic Scotland', remarks one historian, exaggerating only slightly – in the north of India, Bengal, the administration was substantially in Scottish hands.[13]

The concentration of Scots regiments in the Cape expedition was thus partly to be expected, and was partly the result of Baird's patriotic Scottish preferences. The Scots in India were frequently accused of forming a sort of freemasonry, of helping each other too obviously, and the main part of Baird's career had been in India. It was this clannishness which may well have been one of their advantages in Hastings' eyes, for they tended to work very effectively together where the English were more mutually competitive. Baird's conduct in South Africa in grouping the Scots regiments into a Highland Brigade has something of the appearance of favoritism as well, and he undoubtedly thought he was conferring a favour on the 71st by selecting that regiment for the South American expedition. The continued presence of the 93rd, and the effect it had had on the local Church, was also one of the reasons for the emigration of Scottish groups after 1815 (see Chapter 5).

The effects of the various expeditions of 1805–1807 in the South Atlantic were thus very different in the two lands which were invaded, though in each case those effects were profound, and there were repercussions also in Britain. In the River Plate area the momentary successes of Beresford's and Auchmuty's forces in conquering Buenos Aires and Montevideo provided the blows which broke the connections, already weakened by new European ideas and by the long British blockade, between the local communities of the

Plate estuary and the imperial power of Spain. In South Africa the conquest of Cape Town by Baird's army, and the capitulation of Janssens' little army at the Hottetots Hollands Pass, finally broke the direct connection with the Dutch homeland, already weakened by the earlier British occupation and local disenchantment with the republican Batavian regime, so dominated by French interests. This therefore inaugurated a new imperial regime which opened up the small society of white South Africa to a wider world, and began the contradictory processes of anglicization and 'apartheidization'.

Thus these conquests, carried out in large part by the same men, had opposite effects in political terms, just as they had opposite military outcomes; independence for one society and subjugation for the other. Beyond the immediate effects, however, the new regimes opened both countries to commercial, and particularly to British, enterprise, in which small groups of active merchants were especially important. The export of capital from Victorian Britain to both countries was a vital element in their development.

In South Africa the adoption by the Scots of the Dutch Reformed Church of the prevailing local racist attitudes – adopted also by the immigrants from Britain during the next century – led on to the iniquity of *apartheid*; in Argentina, on the other hand, the increased wealth of the coastal area, in part based on trade with Britain, was a foundation for the later wars against the Indians of the interior, a process which very largely exterminated them. They were replaced in the Pampas by great ranches, whose proprietors came to exercise oligarchic power within the state.[14] Note also the idolization of the Argentine army, which did the work of conquest, but which was thereby encouraged to mount repeated *coups d'etat*. One major difference between the two lands can be seen in the people today. Argentina is a land of whites; South Africa is very largely black, though with much of the wealth in white hands.

In accomplishing all this Scots have clearly had a major share. The most obvious element is the intrusion of the Scottish ministers into the Dutch Reformed Church, which revived a distinctly moribund organization and made it a major vehicle for Afrikaner aspirations and self-identity. The presence of the Scots regiments, the 93rd and the 72nd, clearly had a strong effect also, especially the exemplary behaviour of the 93rd. The effect of the Scots of the 71st in South America is less easy to estimate. The reactions of Privates Balfour Kennach and Donald MacDonald to offers of refuge if they deserted (if the offers were really made) – offers which were in effect made to all soldiers and sailors of the various forces, since the deserters were largely welcomed – suggests that there were substantial barriers to be overcome, and that mutual Catholicism was not necessarily enough. Nevertheless several hundred men did ignore these barriers and remained in the land. (But Argentina was not a major emigration target for Scots later, though there is a substantial Welsh colony in the country.)

In both countries, however, religion was only a marginal element in the process of amalgamation. The factor which the stories of both Kennach and MacDonald emphasize is their Scottish patriotism, and this was presumably, together with the social inertia characteristic of closed groups such as regiments, a major factor in persuading the returnees to reject tempting offers of Spanish hospitality. But those who stayed were still Scots, over a hundred of them, and their presence was of some importance.

The behaviour of the men of the 93rd on its return to Plymouth in 1814 was highly unusual, and provoked astonishment locally. The return of the 71st to Cork six years earlier was more typical of the behaviour of British soldiers in such cases. The released men the 71st landed at intervals in December 1807 and January 1808. The men were given a year's pay, and there followed 'such a scene of drunkenness for eight days [as] was never seen in the British or any other Army', according to Ensign Gavin.[15] No one else found it worth commenting on this, presumably because it was not nearly so unusual as Gavin thought. After recovering from the debauch, the regiment marched to Middleton, a few miles east of the port, and there it camped while it recruited its numbers, mainly by receiving transfers from its second battalion in Glasgow, but also taking in any Irish who cared to join. Re-equipped and tidied up, it then received new colours in a ceremony in April. (The old colours remained where Pack and Craufurd saw them, in the church of Santo Domingo in Buenos Aires, and they are still there.) The regiment was thus re-constituted. Four months later, along with other regiments, the Highland Light Infantry embarked at Cork once more, this time for Spain, there to assist a people in rebellion against their legally instituted king and government; how many of the regiment, one wonders, perceived the irony.

Meanwhile in Scotland the great landlords were still clearing lands for sheep. It is difficult to believe they would have done this quite so easily had the large numbers of young men who had been taken into the British army still been at home. It may be a negative result of the South Atlantic expeditions, but it was as profound for the Scottish Highlands as the presence of the 93rd in South Africa or the 71st in Buenos Aires had been for those lands.

All this has led me rather far from the expedition which sailed to retake the Cape in 1805. It seems worth reiterating, however, that these effects, profound though they were in Scotland, South Africa, and the River Plate, were as much the product of the decisions of individuals as of any identifiable greater historical forces. It is very likely, for example, that the British would have at some point retaken the Cape from the Dutch, but it was specifically the persuasiveness of Sir Home Popham in his meeting with the Prime Minister which brought the government to the point of decision. Then it was the appointment of Baird as the land commander in that expedition which ensured that many of the troops involved were Scots, for he had quite deliberately asked for them.

The agency of individuals is even more obvious in the genesis of the Plate expedition. Again it was Popham's persuasiveness operating on Baird which was the catalyst, but this in fact came from the sudden arrival of the American Waine at Cape Town on top of the Admiralty's suggestion that a Royal Navy ship should be sent to interrupt the Spanish trade along the South American coast. Once the River Plate expedition was launched the process of conquest and reaction, and the rapid development of political change in Buenos Aires, was in train, until stopped by Whitelocke's sensible decision to evacuate the whole area, and Liniers' equally sensible decision to release all the prisoners. Both of these decisions were less than popular with some of their followers though to any objective view, even at the time, they made sense; it may have helped that both Liners and Whitelocke were essentially administators, and could generally ignore the military pride of their subordinates. But in both cases the origins of the events lay in minor events and meetings. It is, for example, most unlikely that the British government would have bothered to send an expedition to take Buenos Aires if Popham had not already organized one.

Maps

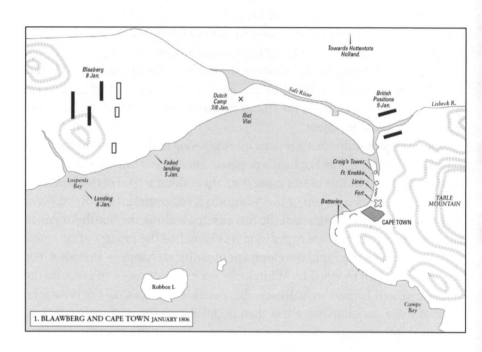

Towards Hottentots
Holland.

Blaaberg
8 Jan.

Dutch
Camp
7/8 Jan.

Salt River

British
Positions
9 Jan.

Lisbeck R.

Riet
Vlei

Failed
landing
5 Jan.

Craig's Tower
Ft. Knokke
Lines
Fort

Lospends
Bay

Landing
6 Jan.

Batteries

CAPE TOWN

TABLE
MOUNTAIN

Robben I.

Camps
Bay

1. BLAAWBERG AND CAPE TOWN JANUARY 1806

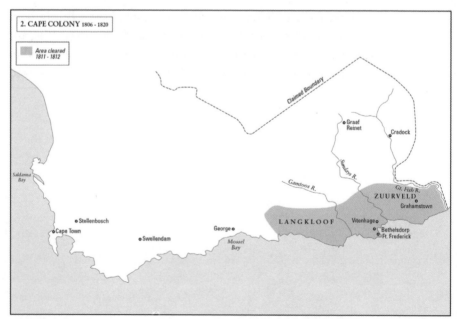

2. CAPE COLONY 1806 - 1820

Area cleared
1811 - 1812

Claimed Boundary

Graaf
Reinet

Cradock

Sundays R.

Gamtoos R.

Gt. Fish R.
ZUURVELD

Grahamstown

Saldanna
Bay

LANGKLOOF

Vitenhage

Stellenbosch

George

Bethelsdorp
Ft. Frederick

Cape Town

Swellendam

Mossel
Bay

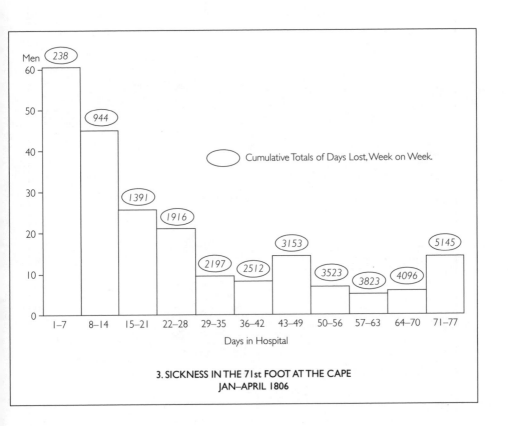

Men
60 —
50 —
40 —   Cumulative Totals of Days Lost, Week on Week.
30 —
20 —
10 —
0 —
      1–7   8–14 15–21 22–28 29–35 36–42 43–49 50–56 57–63 64–70 71–77
                              Days in Hospital

238 944 1391 1916 2197 2512 3153 3523 3823 4096 5145

**3. SICKNESS IN THE 71st FOOT AT THE CAPE
JAN–APRIL 1806**

4. ENGLAND: ORIGINS OF RECRUITS OF 71st FOOT

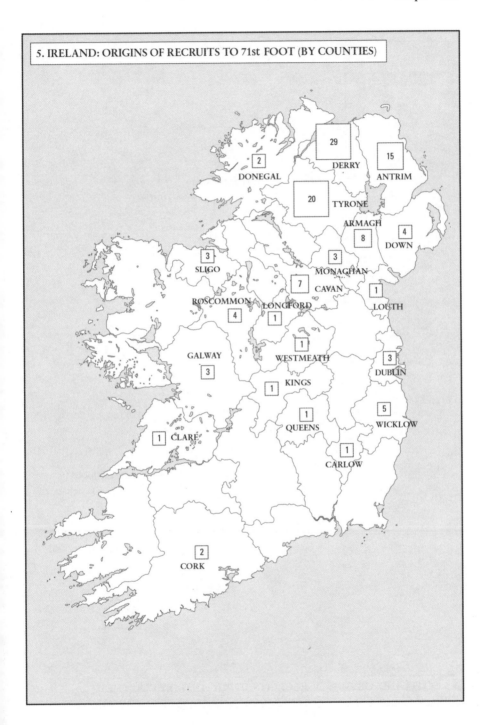

5. IRELAND: ORIGINS OF RECRUITS TO 71st FOOT (BY COUNTIES)

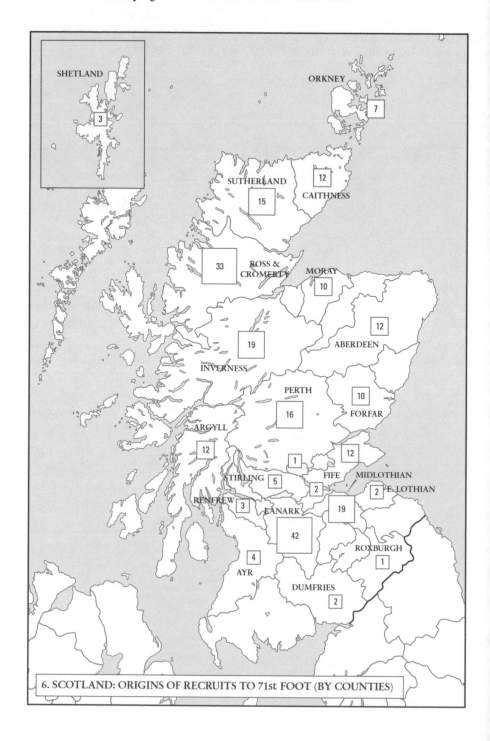

6. SCOTLAND: ORIGINS OF RECRUITS TO 71st FOOT (BY COUNTIES)

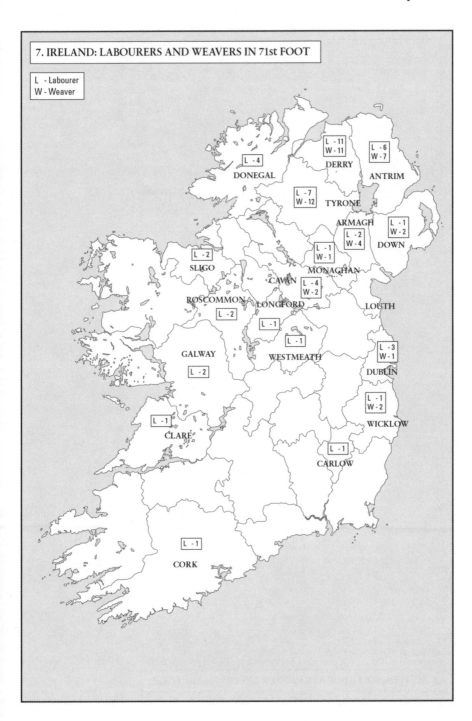

7. IRELAND: LABOURERS AND WEAVERS IN 71st FOOT

L - Labourer
W - Weaver

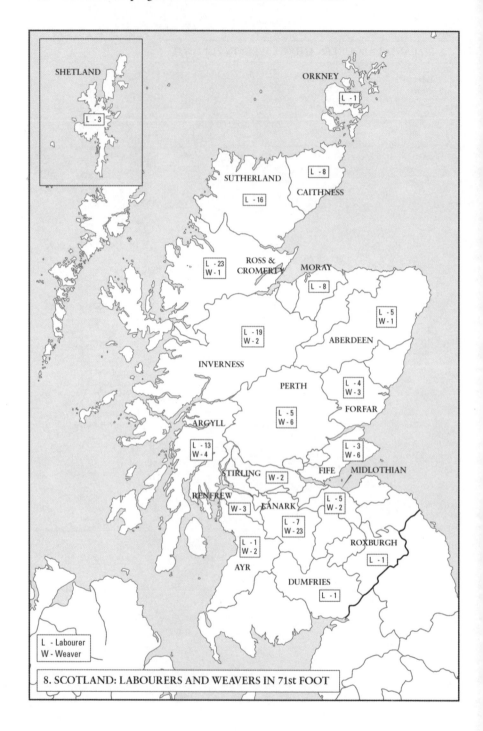

8. SCOTLAND: LABOURERS AND WEAVERS IN 71st FOOT

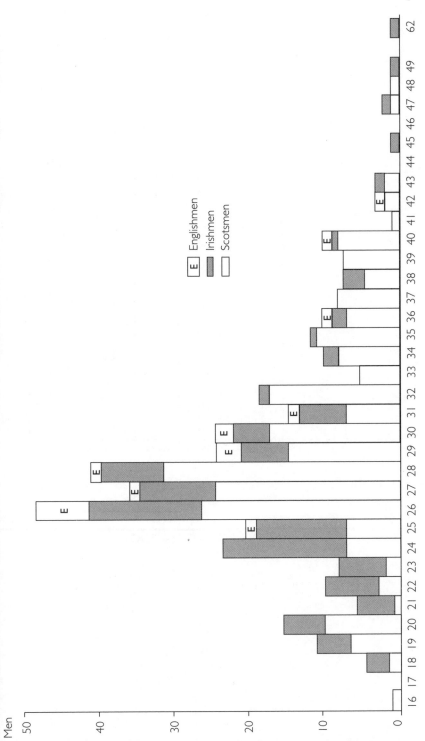

9. AGES OF RANK AND FILE
71st FOOT 1806

Ages

Men

Englishmen
Irishmen
Scotsmen

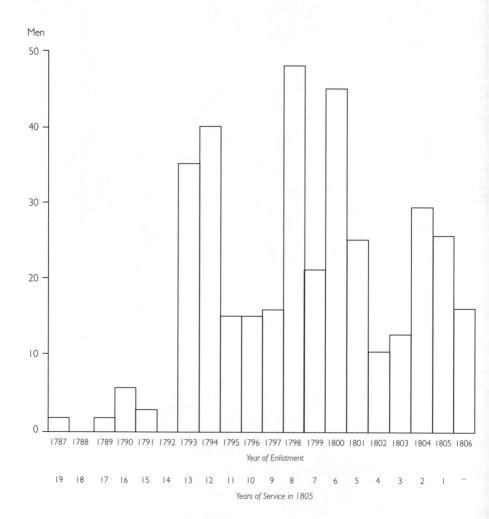

10. SERVICE IN THE 71st FOOT.

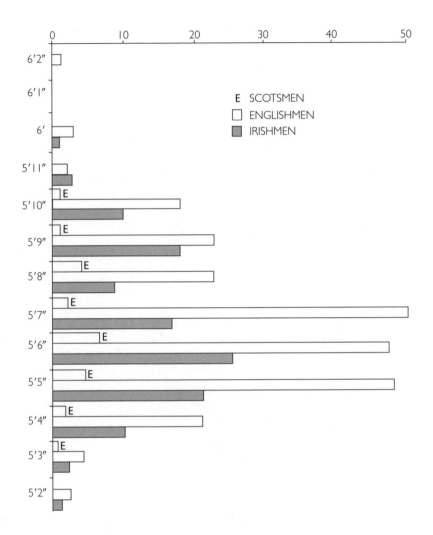

11. HEIGHTS OF SOLDIERS

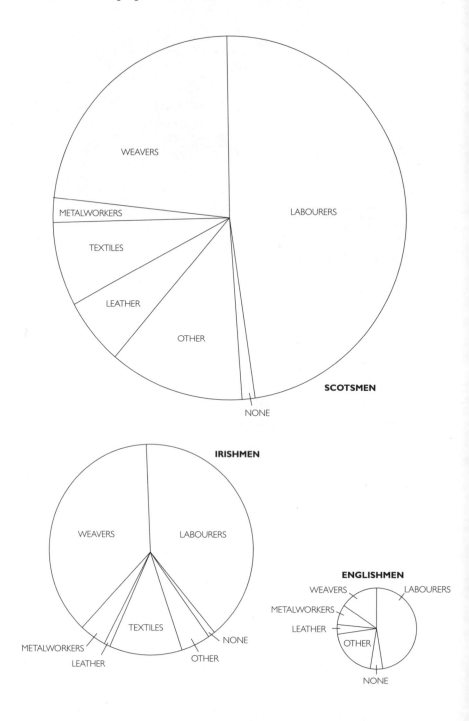

12. CIVILIAN OCCUPATIONS OF SOLDIERS

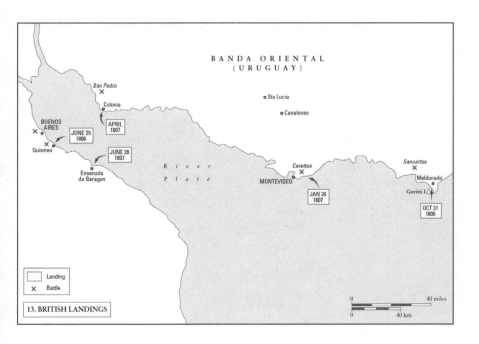

BANDA ORIENTAL
(URUGUAY)

San Pedro
×

○ Sta Lucia

Colonia ○

○ Canalones

APRIL
1807

BUENOS
AIRES
×
JUNE 25
1806

Quismes ○ ×

JUNE 28
1807

R i v e r

P l a t e

Ensenada
de Baragon ○

Carettas
×

Sancartos
×

MONTEVIDEO

Maldonado ○

Goritti I.

JAN 20
1807

OCT 31
1806

☐ Landing

× Battle

13. BRITISH LANDINGS

0   40 miles

0   40 km

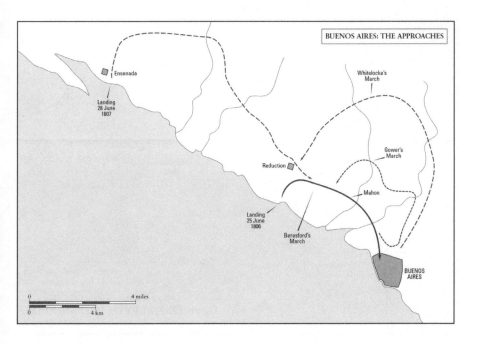

BUENOS AIRES: THE APPROACHES

☐ Ensenada

Whitelocke's
March

Landing
28 June
1807

Reduction ☐

Gower's
March

Mahon

Landing
25 June
1806

Beresford's
March

BUENOS
AIRES

0   4 miles

0   4 km

15. VICEROYALTY OF BUENOS AIRES

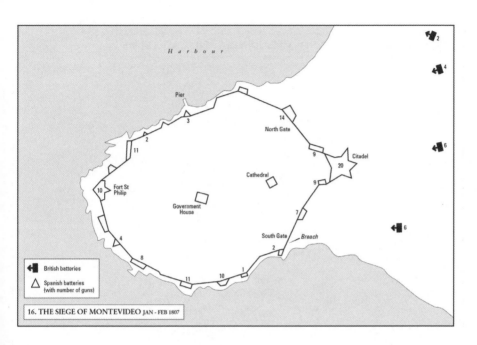

Pier

North Gate

14

3

2

11

Cathedral

9

Citadel

20

Fort St Philip

10

9

Government House

7

South Gate

Breach

2

8

4

1

11

10

British batteries

Spanish batteries (with number of guns)

2

4

6

6

16. THE SIEGE OF MONTEVIDEO JAN - FEB 1807

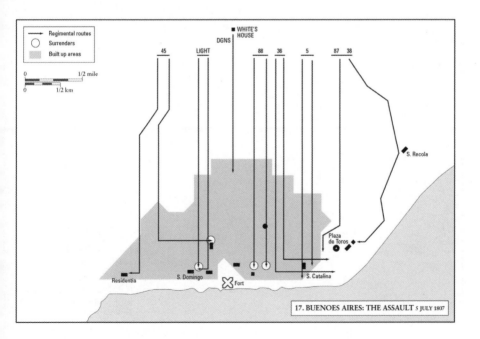

Regimental routes

Surrenders

Built up areas

0   1/2 mile

0   1/2 km

45   LIGHT

DGNS

■ WHITE'S
HOUSE

88   36   5

87   38

■ S. Recola

Plaza
de Toros

Residentia

S. Domingo

Fort

S. Catalina

17. BUENOES AIRES: THE ASSAULT 5 JULY 1807

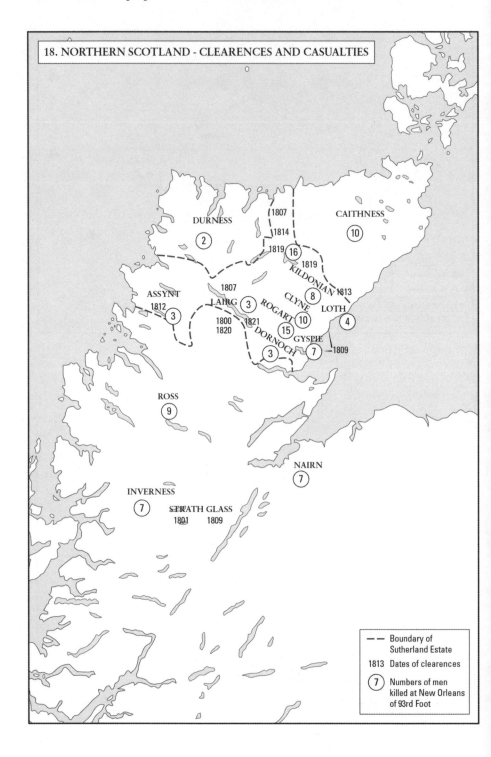

18. NORTHERN SCOTLAND - CLEARENCES AND CASUALTIES

Notes and References

Chapter 1

1. The movements of the fleets are detailed by J.S. Corbett, *The Campaign of Trafalgar* (London 1910).
2. G.J. Marcus, *A Naval History of England*, vol. 2, *The Age of Nelson* (London 1971) 229.
3. WO 1/711, 57–65, and 413.
4. *Popham Court-Martial*, 91 and 165.
5. Corbett, *Campaign of Trafalgar*, 181 and the plan opposite 205.
6. WO 1/341, 1 and 5–8, Baird to Castlereagh, 21 July 1805.
7. M. Fry, *The Dundas Despotism* (Edinburgh 1997).
8. *ODNB*, Sir David Baird.
9. *Hansard* 36, House of Lords, 185.
10. Castlereagh, *Corr.*, VI, 142–146, Castlereagh to Marquess Cornwallis, 10 Sep 1805.
11. *The Times*, 15 July 1805.
12. Cf note 6.
13. Castlereagh, *Corr.* VI, 129–130, Castlereagh to Pitt, 33 July 1805; 131–137, draft instructions for Sir David Baird, 25 July 1805.
14. ADM 2/363, 112–124; *Popham Court-Martial*, Document I, Admiralty to Popham, 29 July 1805.
15. Castlereagh, *Corr.* VI 138–139, Castlereagh to Lord Barham, 26 July 1805; 140, Castlereagh to Baird, 26 July 1805; Baird letters III, 92, Duke of York to Baird, 26 July 1805.
16. *ODNB* Baird.
17. Baird letter book, 5, Baird to Lord Cathcart, 2 August 1805; WO 1/341, Baird to Castlereagh, 2 August 1805; Baird letter book, 10–11 Baird to the Treasury, 3 August 1805; 12–13, Baird to Pole, 4 August 1805; 13, Baird to Lord Cathcart, 5 August 1805.
18. Castlereagh, *Corr.* VI, 140–141, Cooke to Baird, 31 July 1805; 141, Hawkesbury to Baird, 4 August 1805; 141–142, Castlereagh to Baird, 20 August 1805; Baird letter book, 16–17, Baird to Lord Hawkesbury, 4 August 1805; 18–19, Baird to Lord Cathcart, 5 August 1805.
19. Logs of *Diomede* and *Diadem*.
20. Baird letter book, 25–26 and 27–28, Baird to Gordon, 18 August 1805.
21. ADM 1/58, 42–44, Popham to Admiralty, 28 Sep 1805; Graham, II, 134, J. Graham to R. Graham, 31 July 1805; 135, J. Graham to R. Graham, 3 August 1805; Edinburgh University Library DK 7.5383, R. Campbell to A. Campbell, 7 August 1805.
22. National Army Museum 7805–30, 6 August 1805; Landsheit, 138 and 142.
23. Gillespie, 6; Fernyhough, 60.
24. Corbett, *Campaign of Trafalgar*, 301–310.
25. Wilson, 26 Sep 1805.

26. Graham, III, 139, J. Graham to R. Graham, 28 Sep 1805.
27. Master's log of *Raisonable*, 24 August 1805; Walters, 36; ADM 1/58, 42–44, Popham to Admiralty, 28 Sep 1805.
28. *ODNB*, Sir Home Riggs Popham; H. Popham, *A Damned Cunning Fellow* (Tywardraeth, Cornwall, 1991).
29. A fictionalized version of this incident is in C. S. Forester, *The Commodore* (London 1945), one of the Hornblower stories.
30. Annotations in the British Library's copy of the *Popham Court-Martial*, by 'B.T.'. The book belonged to Tom Grenville in his capacity as First Lord, and so B.T. was Benjamin Tucker, Admiralty Secretary 1801–1804 and 1806–1807. Tucker was one of St Vincent's followers and therefore Popham's political opponent, though the tone of the annotations is so splenetic as to make 'opponent' far too weak a term for the relationship.
31. National Library of Scotland, Melville Papers, GD 51.
32. *Popham Court-Martial*, Document II, Admiralty to Popham, 29 July 1805.
33. ADM 1/58, 50, Popham to Marsden, 10 Oct 1805; Captain's log of *Diadem*, 4 Oct 1805.
34. Fernyhough 69.
35. Baird letter book, 54–58.
36. Walters, 38; logs of, e.g., *Diomede*, *Leda*, and *Raisonable*, though December.
37. Wilson, 8 Oct 1805.
38. ADM 1/58, 87, Popham to Admiralty, 4 Oct 1805; Baird letter book, 59–63, Baird to Governor Patten, 2 Ovt 1805.
39. ADM 1/58, 62, protest of Captain W. Bridekirk, of *King George*; 63, protest of Captain Birch of *Britannia*; 62–79; Wilson, 1 and 4 Nov 1805; Baird letter book, 68–72, Baird to Gordon, 18 Nov 1805; Masters' logs of *Leda*, 1 and 4 Nov 1805, *Diomede* and *Belliqueux*, 4 Nov 1805; Gillespie, 9; Fernyhough 72; 'Recollections', 486.
40. Baird letter book, 84–97, Baird to Gordon, 12 Jan 1806.
41. Baird letters III, 89, 'Some Cursory Observations on the probable mode of approach and attack on the Cape'.
42. Graham, II, 138; Wilson, 6 Dec 1805; Gloucestershire Record Office, Rooke Papers 2002/28, 'Standing Orders for the Invading Force'.

Chapter 2

1. ADM 1/58, 92–106, Popham to Marsden, 13 Jan 1806.
2. WO 1/342, 1–24, Baird to Castlereagh, 12 Jan 1806.
3. Masters' logs of *Diomede* and *L'Espoir*, 6 Jan 1806; ADM 1/58, 92–106; WO 1/342, 1–24; Baird letter book, 86–97; Wilson, 7 Jan 1806.
4. National Library of Scotland, Murray of Ochtertyre papers, ADV MS 46.1.21, 17–19, Lt-Col Weir to Lt-Col Murray, 28 Mar 1806.
5. Baird letters III (ref 9923–3), 89, 'Some cursory observations on the probable mode of approach and attack on the Cape' (no date).
6. Gillespie 13.
7. ADM 1/58, 92–106; Masters' logs of *Diadem* and *Encounter*, 7 Jan 1806; Walters 39; Gillespie 14; Graham II, 138, J. Graham to R. Graham, 25 Jan 1806; Baird letter book, 86–97, Baird to Gordon, 12 Jan 1806.
8. Graham II, 138.
9. Ibid.
10. Leibbrandt, *Requesten*, John Jacob Mostert, claim of 3 July 1806.
11. Weir (note 4).

12. ADM 1/56, 123, Capt. Donnelly to Popham, 25 Dec 1805.
13. Lichtenstein 453; Borcherds 250.
14. For the history of the Netherlands at this period, see S. Schama, *Patriots and Liberators* (London 1977).
15. Borcherds 240–249.
16. Brief biographies in *Biografisch Wordenboek der Nederlander* and *Niewe-Nederlandsch biografisch Wordenboek*.
17. Theal, *Records*, V, 218–222, Schimmelpenninck to Janssens, c.June 1805.
18. Borcherds 249; J.D. Grainger, 'The Conquest of the Cape', *Army Quarterly and Defence Journal*, 123, 1993, 316–322.
19. Theal, *History* I, 190.
20. A summary of the political aspects of the whole period from 1794 to 1806 is in T.R.H. Davenport, *South Africa, a Modern History*, London 1977, 29–30; the economic history of the same period is summarized in W.M. Freund, 'The Cape under Transitional Government, 1795–1814', in R. Elphick and H. Giliomee (eds), *The Shaping of South African Society, 1652–1820*, Cape Town 1979, 211–242, but the effects of the much larger British garrison are more or less ignored.
21. R.M.F. Immelman, *Men of Good Hope: the Cape Town Chamber of Commerce, 1804–1954* (Cape Town 1955).
22. M. Arkin, 'John Company at the Cape', *Archives Yearbook for South African History* 23, vol. 2, 1960, 211–213; Theal, *Records*, X, 164, gives the Company's subsequent estimate of its losses in 1803 (not necessarily to be accepted, of course).
23. The names 'Hottentot' and 'Bushman' are now usually replaced by 'Khoi' and 'San'. I continue to use the old terms, since those were the usages of the time.
24. A good concise account of the development of Boer life inland is in N.C. Pollock and S. Agnew, *An Historical Geography of South Africa* (London 1963) 57–68.
25. A good summary of the situation of the 'Eastern Cape' – i.e., to Xhosa (or Nguni) people, both in political and economic matters, is in R. Derricourt, 'Settlement in the Transkei and the Ciskei before the Mfecane', in C. Saunders and R. Derricourt (eds), *Beyond the Cape Frontier* (London 1974) 59–82.
26. A.J. Smithers, *The Kaffir Wars* (London 1973) 60–66.
27. W.M. Freund, 'The Eastern Frontier of the Cape Colony during the Batavian Period (1803–1806)', *Journal of African Studies* 13 (1972) 631–645.
28. Ibid, 641–643; J. Philip, *Researches in South Africa* (London 1828).
29. Theal, *History*, I 191; Theal, *Records* XXXI, 15–18; M. Legassic, 'The Northern Frontier to 1820', in Elphick and Giliomee (note 20), 243–290.
30. Borcherds 240, 249, 255.
31. Master's log of *Leda*, 4–7 Jan 1806.
32. Borcherds 256.
33. Kennach 1–2.
34. Graham II, 138; Weir (note 24); Lichtenstein 454; Borcherds 256–257; WO 1/342, 1–24; Kennach 1.
35. R. Cannon, *Historical Records of the 72nd Regiment*; J. E. Fortescue, *History of the British Army*, vol. VI, 308; Borcherds 258.
36. Baird tended to emphasize this: 'severe fire' in his letter to Col. Gordon (Baird letter book, 86–97) and 'very heavy fire of round shot, grape and musquetry' in his official report (WO 1/342, 1–24); Graham III, 138, notes the cool behaviour of the Dutch gunners.

37. WO 71/205, Court-martial of Captain Aeneas Sutherland; WO 91/1, 79–80, the sentence (cashiering).

38. Borcherds 258.

39. Cannon, *Historical records of 72nd*; Borcherds 258; Gillespie 15; Theal, *History* I, 198.

40. Borcherds 258.

41. Gavin II; Campbell is quoted in Cannon, *Historical Records of 72nd*.

42. The number is repeated in all the memoirs, and had clearly become accepted as accurate by those taking part: Walters, 40; Gillespie 9; Fernyhough 75; but neither Graham nor Weir mention a figure, and they wrote at the time.

43. WO 1/342, 1–24; Baird letter book 86 –97; Castlereagh, *Corr.*, VII, 133–137.

44. WO 1/342, 31, Return of ordnance captured, notes 456 guns taken; Borcherds 258.

45. Weir (note 4), 20; WO 1/342, 1–24; Graham II, 138.

46. WO 1/342, 1–24; Graham II, 138; ADM 1/58, 92–106; Master's log of *Diadem*, 11 Jan 1806.

47. WO 1/342, 21 and 23, casualty returns; the exact figures are 37 killed and four wounded at the landing, 15 killed, 179 wounded and 8 missing in the battle; WO 1/342, 1–24; Baird letter book, 86–97.

48. Theal, Records V, 261–263, Preliminary Articles of Capitulation, and 263–265, Final Articles of Capitulation. WO 103/49 lists the prisoners of war in British hands on 11 January 1806 as 788, of whom 287 were sailors; ADM 1/58, 109, Popham to Marsden, 13 Jan 1806.

49. Walters 41; Wilson, 7 Jan 1806; Masters' logs of *Diomede* and *L'Espoir*, 7 and 8 Jan 1806.

50. Wilson, 7–9 Jan 1806; 'Recollections' 190.

51. Theal, *Records* V, 266–269.

52. WO 1/342, 35–42, Baird to Castlereagh, 12 Jan 1806.

53. ADM 1/58, 127, Popham to Marsden 13 Jan 1806.

54. Theal, *Records* V, 290–291; ADM 1/58, 141, Popham to Marsden, 25 Jan 1806.

55. Detailed in WO 103/49. Of the 794 whose origin is given, 419 were German, 282 French and only 47 Dutch. There were 4 Americans, 3 from Malabar, 12 Scandinavians, 2 Portuguese, 5 Italians, 6 from Austria or Hungary, 10 from 'Brabant', 1 'Scalavonian' and 1 Pole.

56. Article 11 of the Final Articles of Capitulation: Theal, *Records* V, 263–265; 'Recollections' 191.

57. WO 1/342, 35–42, Baird to Castlereagh, 13 Jan 1806; Wilson 10 Jan 1806; Cannon, *Historical Records of 72nd*.

58. *DSANB*, III, John Murray.

59. WO 1/342, 35–42, Baird to Castlereagh, 13 Jan 1806.

60. J. Perceval, *An Account of the Cape of Good Hope*, London 1804, 80.

61. Gavin III; Graham II, 138; Wilson, 21 Jan 1806.

62. Theal, *Records* V, 287–288; WO 1/342, 35–42; Wilson, 21 Jan 1806.

63. Theal, *Records* V, 292–296 and 297, Janssens to Beresford, 16 Jan 1806, and 297–302.

64. Wilson, 21 Jan 1806.

Chapter 3

1. Theal, *History*, I, 207; WO 1/342, 125–135, Baird to Castlereagh, 8 Mar 1806.

2. Graham II, 142, an extract from Baird's orders.

3. Landsheit 154.

4. WO 103/49 and muster rolls and monthly returns of the various regiments.

5. 'Recollections' 191.

6. Monthly Returns.

7. WO 71/205, Sutherland's court-martial, 1 Feb, and WO 91/1, 79–80 and 99–100, summary and royal confirmation of the sentence; WO 71/205, Ramsden's court-martial, 17–18 Feb, and Pococke's court-martial, 19 Feb 1806.

8. ADM 1/58, 134, Popham to Marsden, 14 Jan 1806.

9. Graham II, 138–139; ADM 103/49 shows that 39 men 'volunteered' to join Major Graham; WO 17/212, monthly return of the Cape Regiment.

10. Theal, *Records* V, 338–340, Baird to Captain Cuyler, 14 Feb 1806, and 347, official appointment of Cuyler, 14 Feb; WO 1/342, 53–67, Baird to Castlereagh, 26 Jan 1806.

11. *DSANB*, Jacob Glen Cuyler.

12. WO 1/342, 153–159, Baird to Castlereagh, 20 Mar 1806 (Cuyler); School of Oriental and African Studies, London Missionary Society Correspondence, South Africa, Schoonberg to Ysselstein, 24 March 1806 (van der Kemp).

13. C.N. Parkinson, *War in the Eastern Seas* (London 1954) 271–272.

14. ADM 1/58, 156, Popham to Marsden 28 Jan 1806; Master's logs of *Diomede* and *Encounter*, 22–24 Mar 1806.

15. E.g., Master's Log of *Diomede*, 27 Jan 1806.

16. Master's log of *Diadem*, 2–5 Feb 1806; ADM 1/58, 233, 'Disposition of transports', 21 Mar 1806; ADM 1/58, 178–179, Popham to Marsden, 22 Feb 1806.

17. ADM 1/58, 180–184, Linois' letters captured in *Rollo*.

18. *Leda* had returned two days before *Rollo* was retaken: ADM 1/58, 172; she had taken nine days to reach St Helena, but 23 for the return voyage (Master's log, 15 Jan – 19 Feb 1806).

19. Adm 1/58, 178–179.

20. ADM 1/58, 108, Popham to Marsden, 4 March 1806, enclosing embarkation return; of the 804, 94 were officers, 573 rank-and-file, and the rest civil servants (31) and women and children (106); Theal, *History* I, 207–208

21. ADM 1/58, 190, Popham to Marsden, 4 Mar 1806; Master's log of *Diadem*, 4 March 1806; Thompson 129.

22. Fernyhough, 79–80; Baird letter book, 125–135, Baird to Castlereagh, 8 March 1806.

23. ADM 1/58, 199–204, Popham to Marsden, 7 Mar 1806.

24. Wilson, 6 Mar 1806.

25. ADM 1/58, 199–204.

26. Theal, *Records*, 366–367; 'Recollections' 192; Baird letter book, 137–138, Baird to Popham, 8 Mar 8006; ADM 1/58, 209–212, Popham to Marsden (n.d.) and enclosures; Theal, *Records* 361–362, Popham to Marsden, 5 Mar 1806; Popham gave a separate parole to Lt Steetz, his German friend (ADM 1/58, 234, Popham to Marsden, 28 Mar 1806).

27. ADM 1/58, 213, Popham to Marsden, 10 Mar 1806 (*Volontaire*), and 215, Popham to Marsden, 12 Mar 1806 (*Rollo*). *Volontaire*, a large frigate with a nominal complement of 300 men, was allocated a crew of 157, plus 67 supernumeraries, on 15 Mar. *Rolla*, with a complement of 50, had a crew of 24 and 44 supernumeraries on 28 March – the crew being lascars with white officers. *Volontaire's* men had come largely from the other naval ships at the Cape, and no doubt the captains took the opportunity to remove their worst men. The initial crew was certainly heavily salted with foreigners: 11 Germans, 2 Portuguese, 7 Swedes, 5 Americans, 2 Indians, 5 Hungarians, 2 Danes, 1 Prussian, i

from Riga, 3 from Guinea, 2 from Santo Domingo, and 7 from active enemies – 4 Dutch, 1 East Indian (presumably a Dutch subject), 1 from Martinique, and 1 Spaniard. It is notable, however, that no metropolitan Frenchman is included, though several hundred had been prisoners at the Cape in the previous three months (muster books of *Volontaire* and *Rolla* respectively – *Rolla* was the name used in the Royal Navy for the former *Rollo*).

28. WO 1/342, 125–135, Baird to Castlereagh, 8 Mar 1806; Theal, *Records*, 375; 'Recollections' 192; Wilson, 10 Mar 1806; Theal, *Records* 382–383.
29. ADM 1/58, 224–226, Popham to Marsden, 21 Mar 1806.
30. Wilson, 12 Mar 1806.
31. WO 1/343, 9–20, Baird to Gordon, 29 Mar 1806 (24th in Baird's own copy: Baird letter book 141–152); Weir (note 4, ch 3).
32. *Popham Court-Martial*, document I, Admiralty to Popham, 2 August 1806.
33. Baird letter book 1–11, Baird to Gordon, 24 March 1806.
34. ADM 1/58, 244, Waine to Popham, 24 Mar 1806.
35. Gillespie 22; 'Recollections' 195.
36. Master's log of *Leda*, 4 April 1806. The ship reached South American waters on 12 May; the master was taken prisoner on the 20th, which means his log is interrupted until 3 Aug.
37. ADM 1/58, 238–239, Popham to Marsden, 9 Apr 1806.
38. 'Recollections' 196.
39. Wilson, 14 Apr 1806.

Chapter 4

1. Arkin, 'John Company at the Cape, a History of the Agency under Pringle (1794–1815)', *Archives Year Book of South African History* 23 (1960) 179–344.
2. E.A.G. Clark, '"The Spirit of Private Enterprise", British Merchants and the Establishment of new Ports and Trades in the Cape of Good Hope, 1795–1840', in S. Fisher (ed.), *Innovation in Shipping and Trade*, Exeter Maritime Studies 6 (Exeter 1989) 111–130; *DSANB*, John Murray.
3. Theal, *Records*, VI, 36–38.
4. Liebbrandt, *Requesten*, Andrew MacDonald.
5. Clark, 'Spirit'; see also the long list of British emigrants in E. M. Jones, *Roll of the British Settlers in South Africa*, 2nd ed, Cape Town, 1971, and the even longer list in P. Philip, *British Residents in the Cape, 1795–1819*, Cape Town, 1990; however, note the difference between 'settlers' and 'residents'.
6. Population figures: fig. 10.1, in R. Elphick and H. Giliomee (eds), *The Shaping of South African Society, 1652–1820*, (Cape Town 1979) 236.
7. Theal, *Records*, VI, 58 (wine), V, 57 (sheep), VI 36–38 (harvest), V, 415–420 (cattle).
8. Theal, *Records*, V, 406, 430–431, 433–434, 444, VI, 22–26, 26–27, 44–46, 47–49.
9. BL Add Mss 37852, 312–314, Lord Minto to Windham, 7 Apr 1807.
10. C. N. Parkinson, *War in the Eastern Seas, 1793–1815* (London 1954) 375–411; J. Sym (ed.), *Seaforth Highlanders*, Aldershot 1962.
11. A.J. Smithers, *The Kaffir Wars* (London 1973) 80–88.
12. J. Campbell, *Travels in South Africa* (London 1815) 100.
13. A.J. Smithers, *The Kaffir Wars* (London 1973) 95.
14. A.E.J. Cavendish, *The 93rd Sutherland Highlanders* (London 1926) 35.

15. J. Campbell, *Travels in South Africa* (London 1815) 95.
16. Figures are from the monthly returns, WO 17.
17. A.E.J. Cavendish, *The 93rd Sutherland Highlanders* (London 1926) 37.
18. See the list in Philip, *British Residents*.
19. Jones, *Roll of British Settlers*.
20. H. A. Hockly, *The Story of the British Settlers of 1820 in South Africa*, (Cape Town 1975).
21. A. C. Ross, 'The Dutch Reformed Church of South Africa: a Product of the Disruption?' in S. J. Brown and M. Fry, *Scotland in the Age of the Disruption* (Edinburgh 1993) 151–164, is my source for this section.
22. M. Wilson and L. Thompson (eds), *A History of South Africa to 1870*, London 1979; E. Walker, *The Great Trek*, London 1965; Smithers, *The Kaffir Wars*. The literature on the Great Trek is, of course, very large, and very partisan.

Chapter 5

1. D. Stewart, *Sketches of the Character, Manners and Present State of the Highlands of Scotland with Details of the Military Service of the Highland Regiments*, vol. 2 (Edinburgh 1822 (reprinted 1977)).
2. Ibid.
3. Ibid; cf also, V. Kiernan, 'Scottish Soldiers and the Conquest of India', in G. G. Simpson (ed.), *The Scottish Soldier Abroad* (Edinburgh 1992) 93–110.
4. WO 25/456; this is the basis of much of the rest of this chapter.
5. Regimental pay lists are in WO 12/7855 and 7856.
6. Edinburgh University Library DK 7.53/83.

Chapter 6

1. Muster books of ships; Walters 41–42.
2. Master's log of *Diomede*, 21 April 1806; Gavin III; Walters 42.
3. Master's log of *Encounter*, 22 April 1806; Thompson 130, says that the Commodore signalled to the fleet to sail for St Helena after *Ocean* had parted. It is clear that the fleet did not know its destination.
4. G.C. Kitching, 'The St Helena Regiments of the East India Company', *Journal of the Society of Army Historical Research* 25 (1947) 2–8.
5. India Office Records, F/MIL/13/4, St Helena muster rolls, Oct – Dec 1805.
6. ADM 1/58, 252–254, Popham to Patten, 23 Apr and 1 May 1806; Gillespie 28; ADM 1/58 289–290, Popham to Marsden, 6 July 1806; Thompson 130; Walters 42.
7. Master's log of *Narcissus*, 27 May – 7 June 1806; Gillespie 30; Walters 42; Thompson 130.
8. Thompson 130–131.
9. Ibid.
10. Thompson 131; Gavin III; Master's log of *Encounter*, 12 and 14 June 1806.
11. Gillespie 40, 45.
12. *ODNB*, Beresford.
13. *ODNB*, Popham.
14. Adm 1/58, 289–292; Masters' logs; Walters 42.
15. Gillespie 42–43 (dating the landing to the 25th); Thompson 131–133; Fernyhough 90; Master's log of *Encounter*, 26 Jan 1806.
16. Thompson 133.

17. Gillespie 42–43; ADM 1/58, 289–292, Popham to Marsden, 6 July 1806; Master's log of *Encounter*, 26 June 1806.
18. Gavin IV.
19. Gillespie 45–46; Fernyhough 90–91; Gavin IV; WO 1/161, 65–73, Beresford to Baird, 2 July 1806.
20. A.M. Salas, *Diario de Buenos Aires, 1806–1807*, (Buenos Aires 1981) 16 June 1806.
21. Velasquez 1 in Castlereagh, *Corr.* VII, 302–314. This is a long letter by the intendant of Paraguay to the Minister of War in Madrid, dated 1 Aug. Velazquez took part in the subsequent events and is a good if verbose witness. This letter was intercepted by the British and translated; it is the translation which is in the Castlereagh papers. A later letter, also intercepted and translated, deals with the events of 1807.
22. Ibid.
23. Salas, *Diario*, 17–18 June 1806.
24. E. Costa, *English Invasion of the River Plate*, Buenos Aires 1937, 37–38; some details are also in F. Pigna, *The Myths of Argentine History*, (Buenos Aires 2005), which is curiously inaccurate on almost everything British, but may perhaps be cautiously trusted on things Argentine.
25. WO 1/161, 65–73, Beresford's report to Castlereagh, 2 July 1806; the order of movement of the Spanish troops is evident from this account.
26. As do: D. Rock, *Argentina 1516–1987* (London 1987) 71; H.S. Ferns, *Britain and Argentina in the Nineteenth Century* (Oxford 1960) 27; T. Halperin Donghi, *Politics, Economics and Society in Argentina in the Revolutionary Period* (Cambridge 1975) 126 (by implication). As Ferns says 'few historians' have been 'willing to defend his conduct or even to explain it'. But fewer still, including Ferns himself, have even tried to understand it. From his own point of view, Sobremonte's actions are clear, rational, and sensible; the problem was that his people were not prepared to be equally rational. And, of course, they turned out to be the winners. Sobremonte then became a very useful scapegoat. See the summary of his career in J. Lynch, *Spanish Colonial Adminstration in the Viceroyalty of the River Plate, 1782–1810* (London 1958).
27. Mulhall, 92–94.
28. Beresford omits this approach march in his report (WO 1/161, 65–73) but the two-column order is attested by Gillespie, 47, and Fernyhough, 91.
29. Mulhall 97; Gillespie 47.
30. WO 1/161, 65–73, Beresford to Baird, 2 July 1806.
31. Gillespie 47–48.
32. 'Recollections' appendix 513.
33. WO 1/161, 80, return of killed and wounded and missing, 27 June 1806.
34. Gillespie 48; WO 1/161, 65–73; Gavin IV.
35. Mulhall 93; Gavin V.
36. WO 1/161, 65–73.
37. Gavin V.
38. WO 1/161, 65–73.
39. Gillespie 48–49; see also Roberts 140–144.
40. Gavin V.
41. Gillespie 49.
42. Mulhall 93–94; Roberts 145–146.

43. He was also at Waterloo, where he sustained mortal wounds, as one of Wellington's aides; Wellington gave up his bed for him to die on.
44. Fernyhough 93; WO 1/161, 65–73.
45. A copy of the terns is at WO 1/161, 74–75.
46. Gavin V – VI; Fernyhough 94; Gillespie 50–51.
47. Quoted by Pigna, *Myths*, 177–178.
48. Fernyhough 94; Mulhall 94; ADM 1/58, 289–292, Popham to Marsden, 7 July 1806.

Chapter 7

1. ADM 1/58, 292, Popham to Marsden, 6 July 1806.
2. WO 1/161, 78, Return of Captured Ordnance, 5 July 1806.
3. ADM 1/58, 285–340, letters to the Admiralty. WO 1/161, 102, Popham to Castlereagh, 14 July 1806; National Library of Scotland, Melville Papers 1075, 82–85, Popham to Melville, 12 July 1806; Scottish Record Office, GD 136/496, Popham to Sir John Sinclair, 14 July 1806; R.A. Waite, *Sir Home Riggs Popham, KM, KCG, KCH, FRS, Rear Admiral of the Red Squadron*, Ph.D. thesis, Harvard, 1942, names London, Birmingham, Liverpool, Bristol, Manchester, and Glasgow as targets for Popham's correspondence, to which Leeds can be added. The Birmingham letter is reproduced in *The Times* of 20 Sep 1806, and is representative of the others.
4. *The Times*, 13 Sep 1806.
5. WO 1/342, 235–236, appointment of Beresford as local Major General, by Baird, 14 April 1806.
6. WO 1/161, 88–89 and 90, Proclamations by Beresford, 30 June 1806.
7. WO 1/161, 74–76, a printed version is in ADM 1/58, 295.
8. Gavin V.
9. Ibid.
10. ADM 1/58, 300–304, Popham to Marsden, 8 July 1806.
11. Ibid.
12. WO 1/161, 90, Proclamation by Beresford, 30 June 1806.
13. ADM 1/58, 300–304, Popham to Marsden, 8 July 1806, 'P.S.'; Gillespie 54; Gavin VI says the commander of the party sent for the treasure was Captain Charles Graham, though Graham was actually a lieutenant; Pigna, *Myths*, 177, quoting the *Book of the Lujan Cabildo*, 1806–1814, folio 6.
14. WO 1/161, Account of Money, 16 July 1806.
15. Pococke, 15 July 1806; Waite, *Popham* 150.
16. S. Arcos, *La Plata, Etude Historique*, Madrid 1865, 202.
17. The matter is ignored by H. Popham, *A Damned Cunning Fellow*, (Tywardraeth, Cornwall 1991).
18. Baird letters III, 106, Popham to Baird 6(?) July 1806.
19. Acknowledged by Baird on 12 August: WO 1/161, 12 Aug 1806, Baird to Beresford.
20. Ibid, 105, Popham to the Senior Naval Officer at the Cape, 5 July 1806.
21. Gavin VI.
22. Mulhall 94.
23. Scottish United Services Museum, *Trofeos de la Reconquista de la Cuidad de Buenos Aires en la Ano 1806*, Eng trans in typescript. This is a series of testimonies by participants or their descendents, some no more reliable than their equivalents on the British side, but with useful details.

24. J. Lynch, *Spanish Colonial Administration 1782–1810*; brief biographies are in *Biographie Universelle*, vol. 24, 568–569, and *Gran Enciclopedia Argentina*.
25. Roberts 178–179, 183.
26. Baird letters III, 109, Liniers to the Prince of the Peace, 16 Aug 1806, captured and translated into English.
27. Roberts 177.
28. *Trofeos*, testimony of the grandson of Don Santiago Fernandez de Lorca.
29. Roberts 178.
30. This is evident from casual comments, all clustering at the end of July, in Pococke, Fernyhough (97), Gillespie (87), and Gavin (V).
31. Pococke, 19 July 1806; Fernyhough 91.
32. Gillespie 55; H.V. Livermore, 'Captain Gillespie and the 58 Anglophiles of Buenos Aires in 1806', *Hispanic American Historical Review* 60, 1980, 69–78.
33. Gillespie 88–89.
34. Fernyhough 97.
35. Gavin V.
36. Mulhall 94.
37. L. Butler, 'Minor Expeditions of the British Army from 1803 to 1815: VI Expeditions to South America', *United Services Magazine 31* (1905) 280.
38. ADM 1/58, 349–350, Popham to Marsden 19 July 1806, 294, List of gun vessels captured; this named four ships captured and added that four unnamed gunboats had also been taken; these had to be manned from warships which were already grievously undermanned; ADM 1/58, 289–292; Master's log of *Encounter*, 4 July 1806; even so, *Encounter* was frequently aground, Master's log, *passim;* ADM 1/58, 363, Popham to Marsden, 26 July 1806. Rowley, of *Raisonable*, left all his marines except one at Buenos Aires and more than fifty of his seamen (muster book).
39. ADM 1/58, 449–350, Popham to Marsden, 19 July 1806; Master's log of *Encounter*, July and Aug 1806.
40. Pococke 193–194.
41. Roberts 181–183.
42. Gavin VI.
43. Fernyhough 101; Pococke 195.
44. Liniers to the Prince of the Peace, 16 Aug 1806, a captured and translated account.
45. Roberts 182–184.
46. Pococke 211; ADM 1/58, 393–396, King to Popham, 12 Aug 1806; Master's log of *Leda*, 6 Aug 1806; ADM 1/58, 393–396; Pococke 212.
47. ADM 1/58, 414–423; Roberts 186; Master's log of *Encounter*, 6 Aug 1806.
48. Pococke 211.
49. Ibid 211–212.
50. Gillespie 93; Roberts 186–187; Mulhall 98.
51. Gillespie 94.
52. ADM 1/58, 414–423; Mulhall 98; Pococke 212.
53. Gllespie 94; ADM 1/58, 414–423, Liniers to the Prince of the Peace, 12 Aug 1806. Gillespie says the post was manned by a sergeant and 17 men, of whom only two survived: Liniers claimed 30 to 35 killed and 10 prisoners, five of them wounded; Velazquez says the post was manned by 60 men. The regimental records of the 71st name only four men killed on the 10th. Gavin VI named the picquet commander.

54. Mulhall 99; Pococke 213; ADM 1/58, 414–423.
55. Pococke 213; Mulhall 100 claims Popham urged Beresford to evacuate at once.
56. WO 1/161, 251–276, Beresford to Castlereagh, 4 May 1807.
57. Gavin VI.
58. Gillespie 94–96.
59. Fernyhough 99–100.
60. Ibid 102.
61. WO 1/162, 251–276.
62. Roberts 190–196.
63. Pococke 216
64. Fernyhough 101.
65. WO 1/161, 251–276.
66. Gillespie 97.
67. Pococke 216.
68. Roberts 197, tabulated the Spanish casualties; J.W. Fortescue, *History of the British Army*, vol VII, 71; Butler 'Minor Expeditions', VII 282. The source of the British figure for the Spanish casualties is unknown, though it was presumably based on something; whatever the source; it is clearly a blind guess; Salas, *Diario* 208–209, footnote 92.

Chapter 8
1. WO 1/162, 301–331, Beresford to Castlereagh, 12 May 1807; I have punctuated, Beresford's pen not being equipped for the purpose, it seems.
2. Pococke, 13–16 Aug 1806; Gillespie, 97; Fernyhough, 105.
3. For accounts of the situation in Buenos Aires after the August days, see the books by H.S. Ferns, *Britain and Argentina in the Nineteenth Century* (Oxford 1960) 30–31, T. Halperin Donghi, *Politics, Economics and Society in Argentina in the Revolutionary Period* (Cambridge 1975) 122–135, J. Lynch, *The Spanish American Revolutions, 1806–1826* 2nd ed., (New York 1986) 41–42. Only Haperin Donghi seriously distinguishes between the events of 1806 and those of 1807; all are more concerned to apply revolutionary theory to the events than to recount what happened. Argentine accounts tend to magnify the heroic, but see Roberts for a balanced discussion.
4. Kennach 3.
5. Gavin VII; Pococke 14 and 17 Aug 1806; Kennach 3, Fernyhough 107.
6. Gavin VII.
7. Ibid.
8. Gillespie 98–99.
9. ADM 1/58, 426, Popham to 'the General Commanding the Spanish Forces in Buenos Ayres', 12 Aug 1806.
10. The first letter to Montevideo was dated 15 Aug 1806 (ADM 1/58, 424–425) addressed to the 'Governor-General'. Between 23 August and 14 September, they exchanged 23 letters.
11. There is a letter addressed to the viceroy by Popham dated 24 Aug 1806 (BL Add 32607, 29) but all essential conversation was between Popham and Huidobro, with virtually no reference to Sobremonte.
12. E.g., Pococke, 17, 19, 25 Aug 1806.
13. WO 1/162, 335–338, Pack to Auchmuty, 27, Feb 1807.
14. Pococke 22–23 Aug 1806.

15. ADM 1/58, 490, Huidobro to Popham, 24 Aug 1806.
16. Ibid, 503–504, Beresford to Liniers, 24 Aug 1806.
17. Ibid, 511, Beresford to the Masters of the Transports, 28 Aug 1806.
18. Pococke 29 Aug 1806; Gillespie 98.
19. ADM 1/58, 513, de la Concha to the Commander of the British ships 29 Aug 1806; 519, Captains Honeyman, Edmonds and King reported on the investigations to Popham, 8 Sep 1806.
20. Gavin VII.
21. Pococke 2, 3, 5, 6, and 24 Sep 1806.
22. Kennach 3.
23. Gavin VII.
24. Fernyhough 106.
25. Kennach 3–4.
26. Figures from A. Graham-Youll, *The Forgotten Colony* (London 1976) 45–46; Gavin IX.
27. Fernyhough 108–111.
28. Gillespie 124–130 and 137–139.

Chapter 9
1. Baird reported their arrival on 31 Aug 1806, Baird letter book, 222–223, Baird to Gordon.
2. Originally published in 1819; sometimes attributed to Pococke, in one recent edition to Joseph Sinclair.
3. Landsheit, 160.
4. Muster roll of 20 Light Dragoons, August, according to the embarkation return produced when the detachment sailed for the River Plate: Theal, *Records*, VI, 33. There were also 9 women and 14 children, and 8 of each with the 20th.
5. The precise figures are from the muster rolls of these regiments for August 1806:
   34 Foot 538
   72 Foot 625
   83 Foot 739
   93 Foot 664
   38 Foot 897 (Embarkation return).
   These figures include the sick but exclude those 'on command'. Of the total of 3,463, 208 were sick, though no figures are available for the 38th. Theal, *Records*, VII 33, shows this figure embarked for South America.
6. Of the 111 from the 2nd Foot originally captured, only 74 finally rejoined the regiment in April 1807 (Muster book of the 2nd Foot). Of the 54th Foot, 114 went to the River Plate (Theal, *Records*, VII 33).
7. In August 1806, the total on muster was 616, but 97 were sick or on command (Muster of Cape Regiment).
8. Master's logs of *Howe* and *Medusa*, 16 Aug 1806. *Howe* was carrying no less than 370 supplementary personnel and *Medusa* another 100 (Muster books; Baird letter book, 240–242, Baird to Beresford, 24 Aug 1806; Master's log of *Rolla*, 22 Aug 1906; Theal, *Records*, VI, 33, embarkation returns.)
9. *Later Correspondence of George III*, IV, 3274, Cabinet Minute enclosed in Windham to the King, 27 June 1806.
10. Theal, *Records*, V, 446, Grey's instructions, 26 July 1806.
11. WO 6/3, 3–7, 7–9, Windham to Auchmuty, 24 July 1806; ADM 2/1364, 37–39, Admiralty Board to Stirling, 28 July 1806.

12. BL Add Mss, 37842, 152, Duke of York to Windham, 1 July 1806; HMC Fortescue Mss, VIII, 209–210.

13. WO 6/3, 14, Windham to Duke of York, 1 August 1806, and 16, Windham to Auchmuty, 6 Aug 1806; a diary note of Sir William Watkins Wynn of 1 August records the discussion over dinner of the measures to be taken and the alternative scenarios expected (Aberystwyth, National Library of Wales, Coed-y-Maen Ms 504).

14. ADM 1/58, 399 and 400, Stirling to Marsden, 28 Aug 1806; Stirling, 28–31 Aug 1806.

15. Mrs. M. Baring (ed.), *Diary of the Rt Hon William Windham*, London 1866, 12 Sep 1806; Huntington Library, STG 45, 57, Windham to Buckingham, 12 Sep 1806; *The Times*, 13 Sep 1806.

16. *British Volunteer and Manchester Weekly Express*, 20 Sep 1806.

17. BL. Add 31884, 9, Lord Selkirk to Windham, 7 June 1806, the covering note for 11–22, 'Observations on the Proposed Expeditions against Spanish America'; BL Add 59079, 58, 'Antigallican' to Lord Grenville, 29 Sep 1806.

18. *The Times*, 20 Sep 1806; *British Volunteer and Manchester Weekly Express*, 20 Sep 1806.

19. *The Courier*, 18 Sep 1806 – one example of contemporary newspaper reports.

20. *Evening Courant*, 18 Sep 1806; W. R. Crump (ed.), *The Leeds Woollen Industry, 1780–1820*, Publications of the Thoresby Society 32 for 1929, Leeds 1931 (the Gott Papers), 108–109; Kent Record Office, U 840, Pratt Ms, C 117/2, Lord Lowther to Lord Camden, 29 Sep 1806.

21. As was, e.g. the *British Volunteer* and *Manchester Weekly Express*, 20 and 27 Sep 1806.

22. Eastwicke, 220–221.

23. Humphreys, *Liberation*, 7–8.

24. Robertson, *Paraguay*, vol 1, 8.

25. School of Oriental and African Studies, London Missionary Society Archives, America, 1799–1896, folder 3, 1, Letter of Instructions to Rev'd Creighton, Missionary to Buenos Aires, 6 Oct 1806.

26. WO 1/161, 118–121, Windham to Auchmuty, 22 Sep 1806.

27. WO 1/161, 122–131, Windham to Beresford, 21 Sep 1806.

28. BL Add 59286, 171, Troops for Embarkation, 21 Sep 1806; WO 6/3, 41–47, Windham to Auchmuty, 22 Sep 1806; WO 1/161, 122–131, Windham to Beresford, 21 Sep 1806.

29. BL Add 59028, 201, R. Craufurd to Lord Grenville, 30 June 1806.

30. WO 6/3, 60–71, Windham to Craufurd, 30 Oct 1806.

31. WO 6/3, 122–123, Windham to Governor Bligh, 26 Nov 1806.

32. *ODNB*, Auchmuty, Craufurd, Murray, Stirling.

33. WO 6/3, 2, Admiralty to Murray, 17 Nov 1806.

34. Huntington Library, STG 37, 32, Tom Grenville to Buckingham, 8 Nov 1806; ADM 50/47, Murray's Journal, 24–31 Dec 1806.

35. Baring, *Diary of Windham*, 12 Feb 1807; Durham University, Grey Papers, First Earl, 2214, Memo on the question of retaining Buenos Aires; Fortescue suggested Popham as the author of this paper, but it is not his style at all, being much more judicious.

36. Huntington Library, STG 136, 5, John Barlinder to Lord Grenville, 21 Jan 1807; the fact that this letter is in this collection suggests that it was handed on to Tom Grenville as First Lord.

37. BL Add 59079, 120, Military strength of the Kingdom of Buenos Aires; there is another copy in the Grey Papers at Durham, 52/7.

38. BL Add Mss 37847, 186–187, Minute by Lord Grenville (n.d).

39. H.M.C. Fortescue Mss, IX, 1–2, Lord Grenville to Windham, 1 Jun 1807; BL Add 59288, 56, Memorandum relating to the Inspector-General's Office, Mar 1807.

40. Sir Robert Steele, *The Marine Officer, or Sketches of Service* (London 1840) 67; Capt. John Hawley, *The Veteran, or Fifty Years in the British Service* (London 1838) 181; 'Recollections', 215; *ODNB*, Whitelocke.

41. WO 1/162, 176, Whitelocke to Windham, 27 May 1807.

Chapter 10

1. The figures for captured seamen are based on the ships' musters:

	Captured	Killed	Run	Discharged
Diadem	114	2	0	9
Raisonable	117	2	0	4
Diomede	63	8	0	6
Leda	34	2	0	6
Encounter	0	1	0	1

putting seamen and marines together: total 328 captures.

2. ADM 1/58, 484–498, Popham to Marsden, 9 Oct 1806; 536, Popham to Marsden, 11 Oct 1806; 549–549, Popham to Marsden, 30 Oct 1806; Landsheit, 168–169; 'Recollections', 201.

3. J. Street, *Artigas and the Emancipation of Uruguay* (Cambridge 1959) 87–90.

4. The lengthy and extraordinary exchange of letters between Popham – increasingly petulant – and Stirling – stolidly consistent – is published in my Navy Records Society volume, *The Royal Navy in the River Plate, 1806–1807* (1996) nos 225–245.

5. WO 1/162, 28–30, Auchmuty to Windham, 7 Feb 1807; Stirling, Jan 1807.

6. Stirling, 13 Jan 1807.

7. BL Add 32607, 67–70, Proclamations by the viceroy to arm Montevideo and put the city in a state of siege, 20 and 23 December 1806.

8. Stirling, 16 Jan 1807.

9. WO 1/162, 56–59, Auchmuty to Windham, 7 Feb 1807.

10. 'Recollections', 490.

11. Stirling, 17 Jan 1807.

12. Roberts 274–276, and his plan, opposite p. 312.

13. WO 1/162, 29–40, Auchmuty to Windham, 6 Feb 1807.

14. Landsheit, 192–195.

15. *A Narrative of the Operations*, 8.

16. WO 1/162, 29–40.

17. Jennings, 83.

18. Stirling, 20 Jan 1807.

19. WO 1/162, 52–53, Return of killed, wounded and missing, 16–20 Jan 1807; a letter from a soldier to the Cabildo of Buenos Aires cannot provide the number of dead, but speaks of 200 wounded and 300 prisoners; proportionately the Montevideans probably lost less than a hundred dead (Costa, *English Invasion*, 82–83).

20. Stirling, 21 Jan 1807.

21. *Journal of a Soldier of the 71st or Glasgow Regiment* (Edinburgh 1819) 34.

22. Stirling, 22 Jan 1807.

23. Stirling, 30 Jan 1807; Street, *Artigas*, 89.

24. Roberts 282.

25. Stirling, 23, 28, 30 Jan and 1 Feb 1807.
26. Stirling, 24 and 28 Jan, 1 Feb 1807; WO 17/1219, Auchmuty Expedition Monthly Return, 1 Feb 1807.
27. Jennings, 85–88.
28. Lawrence, 23.
29. WO 1/162, 29–40.
30. Lawrence, 24–25.
31. WO 1/162, 26–27, Return of Casualties, 16 Jan – 3 Feb 1807; WO 1/162, 15–20; ADM 103/242, Prisoners captured at Montevideo, 3 Feb 1807.
32. 'Recollections', 495–496.
33. *Authentic Narrative*, 102–104.
34. Jennings, 88–89.
35. Stirling, 3 Feb 1807.
36. WO 1/162, 29–40.
37. BL Add 37886, 38–39, Bourke to Windham, 9 Feb 1807.

Chapter 11

1. *Authentic Narrative*, 110.
2. WO 1/162, 54–58, Auchmuty to Windham, 2 Mar 1807.
3. WO 1/162, 301–331, Beresford to Castlereagh, 12 May 1807.
4. 'Billy Pitt', *The Cabin Boy* (London 1840) 124.
5. WO 1/162, 164, Auchmuty to Sir George Shee, 20 Mar 1807.
6. Lawrence, 29–31.
7. J. Mawe, *Travels in the Interior of Brazil* (London 1820) 20–33.
8. Stirling, 'Remarks' .
9. ADM 1/59, 23, Stirling to Marsden, 8 Mar 1807.
10. Robertson, *Paraguay*, I, 101.
11. Humphreys, *Liberation*, 9.
12. Gillespie, 138–139.
13. Fernyhough, 114–115.
14. Gillespie, 166–167.
15. Gavin, VIII.
16. Pococke, 594.
17. Gavin VIII.
18. WO 1/162, 175–178, Major D. Campbell to Auchmuty (n.d).
19. Lawrence, 21
20. Lawrence, 22.
21. 'Recollections', 212–213.

Chapter 12

1. ADM 1/59, 37, Murray to Marsden, Polyphemus, Table Bay, 23 Mar 1807.
2. WO 1/162, 179, Craufurd to Windham, Cape Town, 27 Mar 1807.
3. *ODNB*, Whitelocke; copies of *The Southern Star* are in the Bodleian Library, Oxford.
4. WO 1/162, 387–388, Lieutenant-Colonel Pack to Whitelocke to Windham, Colonia, 8 June 1807.
5. Roberts 322–323.
6. *Authentic Narrative*, 113–114.
7. *Whitelocke Court-Martial*, 39, Evidence of Brigadier-General Craufurd.

8. *Whitelocke Court-Martial*, 24, Evidence of Lieutenant-Colonel Bourke.

9. *Journal of a Soldier of the 71st*, 40.

10. Holland, 55–56.

11. Lawrence, 36–37.

12. WO 1/162, 457–459, Gower to Major Henry Torrens, Coral of Miserere, 3 July 1807.

13. *A Narrative of the Expedition*, 12.

14. *Whitelocke Court-Martial*, 44, Evidence of Brigadier-General Craufurd.

15. 'Minor Expeditions.'

16. Tabulated by Roberts 232–233; the figures are precise, but must be taken as usual as only approximate; see also I. Fletcher, *The Waters of Oblivion* (Stroud 2006) 139–142.

17. F. Whittingham, *A Memoir of the Services of Lt-Gen Sir Samuel Ford Whittingham* (London 1868).

18. National Army Museum, 6403–14, Major Henry King's Diary.

19. Holland, 61–62.

20. *Whitelocke Court-Martial*, 125–128, Evidence of Brigadier-General Craufurd.

21. WO 1/162, 222–223, Casualty Return.

22. *Whitelocke Court-Martial*, 166, Evidence of Lieutenant-Colonel Bourke.

23. *Gazeta de Madrid*, 26 November 1807; a copy is in BL Eg 383, 70 75.

24. WO 1/162, 224–225, copy of the Definitive Treaty.

Chapter 13

1. Holland, 61–62.

2. *Journal of a Soldier of the 71st*, 42–43.

3. *Authentic Narrative*, 167.

4. Holland, 62–63.

5. 'Tom Plunkett', *United Services Journal*, 1842, 70.

6. *Authentic Narrative*, 172.

7. *Journal of a Soldier of the 71st*, 43.

8. Fernyhough, 117, 119, 120, 121.

9. H. V. Livermore, 'Captain Gillespie and the 59 Anglophiles of Buenos Aires in 1806', *Hispanic American Historical Review* 60 (1980) 69–78.

10. Gillespie, 194, 260–261.

11. Kennach, 4–5.

12. Fernyhough, 121–122.

13. Ibid, 122–124.

14. Ibid, 124–125.

15. Gillespie, 264.

16. Gavin, VIII.

17. Kennach, 5–7.

18. *Authentic Narrative*, 203–203.

19. The figures are based on the summary of the army musters in WO 1/1219; the navy's figures are from the equivalent monthly musters of each ship.

20. Gavin, IX.

21. Gillespie, 278–279.

22. J. Mawe, *Travels in the Interior of Brazil* (London 1820) 55–56.

23. WO 1/162, 523–538, Whitelocke to Castlereagh, 10 Sep 1807.

24. *Whitelocke Court-Martial*, Whitelocke's Defence.

Chapter 14

1. *Authentic Narrative*, 205.
2. WO 1/162, 260–261, Whitelocke to Castlereagh, 29 July 1807.
3. Monthly returns of the regiments and ships.
4. WO 12/7856.
5. [Anon], *Regimental Records of the First Battalion, Highland Light Infantry*, Dinapore (1908) 45; H. J. T. Hildyard, *Historical Records of the 71st Regiment, Highland Light Infantry* (London 1876); L. B. Oatts, *Proud Heritage*, vol 1 (London 1952).
6. M. Newitt (ed.), *War, Revolution and Society in the Rio de la Plata, Thomas Kidder's Narrative of a Journey to Madeira, Montevideo and Buenos Aires* (Oxford 2010) 172.
7. H.S. Ferns, *Britain and Argentina in the Nineteenth Century* (Oxford 1960) 77.
8. For instance, see the figures quoted in A.E.J. Cavendish, *The 93rd Sutherland Highlanders* (London 1926).
9. *Gran Enciclopedia Argentina*, Brown, Guillermo.
10. J.P. Robertson, *Letters from Paraguay*, Vol. I, London 1843, 178.
11. Ibid.
12. R. Humphreys, *Liberation in South America, 1806–1827, the career of James Paroissien* (London 1952).
13. Ferns, *Britain and Argentina*.
14. Scottish United Services Museum, *Trofeos de la Conquista*.
15. Fernyhough, 112.
16. Newitt (ed.) *War, Revolution*, 127.
17. This is much studied; see the books by Halperin Donghi, Lunch, Rock, and others in the bibliography.
18. J. Street, *Artigas and the Emancipation of Uruguay* (Cambridge 1959).
19. D. Rock, *Argentina 1516–1987* (London 1987) 82–83.
20. Marquis de Sassenay, *Napoleon Ier et la fondation de la Republique Argentine (*Paris 1892).

Chapter 15

1. The Vellore mutiny is much less famous than the greater one fifty years later, but had much the same causes and results; see P. Mason, *A Matter of Honour* (London 1974) 237–242; R. Holmes, *Sahib* (London 2005) 237; J. Rosselli, *Lord William Bentinck* (London 1974) 139–145.
2. D. Gates, *The Spanish Ulcer* (London 1966) 82–91; J. Weller, *Wellington in the Peninsula* 2nd ed., (London 1992) 29–58.
3. G.C. Moore Smith (ed.), *Autobiography of Sir Harry Smith* (London 1901); this is less an autobiography that a reconstructed life; Harry Smith's diary for 1806–1807 is meagre in the extreme, and the account of these years rests on other sources.
4. A.E.J. Cavendish, *The 93rd Sutherland Highlanders* (London 1926), 40.
5. Cavendish, *Sutherland Highlanders*, states the casualties as 116 killed, 359 wounded, and 72 missing (most of whom apparently died); this is seventy-five per cent of the regiment's strength; R. H. Burgoyne, *Historical Records of the 93rd Sutherland Highlanders* (London 1883), lists the killed by name and origin, producing a total of 128 dead.
6. The main clearances are listed conveniently in J. Prebble, *The Highland Clearances* (London 1963) 307–310. A more balanced view of the events is by E. Richards, *A History of the Highland Clearances* (London 1982); a summary of the problem is by T.M. Devine, 'The Highland Clearances', *Exploring the Scottish Past* (East Linton, 1995) 133–141;

for the economic background, B. Lenman, *An Economic History of Modern Scotland* (London, 1977) – the relevant chapter is entitled 'The Triumph of Commercialization and Industry'.

7. J. Prebble, *Mutiny* (London 1975) – but this book goes no farther than 1804.

8. *Annual Register*, 1816.

9. B. Bailyn, *Voyagers to the West* (New York 1986), suggests some numbers; N. Landsman, *Scotland's first American Colony, 1683–1765,* (Princeton NJ 1985), discusses New Jersey; A.J. Youngson, *After the Forty-Five* (Edinburgh 1973), looks at reasons and numbers; M. I. Adam, 'The Causes of the Highland Emigration of 1783–1803', *Scottish Historical Review* 17, (1919–1920), is still useful, and succinct; I. Adams and M. Somerville, *Cargoes of Despair and Hope, Scottish Emigration to North America 1603–1803* (Edinburgh 1993); A. L. Karras, *Sojourners in the Sun, Scottish Migrants in Jamaica and the Chesapeake, 1740–1800* (Ithaca, NY 1992).

10. T. M. Devine, 'The Paradox of Scottish Emigration', *Exploring the Scottish Past* (East Linton, 1995) 238–250; the same author has also produced two more detailed overlapping discussions: *Scotland's Empire 1600–1815* (London 2003), and *To the Ends of the Earth, Scotland's Global Diaspora 1750–2010* (London 2011); see also M. Fry, *The Scottish Empire* (East Linton and Edinburgh, 2006).

11. Adam, 'Causes'.

12. R. Clyde, *From Rebel to Hero, the Image of the Highlander 1745–1830* (East Linton, 1995).

13. V. Kiernan, 'Scottish Soldiers and the Conquest of India', in G. G. Simpson (ed.), *The Scottish Soldier Abroad* (Edinburgh 1992) 93–110.

14. For the process, see J.R. Scobie, *Revolution in the Pampas, the Social History of Argentine Wheat, 1860–1910* (Texas 1964).

15. Gavin IX.

Sources and Bibliography

I. Manuscript sources.

The National Archives, London
ADM 1/58 and 59, 2/1363 and 1364
ADM 50 Admirals' Journals, 51 Captains' logs, 53 Masters' logs
WO 1/161 and 162 War Office In-letters
WO 1/341, 342, 342 Despatches from South America
WO 6/3 War Office out-letters
WO 17 Muster rolls and monthly returns
WO 1/711, 1219 12/7855 and 7856; WO 25; WO 103
WO 71 Court-martials and 91 Court martial sentences

British Library, London
BL Add Mss 30096 Papers of General Wilson
BL Add Mss 31884 Windham Papers
BL Add Mss 32607
BL Add Mss 37842, 37847, 37852 Windham Papers
BL Add Mss 59028, 59079, 59286 Grenville Papers
BL Eg Mss 383
India Office Records, F/MIL/13/4

Bodleian Library, Oxford
MS Eng. Misc. d 242, Journal of Richard Thompson, Surgeon RN (1799–1810)

Durham University
52/7 Grey Papers

Edinburgh University Library
DK 7.5383
DK 7.53/83

Gloucestershire Record Office
Rooke Papers 2002/28, 'Standing Orders for the Invading Force'

Huntington Library, San Marino
Stowe Papers

Kent Record Office, Maidstone
U 840, Pratt Ms, C 117/2

National Army Museum, London
7805–30
6403–14 Major Henry King's Diary.
8301–102 Diary of Captain P. R. Jennings, 40th Foot.

National Library of Scotland, Edinburgh
GD 51, Melville Papers
ADV MS 46.1.21, Murray of Ochtertyre papers.

National Library of Wales, Aberystwyth
Coed-y-Maen Ms 504).

Scottish Record Office
GD 136/496, Melville Papers.

Scottish United Services Museum
Baird letter book
Kennach, *The Campaigns of Corporal Balfour Kennach*, typescript.
Trofeos de la Reconquista de la Cuidad de Buenos Aires en la Ano 1806, English translation in typescript.

School of Oriental and African Studies, University of London
London Missionary Society Correspondence, South Africa and America.

II. Collections of Original Sources.
(These are usually referred to by abbreviated titles.)
Castlereagh, *Corr.* – Marquis of Londonderry, *Correspondence, Despatches and other Papers of Viscount Castlereagh*, second series, Military and Miscellaneous, vol. VI (London 1851).
W.R. Crump (ed.), *The Leeds Woollen Industry, 1780–1820*, Publications of the Thoresby Society 32 for 1929 (Leeds 1931) (the Gott Papers).

Historical Manuscripts Commission:
Fortescue Mss.
Graham of Fintry Mss
Later Correspondence of George III
Liebbrandt, *Requesten* – H. C. Liebbrandt, *Precis of the Archives of the Cape of Good Hope: Requesten (Memorials)*, 5 vols (Cape Town, 1905–1988).
Popham Court-Martial – Anon., *The Court-Martial of Captain Home Popham*, The National Archives G 19449.
Theal, *Records* – G.M. Theal, *Records of South Africa* (Cape Town, 1897–1905).
Whitelocke Court-Martial – Anon., *Trial of Lt-General John Whitelocke*, (London 1808).

III. Contemporary or Near-Contemporary Accounts.

A. Newspapers
British Volunteer and Manchester Weekly Express
The Courier
Evening Courant
The Southern Star (in the Bodleian Library, Oxford)
The Times

B. Literary Accounts
Authentic Narrative – Anon, *An Authentic Narrative of the Proceedings of the Expedition under the Command of Brigadier-General Craufurd* ..., by an officer of the Expedition (London 1808).

Borcherds, P. A., *An Autobiographical Memoir* (Cape Town 1861).

Campbell, J., *Travels in South Africa* (London 1815).

Eastwicke, Capt. Robert, *A Master Mariner* (London).

Fernyhough, R., *Military Memoirs of Four Brothers* (London 1829).

Gavin, Sir Charles Oman (ed.), 'Diary of William Gavin', *H.L.I. Chronicle*, XX, 1920.

Gillespie, A., *Gleanings and Remarks collected during many months of Residence at Buenos Ayres* ... (Leeds 1818).

Hawley, Capt. John, *The Veteran, or Fifty Years in the British Service* (London 1838).

Holland, Diary of Lieutenant-Colonel Lancelot Holland, MS room (University College, London).

Journal of a Soldier of the 71st – Anon., *Journal of a Soldier of the 71st or Glasgow Regiment* (Edinburgh 1819).

Landsheit, C. G. Gleig (ed.), *The Hussar* (London 1837).

Lawrence, G. N. Bankes (ed.), *Autobiography of Sergeant W. Lawrence* (London 1886).

Lichtenstein, H., *Travels in Southern Africa*, trans. A. Plumtre (Cape Town 1930).

Mawe, J., *Travels in the Interior of Brazil* (London 1820).

A Narrative of the Expedition to and the Storming of Buenos Ayres by the British Army Commanded by Lieutenant-General Whitelocke, by an officer attached to the Expedition (Bath 1807).

Newitt, M. (ed.), *War, Revolution and Society in the Rio de la Plata, Thomas Kidder's Narrative of a Journey to Madeira, Montevideo and Buenos Aires* (Oxford 2010).

Perceval, J., *An Account of the Cape of Good Hope* (London 1804).

Philip, J., *Researches in South Africa* (London 1828).

'Billy Pitt', *The Cabin Boy* (London 1840).

Plunkett, Tom, *United Services Journal* (1842).

Pococke, 'Copy of the Journal of Captain Pococke, 71st Highland Regiment', *H.L.I. Chronicle*, (1894–1895).

Steele, Sir Robert, *The Marine Officer, or Sketches of Service* (London 1840).

Stewart, D., *Sketches of the Character, Manners and Present State of the Highlands of Scotland with Details of the Military Service of the Highland Regiments*, vol. 2, (Edinburgh 1822 (reprinted 1977)).

Walters, C. N. Parkinson (ed.), *Memoirs of Lieutenant Samuel Walters R.N.* (Liverpool 1949).

Wilkie, F., 'Recollections of the British Army in the Early Campaigns of the Revolutionary War', United Services Journal (1856).

IV. Reference Books
Annual Register
Biografisch Wordenboek der Nederlander
Biographie Universelle
DSANB – Dictionary of South African National Biography.
Gran Enciclopedia Argentina
Jones, E. M., Roll of the British Settlers in South Africa, 2nd ed, (Cape Town, 1971).
Niewe-Nederlandsch biografisch Wordenboek
ODNB – Oxford Dictionary of National Biography
Philip, P., British Residents in the Cape, 1795–1819 (Cape Town, 1990).

V. Modern Bibliography
Adam, M. I., 'The Causes of the Highland Emigration of 1783–1803', Scottish Historical Review 17 (1919–1920).
Adams, I. and M. Somerville, Cargoes of Despair and Hope, Scottish Emigration to North America 1603–1803 (Edinburgh 1993).
[Anon], Regimental Records of the First Battalion, Highland Light Infantry (Dinapore, India, 1908).
Arcos, S., La Plata, Etude Historique (Madrid 1865).
Arkin, M., 'John Company at the Cape, a History of the Agency under Pringle (1794–1815)', Archives Year Book of South African History 23 (1960) 179–344.
Bailyn, B., Voyagers to the West (New York 1986).
Baring, Mrs. M. (ed.), Diary of the Rt Hon. William Windham (London 1866).
Burgoyne, R. H., Historical Records of the 93rd Sutherland Highlanders (London 1883).
Butler, L., 'Minor Expeditions of the British Army from 1803 to 1815: VI Expeditions to South America', United Services Magazine 31 (1905).
Cannon, R., Historical Records of the 72nd Regiment (London 1837).
Cavendish, A. E. J., The 93rd Sutherland Highlanders (London 1926).
Clark, E. A. G., '"The Spirit of Private Enterprise", British Merchants and the Establishment of new Ports and Trades in the Cape of Good Hope, 1795–1840', in S. Fisher (ed.), Innovation in Shipping and Trade, Exeter Maritime Studies 6 (Exeter 1989) 111–130
Clyde, R., From Rebel to Hero, the Image of the Highlander 1745–1830 (East Linton, 1995).
Corbett, J. S., The Campaign of Trafalgar (London 1910).
Costa, E., English Invasion of the River Plate (Buenos Aires 1937).
Davenport, T. R. H., South Africa, a Modern History (London 1977).
Derricourt, R., 'Settlement in the Transkei and the Ciskei before the Mfecane', in C. Saunders and R. Derricourt (eds), Beyond the Cape Frontier (London 1974) 59–82.
Devine, T. M., 'The Highland Clearances', Exploring the Scottish Past (East Linton, 1995) 133–141.
Devine, T. M., 'The Paradox of Scottish Emigration', Exploring the Scottish Past (East Linton, 1995) 238–250.
Devine, T. M., Scotland's Empire 1600–1815 (London 2003).

Devine, T. M., *To the Ends of the Earth, Scotland's Global Diaspora 1750–2010* (London 2011).

Ferns, H. S., *Britain and Argentina in the Nineteenth Century* (Oxford 1960).

Fletcher, I., *The Waters of Oblivion* (Stroud 2006).

Forester, C. S., *The Commodore* (London 1945).

Fortescue, J. E., *History of the British Army*, vol. V, (London 1921).

Freund, W. M., 'The Cape under Transitional Government, 1795–1814', in R. Elphick and H. Giliomee (eds), *The Shaping of South African Society, 1652–1820* (Cape Town 1979) 211–242.

Freund, W. M., 'The Eastern Frontier of the Cape Colony during the Batavian Period (1803–1806)', *Journal of African Studies* 13 (1972) 631–645.

Fry, M., *The Dundas Despotism* (Edinburgh 1997).

Fry, M., *The Scottish Empire* (East Linton and Edinburgh, 2006).

Gates, D., *The Spanish Ulcer* (London 1966).

Graham-Youll, A., *The Forgotten Colony* (London 1976).

Grainger, J. D., 'The Conquest of the Cape', *Army Quarterly and Defence Journal*, 123 (1993) 316–322.

Halperin-Donghi, T., *Politics, Economics and Society in Argentina in the Revolutionary Period* (Cambridge 1975).

Hildyard, H. J. T., *Historical Records of the 71st Regiment, Highland Light Infantry* (London 1876).

Hockly, H. A., *The Story of the British Settlers of 1820 in South Africa* (Cape Town 1975).

Holmes, R., *Sahib* (London 2005).

Humphreys, R., *Liberation in South America, 1806–1827: the Career of James Paroissien* (London 1952).

Immelman, R.M.F., *Men of Good Hope: the Cape Town Chamber of Commerce, 1804–1954* (Cape Town 1955).

Karras, A.L., *Sojourners in the Sun, Scottish Migrants in Jamaica and the Chesapeake, 1740–1800* (Ithaca, NY 1992).

Kiernan, V., 'Scottish Soldiers and the Conquest of India', and 'Scottish Soldiers and the Conquest of India' in G. G. Simpson (ed.), *The Scottish Soldier Abroad* (Edinburgh 1992) 93–110.

Kitching, G.C., 'The St Helena Regiments of the East India Company', *Journal of the Society of Army Historical Research* 25 (1947) 2–8.

Landsman, N., *Scotland's first American Colony, 1683–1765* (Princeton NJ 1985).

Legassic, M., 'The Northern Frontier to 1820', in R. Elphick and H. Giliomee (eds), *The Shaping of South African Society, 1652–1820* (Cape Town 1979) 243–290.

Lenman, B., *An Economic History of Modern Scotland* (London 1977).

Livermore, H.V., 'Captain Gillespie and the 58 Anglophiles of Buenos Aires in 1806', *Hispanic American Historical Review* 60 (1980) 69–78.

Lynch, J., *Spanish Colonial Adminstration in the Viceroyalty of the River Plate, 1782–1810* (London 1958).

Lynch, J., *The Spanish American Revolutions, 1806–1826*, 2nd ed., (New York 1986).

Marcus, G. J., *A Naval History of England*, vol. 2, *The Age of Nelson* (London 1971).

Mason, P., *A Matter of Honour* (London 1974).

Mulhall, M.G. and E.T., *Handbook of the River Plate* (Buenos Aires, 1885).

Oatts, L.B., *Proud Heritage*, vol 1 (London 1952).

Parkinson, C.N., *War in the Eastern Seas* (London 1954).

Pigna, F., *The Myths of Argentine History* (Buenos Aires 2005).

Pollock, N.C. and S. Agnew, *An Historical Geography of South Africa* (London 1963).

Popham, H., *A Damned Cunning Fellow* (Tywardraeth, Cornwall, 1991).

Prebble, J., *The Highland Clearances* (London 1963).

Prebble, J., *Mutiny* (London 1975).

Richards, E., *A History of the Highland Clearances* (London 1982).

Roberts, C., *Las Invasiones Inglesias de la Rio de la Plata* (Buenos Aires 1938).

Robinson, J. P., Letters on Paraguay, 3 vols (London 1843).

Rock, D., *Argentina 1516–1987* (London 1987).

Ross, A. C., 'The Dutch Reformed Church of South Africa: a Product of the Disruption?' in S. J. Brown and M. Fry, *Scotland in the Age of the Disruption* (Edinburgh 1993) 151–164.

Rosselli, J., *Lord William Bentinck* (London 1974).

Salas, A.M., *Diario de Buenos Aires, 1806–1807* (Buenos Aires 1981).

Sassenay, Marquis de, *Napoleon Ier et la fondation de la Republique Argentine* (Paris 1892).

Schama, S., *Patriots and Liberators* (London 1977).

Smith, G.C. Moore (ed.), *Autobiography of Sir Harry Smith* (London 1901).

Smithers, A.J., *The Kaffir Wars* (London 1973).

Street, J., *Artigas and the Emancipation of Uruguay* (Cambridge 1959).

Sym, J. (ed.), *Seaforth Highlanders* (Aldershot 1962).

Theal, G. M., *The History of South Africa since 1795* (Cape Town, 1908–1910).

Wilson, M. and L. Thompson (eds), *A History of South Africa to 1870* (London 1979).

Waite, R.A., *Sir Home Riggs Popham, KM, KCG, KCH, FRS, Rear Admiral of the Red Squadron*, Ph.D. thesis (Harvard, 1942).

Walker, E., *The Great Trek* (London 1965).

Weller, J., *Wellington in the Peninsula*, 2nd ed., (London 1992).

Whittingham, F., *A Memoir of the Services of Lt-Gen Sir Samuel Ford Whittingham* (London 1868).

Youngson, A. J., *After the Forty-Five* (Edinburgh 1973).

Index